THE MEANING OF LIFE

Books by A. J. Ayer

THE MEANING OF LIFE

A. J. AYER

A ROBERT STEWART BOOK

Charles Scribner's Sons
New York

Maxwell Macmillan International
New York   Oxford   Singapore   Sydney

Introduction copyright © 1990 by Ted Honderich

Originally published by George Weidenfeld & Nicolson Ltd, London

Charles Scribner's Sons
Macmillan Publishing Company
866 Third Avenue, New York, NY 10022

Collier Macmillan Canada, Inc.
1200 Eglinton Avenue East, Suite 200
Don Mills, Ontario M3C 3N1

Library of Congress Cataloging-in-Publication Data

Ayer, A. J. (Alfred Jules), 1910–89.
The meaning of life / A. J. Ayer.
p.   cm.
"A Robert Stewart book."
ISBN 0-684-19195-4
1. Philosophy.   I. Title.
B1574.A94M42   1990   90-33123   CIP
192—dc20

10 9 8 7 6 5 4 3 2 1

Printed in the United States of America

Contents

Acknowledgements

The publishers are grateful to the following for permission to quote published material from the writings of A. J. Ayer:

The Free Press and Father F. C. Copleston SJ: *Logical Positivism*, ed. A. J. Ayer, 1959.

McGraw-Hill Book Company: *The Owl of Minerva: Philosophers on Philosophy*, ed. Charles J. Bontemps and S. Jack Odell, 1975.

University of Notre Dame Press: three lectures from *The Nature of Philosophical Inquiry*, ed. Joseph Bobik, 1975.

Souvenir Press and Professor Arne Naess of Oslo University: 'The Glass is on the Table' from *Reflexive Water: The Basic Concerns of Mankind*, ed. Fons Elders, 1974.

Gerald Duckworth & Co Ltd: Introduction to J. S. Mill, *On the Logic of the Moral Sciences*.

The British Academy: *Bertrand Russell as a Philosopher* (Lecture on a Master Mind), Proceedings of the British Academy, vol. LVIII, 1972. © The British Academy 1972.

Barrie & Jenkins and The Advisory Council of the British Humanist Association: Introduction to *The Humanist Outlook*, ed. A. J. Ayer, published by Pemberton with Barrie & Rockcliff, 1968.

South Place Ethical Society and Nicholas Hyman: *The Meaning of Life*; 64th Conway Memorial Lecture, 1988; © 1988 South Place Ethical Society and A. J. Ayer.

The Spectator: 'Postscript to a Postmortem', *The Spectator*, 15 October 1988.

Introduction

Language, Truth and Logic was in the late 1950s what it will remain, very reassuring to anyone not fond of philosophy with angels' wings. It was reassuring despite being a little breathtaking itself, even breathless. First chapter: 'The Elimination of Metaphysics'. Last chapter: 'Solutions of Outstanding Philosophical Disputes'. All of it was indeed from a young man with his spurs on, not making accommodations.

When I first met Freddie, in 1959, in the house in Gordon Square in which the philosophers of University College London reside, he had had second thoughts, rueful ones. But he was not abashed. He could take with aplomb the idea that a postgraduate had preferred him to all of Harvard. He took me, I think, for a sensible fellow.

He never recanted the intention of *Language, Truth and Logic*. He never recanted its fundamental commitment. To do so would have been too close to putting aside as *wrong*, which is unlikely, the greatest of traditions in philosophy in the English language. It is also the tradition in modern philosophy as a whole to which others can only be reactions. It is the one which has Locke, Berkeley, Hume, Mill and Russell in it, and Voltaire and William James as foreign members. Freddie adorned it too. At the Monday evening seminars which remained in 1959 before he left University College for another place, he was still a kind of hussar against nonsense.

That description is too negative. He was a philosopher whose audacity was *being true to truth*. He was true to *the truth of sense*, not the truth of aspiration, predilection, or theory. This empiricism of his twelve or thirteen purely philosophical books, and of the others, if he did not mind discomfiting bishops by it, and sedentary dons, and earning a guinea or two from it – this pellucid empiricism was what he really could believe. It was also what he could give clear reasons for believing.

He did not write to intimate or evoke, or as the apostle of a specialism, or to elaborate a style, or strike a prolonged pose, or to do any of the things that are better done by choosing a calling other than philosophy. He would have eschewed – perhaps *did* eschew what he could in fact have displayed – the kinds of originality which have given greater fame to one or two others. He went on saying the truth of sense when, as truth recurrently does, it became a little dull.

Nor was he ever taken over by the recurrent illusion that the central questions of philosophy, the questions that are the very subject, can be answered or managed by recourse to some other discipline. He believed, certainly, that philosophy which is blind to science is futile. But he never thought that the nature of knowledge is revealed by computer programmes or that of causation by Quantum Theory. Nor did he think that what philosophy has to say of the meaning of life can be imported. It was thought for a moment that a meeting in memory of him should be in Westminster Abbey. That *would* have reflected his attainment. It would not have reflected him.

He also did more than write philosophy. Some say, with reason, that it existed in University College before him. They can also say that philosophy had been heard of outside our universities before his broadcasting. Things were very different afterwards.

Still, it is a whole man, and not only a man of a calling, whose life has ended. I knew him best in its last twelve years.

Some linger too long with the idea that he was proud of himself. The fact could not be missed by, say, a publisher who received his instructions, or by the provost of a college. That he could be full of the logic of what he was about to say was not missed either, I fancy, by Miss Oughterson, the matron of his school. She reported to the boys to whom she was giving tea, as *he* reported thereafter, that an anonymous telephone caller had been disturbing her sleep. 'I can't think why anyone would want to do that,' she said. 'Can you?' Answer there came. 'It depends on how much they disliked you, Miss Oughterson.'

He was full enough of something other than himself. He was full enough of what was more important, an unconfused and cool concern for others. In his politics, he never fell into forgetfulness of the desires and the hurts of the unlucky. If he never wrote much about social justice, he knew what it was. If he had been elected, he would have let Westminster Council know about it. He would not have made accommodations there either.

He also had that other side of decency, the private rather than the public side. He was loyal to friends, resolutely so to me. He was responsible with students. He was fairer to personal adversaries than they were to him. He could write an obituary and keep his politics out of it. It would surprise me if he was careless about others in his personal affections. He did not have to be a prig to be careful. He could also forgive affronts, and make amends himself.

I remember him best in two settings, both of them places in which he was happy in great personal attachments, to Vanessa and to Dee. One was his York Street sitting room, with the bookshelves around his desk, and the big book on him prominently next to the big book on Hegel. The other place was Le Beausset in the Var, in the shade of the lime tree, before lunch. Talk in both places was lovely, if bracing – talk of the 400 words he had written in the morning, of my confounded weakness for natural necessity in causation, of a bet about whether Jane Austen gives the very words in which Mr Darcy proposes for the second time, of what university committee for the election of a professor must have been out of its mind, and of children, his own and others. His last line of autobiography, about his love for Nick, is exact.

He himself could always recover the exuberance of boyhood. It was never far away. There was a good deal of the logical elf left at the end. There was also fortitude, and no breath of apostasy. It was inconceivable that there should have been any bad news for the good atheists of the South Place Ethical Society. What I last had from him, in return for another detective story, the one he never read, was a beaming smile.

He sought only truth and wrote it down beautifully, he lived fully, he died well.

The above words were spoken at the memorial meeting for the author of the essays in this book. If personal, they will do as well as anything else I might write to introduce what is his last book. He was at work assembling it shortly before his death on 27 June 1989 in London.

It falls into four parts. The first has most to do with Logical Positivism, the second with the nature of philosophy, the third with more particular subjects, and the fourth, which follows naturally from what has gone before, with the meaning of life. Several of the essays, lectures, articles and transcripts of discussions are what might be called principal statements of a doctrine or position. Most of them derive from principal statements elsewhere, and are admirable if brisk summations of them. Together they convey much of a philosophical life.

The earliest of the essays was written in 1947, after his return to Oxford from the war, and the latest of them near the end of his life. He proposed to write a brief foreword to each of them, but finished only one. About the first essay, on 'The Claims of Philosophy', he wrote as follows:

It may seem strange that I should reprint an essay that was originally published over forty years ago. My reasons for doing so are, first, that when I reread the essay after all that time I thought it worth rescuing from oblivion and, secondly, that it expounds in a bold and simple fashion a conception of philosophy that still seems to me to be substantially correct. For instance, I have no fault to find with its account of moral and political philosophy, and what I then said about the meaning of life encapsulates the more discursive lecture, delivered only about a year ago, which I am also reprinting in this volume. And while in my essay 'Metaphysics and Common Sense', first published in 1966 and included by me in 1969 in a book of that title, I treated metaphysics less harshly than I had previously done, I made no concession to the brand of metaphysics which 'The Claims of Philosophy' picks out for attack.

The only part of the essay that I have thought of pruning is the second section where I wrote about Moore and Wittgenstein. With regard to Moore, I am ashamed to have given the impression that I did not take his work seriously. On the contrary, the question of the relation of physical objects to sense data, which preoccupied him, has preoccupied me also throughout my philosophical career. I have, indeed, taken issue with his celebrated defence of common sense but I do not deny that it played a very important part in the development of analytical philosophy. Where I differ from some of Moore's followers, if not from Moore himself, is in regarding analysis as a means towards the critical assessment of our beliefs rather than as an end in itself, and this is my excuse for letting my comments stand.

In writing about Wittgenstein, during his lifetime, one needed to be very careful not to say anything that he would regard either as plagiarizing or as misrepresenting his unpublished views. I was particularly alive to this danger as, ever since the summer of 1932 when my tutor Gilbert Ryle had taken me to Cambridge to introduce me to him, he had done me the honour of treating me as a protégé. I was so far unsuccessful in avoiding the danger that when one of Wittgenstein's pupils brought my essay to his attention, he broke off relations with me and subsequently pretended never to have heard of me. I was told much later that what had offended him was not my rather flippant comment on the legacy of the *Tractatus* but my implying that his way of doing philosophy was tending to turn it into a form of psychoanalysis.

The offence with which Wittgenstein charged me at the time was that of feigning ignorance of his current work. That charge was unjust. Not long before the war I had read the so-called *Blue and Brown Books*, notes taken by pupils of lectures that he gave in the early 1930s, but by 1947 I had almost forgotten what was in them and I had no opportunity of acquiring any knowledge of his later work. When I read the posthumous *Philosophical Investigations* I realized that Wittgenstein's view of philosophy had not been so close to Wisdom's as I had supposed, but it had been close enough for my comments not to be seriously misleading. That is my justification for preserving them.

More generally 'The Claims of Philosophy' has to do with the aspirations of what Ayer takes as the two classes of philosophers, pontiffs and journeymen. The pontiffs, who seek to enlighten us about what they may call ultimate reality, are typified by Hegel and Heidegger, of whom no kind words are spoken. The journeymen, who deal with particular problems of several kinds, include in their number Moore and Wittgenstein – Moore comfortably, as it seems to me, and Wittgenstein not so comfortably. Neither camp satisfies the public's expectation of its philosophers, which is that they should answer questions about the meaning of life and about how we ought to live. Ayer's response to these questions, and to the expectation, as he remarks in his foreword, prefigures but is less developed than what he says in his last pieces, reprinted at the end of the book.

These several views about two kinds of philosophers and their possible contributions have their basis, of course, in the empiricism which Ayer sought to reformulate in *Language, Truth and Logic*, first published in 1936. That reformulation was in its essentials defended against a resourceful and determined metaphysician, Father Copleston, in a BBC radio debate, the likes of which are now heard but rarely. Its transcript is the second item in this book.

The central idea of that reformulation, perhaps a bit overstated in it, is that only two sorts of utterances are either true or false, or, to speak differently, have the recommendation of being possibly true. Only these two sorts are meaningful in exactly the sense of being possibly true. These sorts, the empirical and the logical, do not include the typical utterances of metaphysicians or of their close relatives, the believers of orthodox religion. The history of the idea is no short one beginning with some Viennese in the 1930s, as some have supposed, but rather goes back to Hume.

The debate is no piece of popularizing, but is philosophical discussion. In it, Ayer perseveres in the conviction, among others, that all necessarily true statements are simply those whose truth depends only on the meaning of words. They do not, so to speak, report necessities in reality. His fundamental endeavour, however, is to protect his limiting of true or false utterances to the empirically verifiable and the logical. He will not have it that what he is doing in effect is no more than offering a particular and perhaps arbitrary definition of 'true or false utterance', which definition might readily be replaced by another. In this defence of the Verification Principle he strikes a note, having to do with the matter of an utterance being explanatory, not heard in the introduction to a revised edition of *Language, Truth and Logic*, which appeared at about the same time. Nor, in his defence of the principle, is he called upon to make certain concessions made in that introduction.

The debate does have much to do with the very nature of philosophy, which subject is more thoroughly inquired into in the second group of selections in this book. The opening one, 'Philosophy', was published in 1975, and begins with an explanation of how Ayer and others came to suppose, mistakenly, that the business of philosophy is to do no more than *furnish us with definitions*. What follows serves as a kind of prelude to the more ample reflections in the three lectures which follow, given in 1967.

The first lecture is initially concerned with disputable characterizations of the propositions of philosophy: that they are peculiarly general, that they comprise a world-picture, and so on. The best of these generalizations takes philosophy to consist in judgments on claims to knowledge. This, however, faces a kind of objection derived from Moore's defence of common sense. That was a defence of the existence of what we take to be ordinary reality, and involved Moore's holding up his two hands for the inspection of his audience. The performance was regarded as splendid by some, not so splendid by others.

Ayer proposes that Moore's defence rests on the proposition that there do exist recognized or accredited criteria for deciding various classes of questions. What may seem to follow from *that* is that there is no need for or possibility of judgments by philosophers on various kinds of claims to knowledge. What is left to philosophers, if this is so, is one or more of certain lesser jobs of clarification or analysis. What is left to them is something *much* less grand than the proof and delineation of the Transcendent, or the Absolute, or God.

The second 1967 lecture, partly by effectively dealing with Moore's performance and the underlying proposition, provides a more satisfactory account of the nature of philosophy. It is concerned with the examination or indeed the devising of what are called conceptual schemes. It may be concerned, in particular, with a conceptual scheme which does not rest on physical objects, understood as entities which are taken to exist when unperceived and also to have certain other properties. It operates with what seems to be somehow more immediate and secure, the contents of our experience. These were what were historically called ideas and more recently sense data. Ayer himself, like his great philosophical forbears, remained attracted to this scheme despite its problems. He first set it out in *The Foundations of Empirical Knowledge* in 1940, and gave his final and most accessible account of it in a chapter of *The Central Questions of Philosophy*.

The third 1967 lecture expounds a version of the scheme, and also looks at physicalism, which consists in doctrines to the effect that mental states and processes somehow come to no more than physical or neural states and processes. What we have as a conclusion to the lectures, in part, is that philosophy certainly attempts more than the humble task suggested by saying that it consists in clarification or analysis.

'The Glass is on the Table' is another debate, in this case one which took place on Dutch television in 1971. It is rather less orderly than the earlier one, and its title is no great guide to its contents. It is as much about the nature of philosophy as anything else, but, to say the least, it ranges widely. Some of what is said has to do with scepticism, and Ayer's treatment of it in what he sometimes spoke of as his best book, *The Problem of Knowledge*. Some has to do with personal identity, but not in the measured way of *The Concept of a Person and Other Essays*. Some has to do with the connection between empiricism and politics. Some has to do with the idea of a fact, some with the coherence of an individual's views. All of it serves as a reminder of Ayer as happy controversialist, the philosopher well and truly out of the quiet of his study, not minding the hubbub and not reluctant to add to it.

What follows, the third part of the book, is wholly different. The first of three particular philosophical subjects treated is that of individual freedom. In 'The Concept of Freedom', dating from 1944, Ayer provides a conception of individual freedom as sharp and concise as can be asked. In the course of doing so, he makes plain the political commitment referred to at the beginning of this introduction. The essay at least complements what is better known, the essay on freedom and necessity in *Philosophical Essays*.

Something the same can be said of what follows. It is the introduction to that part of John Stuart Mill's *A System of Logic* which has to do with what can be called a science of man, the application of the scientific method to our thoughts, feelings, decisions and actions. Mill as a good determinist was in no doubt that our existence is in fact nomic or subject to law, but was pessimistic about our uncovering the laws or coming to be able to predict thoughts and the like – as one might be sure that an avalanche will be a matter of strict cause and effect but be pessimistic about settling where each boulder and pebble will come to rest.

Ayer's discussion of Mill's view issues in several statements of his own attitude to the question of the truth of determinism, as distinct from difficulties in the way of establishing or using it. As in a related discussion, in his *Freedom and Morality and Other Essays*, it may be fair to say that he hesitates between agnosticism and denial with respect to determinism. In this he departs from the empiricist tradition.

The last of the three particular subjects in this part of the book is the philosophy of Bertrand Russell. There is nothing new and nothing false in the opinion that one is very likely to get the best account of a great body of thought from someone having affection for it but also capable of independent judgment. The case of Ayer on Russell gives support to that opinion. The lecture on Russell is splendid, no doubt as excellent a brief account as exists. This is as true of what is said of the Theory of Descriptions as of Russell's moral and political thinking. It derives, of course, from the longer studies mentioned in footnote, particularly *Russell and Moore: The Analytical Heritage*.

Reading it put me in mind of a judgment by the very ablest of judges, Professor Sir Peter Strawson, at the memorial meeting mentioned earlier. That was that if we put aside Russell's work in pure logic and logical theory, and consider the theory of knowledge and general metaphysics, Ayer is in no way Russell's inferior, and indeed in clarity, order and coherence may reasonably be said to be his superior.

The fourth part of this book begins by setting out in simple terms the humanist outlook. It is taken to have as intrinsic to it the propositions, certainly still in need of being heard, that morality cannot rest on authority, divine or otherwise, and, since the facts of situations do not speak out what is right, that each of us must choose the right. The humanist outlook has in it, too, an acceptance that one's existence does end with one's death, and a political corollary about doing all that is possible to secure decent lives for all. We have no other lives.

The lecture 'The Meaning of Life', written about a year before he died, enlarges on these and other themes. It is, I think, his fullest treatment of the subject. One theme has to do with the very intelligibility of speaking of a person surviving death. Another has to do with the grounds for fear of death. As for the meaning of life, it is true that we can do what is called give meaning to our lives. We can, at any rate, give them direction, perhaps by pursuing fame or credit. We cannot discover a grander meaning of life, where that is a larger design or destiny fixed for all of us, for there is none.

The last two pieces are a report on the experience of having come near to death, and a later reflection on that report. As does so much of the writing in this book, they show his spirit.

Ted Honderich   LONDON 1990

THE MEANING OF LIFE

ONE

The Claims of Philosophy[1]

I

Contemporary philosophers may be divided into two classes: the pontiffs and the journeymen. As the names that I have chosen indicate, the basis of this division is not so much a difference of opinion as a difference of attitude. It is not merely that the journeyman denies certain propositions which the pontiff asserts, or that he asserts certain propositions which the pontiff denies. It is rather that he has a radically different conception of the method of philosophy and of the ends that it is fitted to achieve. Thus, it is characteristic of those whom I describe as pontiffs that they think it within the province of philosophy to compete with natural science. They may, indeed, be willing to admit that the scientist achieves valuable results in his own domain, but they insist that he does not, and cannot, attain to the complete and final truth about reality; and they think that it is open to the philosopher to make this deficiency good. In support of this view, they may, for example, argue that every scientific theory is based upon presuppositions which cannot themselves be scientifically proved; and from this they may infer, in the interests of their own 'philosophical' brand of irrationality, that science itself is fundamentally irrational; or else they may have recourse to metaphysics to supply the missing proof. Alternatively, they may hold that the scientist deals only with the appearances of things, whereas the philosopher by the use of his special methods penetrates to the reality beyond. In general, the ideal of the pontiff is to construct a metaphysical system. Such a system may actually include some scientific hypotheses, either as premises or, more frequently, as deductions from metaphysical first principles. It may, on the other

[1] 'The Claims of Philosophy' was first published in *Polemic*, No. 7, March 1947; repr. in *Reflections on Our Age* (New York, UNESCO, 1947).

hand, be uncompromisingly metaphysical. In either case, the aim is to give a complete and definitive account of 'ultimate' reality.

Unfortunately, as the journeymen on their side have been at pains to show, this 'ultimate' reality is a fiction, and the ideal of a metaphysical system that is anything other than a scientific encyclopaedia is devoid of any basis in reason. To some extent, indeed, this fact has been borne in upon the pontiffs, and the result is that they now tend to desert reason and even to decry it. This separates them sharply from their philosophical ancestors, who at least professed to reason, even if they did not always reason well. Few men, indeed, can ever have reasoned worse than Hegel, the arch-pontiff of the nineteenth century, but at least he claimed the support of reason for his fantasies. His ground for thinking that a mobile logic is needed to describe a mobile world may have been no better than the principle that 'who drives fat oxen must himself be fat'; but at least, if he rejected the 'static' Aristotelian logic, he did so in favour of what he, no doubt mistakenly, believed to be a superior logic of his own. Though he misused logic abominably, he did not affect to be above it. But now if we turn to Heidegger, the high priest of the modern school of existentialists, and the leading pontiff of our times, we find ourselves in a country from which the ordinary processes of logic, or indeed reasoning of any kind, appear to have been banished. For what we learn from him is that it is only in the clear light of Nothing that Being has being, and consequently that it is the supreme privilege of the philosopher to concern himself with Nothing.[2] For this he requires no special intellectual discipline. It is sufficient that he experiences anguish, provided always that it is an anguish without any special object. For it is thus, according to Heidegger, that the Nothing reveals itself. This strange thesis is indeed backed by a pretence of argument, but since the argument depends upon the elementary fallacy of treating 'nothing' as a name, it is hardly to be taken seriously. Nor does Heidegger himself appear to attach very much weight to it. For it is not by logic that he seeks to convince: nor is his the Socratic method of following an argument wherever it may lead. Like the sermons of Dr Dodd,[3] his work is addressed to the passions; and it is no doubt for this reason that it has succeeded in becoming fashionable.

Now just as William James thought that all prigs must sooner or later end by becoming Hegelians, so it seems to me that the fate of the

[2] See *Was ist Metaphysik* (Bonn, Friedrich Cohen, 1929).

[3] See Boswell's *Life of Johnson*. 'A clergyman (whose name I do not recollect): "Were not Dodd's sermons addressed to the passions?" Johnson: "They were nothing sir, be they addressed to what they may."'

contemporary pontiff must be to go the way of Heidegger. I do not mean by this that he will have to subscribe to Heidegger's doctrines. There are other types of 'deeply significant nonsense' available. But inasmuch as his quest for ultimate reality cannot be made to prosper by any rational means, he is likely, if he adheres to it, to seek some nonrational source of enlightenment. At this point he devolves into a mystic or a poet. As such he may express an attitude to life which is interesting in itself and even a source of inspiration to others; and perhaps it would be churlish to refuse him the title of philosopher. But it is to be remarked that when philosophy has been brought to this stage then, whatever its emotional value, it has ceased to be, in any ordinary sense, a vehicle of knowledge.

II

The history of philosophy, as it is taught in the textbooks, is largely a parade of pontiffs; and it might be thought that the only course open to the budding philosopher was either to enrol himself under one of their banners, or else to try to become a pontiff in his own right. But in this, as in so many other cases, the textbooks are behind the times. For, at least in England and America, the philosophical scene has been dominated for the last fifty years, not by the pontiffs, but by those whom I describe as journeymen. Unlike the pontiffs, the journeymen do not set out in quest of ultimate reality. Nor do they try to bring philosophy into competition with the natural sciences. Believing, as they do, that the only way to discover what the world is like is to form hypotheses and test them by observation, which is in fact the method of science, they are content to leave the scientist in full possession of the field of speculative knowledge. Consequently they do not try to build systems. The task of the philosopher, as they see it, is rather to deal piecemeal with a special set of problems. Some of these problems are historical, in the sense that they involve the criticism and interpretation of the work of previous philosophers; others are primarily mathematical, as belonging to the specialized field of formal logic; others again are set by the sciences: they involve the analysis of scientific method, the evaluation of scientific theories, the clarification of scientific terms. It is, for example, a philosophical problem to decide what is meant by 'probability': and the journeymen have already contributed much towards its solution. Finally, there are a number of problems, such as the problem of perception, the problem of our knowledge of other minds, the question of the significance of moral judgments, that arise out of the common usages and assumptions of everyday life. In a broad sense, all these problems are semantic: that is to say, they can all be represented as concerned with the use of language. But since the term 'semantics' is technically applied to a particular formal discipline which does not, even for the journeymen, comprehend the whole of philosophy, I think it better to resume their philosophical activities under the general heading of logical analysis.

Essentially, the journeymen are technicians; and from this point of view the comparison with the pontiffs is very much to their advantage. They suffer, however, from a certain thinness of material. Consider, for example, the so-called philosophers of common sense, who follow the distinguished leadership of Professor G. E. Moore. In the opinion of this school, it is not sensible for a philosopher to question the truth of such common-sense statements as that this is a sheet of paper or that I am wearing shoes on my feet. And if anyone were to question it they would reply simply that, on the relevant occasions, they knew for certain that statements of this sort were true. Thus, Professor Moore himself has proved, to his own satisfaction, the existence of external objects, a question much canvassed by philosophers, by the simple method of holding up his hands and saying that he knows for certain that they exist;[4] and indeed there is no denying that in its way this is a valid proof. At the same time these philosophers confess to being very doubtful of the correct analysis of the common-sense propositions which they know to be true. The question whether or not this really is a sheet of paper does not puzzle them at all; but the question of what precisely is implied by saying that it is puzzles them a great deal. In technical language, it is a matter of discovering the relationship between the sense data which are immediately experienced and the physical objects which it is their function to present; and this is a problem which, in the opinion of our common-sense philosophers, has not yet been satisfactorily solved. Now I do not wish to suggest that this is not a difficult problem, or to belittle the ingenuity with which the journeymen have tackled it. But I am afraid that a layman who was told that a question of this sort was of sufficient interest to a modern philosopher to occupy him for a lifetime would be inclined to think that modern philosophy was degenerating into scholasticism. If he were told, as he might be by a pontiff, that there was serious doubt of the existence of this piece of paper he would be very properly incredulous, but he might also be impressed: he might even be brought to think that he himself had been excessively naive in taking such a thing for granted.

[4] See his 'Proof of an external world'. *Proceedings of the British Academy*, Vol. XXV.

But once he had been assured that the truth of his common-sense assumption that the paper existed was not after all in doubt, I think it would be difficult to interest him in a meticulous analysis of its implications. He would remark that he understood very well what he meant by saying that this was a piece of paper, and that he did not see what was to be gained by a laborious attempt at further clarification. To this it could, indeed, be objected that he might think very differently if he had been properly educated in philosophy; and that in any case there is no reason why the layman's judgments of value should be binding upon the philosopher. But even so it is difficult not to feel some sympathy for our layman. It is difficult not to suspect that the philosopher of common sense must sometimes be inclined to say to himself what the poet Clough said when he found himself exclusively engaged in doing up parcels for Florence Nightingale: 'This that I see is not all, and this that I do is but little. It is good but there is better than it.'

Another prominent set of journeymen are the followers of Ludwig Wittgenstein, who has succeeded G. E. Moore as professor of philosophy at the University of Cambridge. More than twenty years ago, Professor Wittgenstein came to the conclusion, at the end of his remarkable *Tractatus Logico-Philosophicus*, that 'the right method of philosophy would be the following: to say nothing except what can be said, i.e. the propositions of natural science, i.e. something that has nothing to do with philosophy: and then whenever someone wished to say something metaphysical, to demonstrate to him that he had given no meaning to certain signs in his proposition. This method would be unsatisfying to the other – he would not have the impression that he was learning philosophy – but it would be the only strictly correct method.' In other words, the philosopher is reduced, or elevated, to the position of a park keeper whose business it is to see that no one commits an intellectual nuisance; the nuisance in question being that of lapsing into metaphysics. I do not know whether Wittgenstein is still of this opinion; and even if his point of view has remained substantially the same I doubt if he would now express it in such terms as I have quoted. But what I do know is that the effect of his teaching upon his more articulate disciples has been that they tend to treat philosophy as a department of psychoanalysis. In their eyes, the *raison d'être* of the philosopher is the fact that people continually get themselves into states of metaphysical doubt. They are inclined to say, for example, that they can never really be sure of the existence of the material world, or that they can never really know what goes on in another person's mind, or even, more seriously, that he has a mind. Now these, according to the

Wittgensteinians, are intellectually neurotic doubts; and it is the business of the philosopher to effect their cure. Admittedly, the people who feel them are usually those who have studied some philosophy: but equally the psychoanalyst finds his most profitable patients among those who have delved a little into psychoanalysis. In both cases, the method of cure is to enter sympathetically into the patient's neurosis and try to talk it out. As Mr Wisdom puts it,[5] 'the treatment is like psychoanalytic treatment in that the treatment is the diagnosis and the diagnosis is the description, the very full description, of the symptoms.' That the description is full will hardly be denied by anyone who has read Mr Wisdom. Whether it is effective is perhaps more doubtful; but, in his hands at any rate, it is a work of fascinating subtlety. Nevertheless one is again tempted to ask: 'Is this all that the philosopher is fitted to achieve?'

Not all the contemporary philosophers whom I should classify as journeymen hold the views that I have quoted; but I think it can fairly be said that in the case of nearly all of them there is an unfortunate disparity between the richness of their technique and the increasing poverty of the material on which they are able to exercise it. The principal exceptions are those who, like Bertrand Russell and Professor Whitehead, at least in the days before he became a pontiff, combine a mastery of logic with an understanding of mathematics and natural science. And this suggests that the salvation of the journeymen may be the reunion of philosophy with science, just as the final resource of the pontiff is the passage of philosophy into mysticism, or at least into imaginative literature. In the meantime, however, there remain a number of logical puzzles which the journeyman, who is relatively ignorant of science, may reasonably feel called upon to solve. The importance of his work may not indeed be immediately obvious to the layman; and there may be times when the philosopher himself is reduced to wishing that the field of his achievement were rather more spectacular; but he may perhaps console himself with the words of John Locke that 'it is ambition enough to be employed as an under-labourer in clearing the ground a little, and removing some of the rubbish that lies in the way to knowledge.'[6]

III

On the side of the pontiffs, imaginative literature. On the side of the journeymen, the reintegration of philosophy with science, or the

[5] In the first of his series of articles on 'Other Minds'. See *Mind*, Vol. XLIX, p. 370.
[6] See 'An Essay concerning Human Understanding'. Epistle to the reader.

piecemeal solution of logical or linguistic puzzles. Surely, it will be said, this is not what the public expects of its philosophers. Surely, the business of the philosopher is to make clear the meaning of life, to show people how they ought to live. Call him a pontiff or a journeyman, according to his method of approach; the distinction is not of any great importance. What is important is the message that he has to give. It is wisdom that is needed, not merely scientific knowledge. Of what use to us is the understanding of nature if we do not know the purpose of our existence or how we ought to live? And who is to answer these supremely important questions if not the philosopher?

The reply to this is that there is no true answer to these questions; and since this is so it is no use expecting even the philosopher to provide one. What can be done, however, is to make clear why, and in what sense, these questions are unanswerable; and once this is achieved it will be seen that there is also a sense in which they can be answered. It will be found that the form of answer is not a proposition, which must be either true or false, but the adoption of a rule, which cannot be properly characterized as either true or false, but can nevertheless be judged as more or less acceptable. And with this the problem is solved, so far as reasoning can solve it. The rest is a matter of personal decision, and ultimately of action.

Let us begin them by considering the purpose of our existence. How is it possible for our existence to have a purpose? We know very well what it is for a man to have a purpose. It is a matter of his intending, on the basis of a given situation, to bring about some further situation, which for some reason or other he conceives to be desirable. And in that case it may be said that events have a meaning for him according as they conduce, or fail to conduce, towards the end that he desires. But how can life in general be said to have any meaning? A simple answer is that all events are tending towards a certain specifiable end: so that to understand the meaning of life it is necessary only to discover this end. But, in the first place, there is no good reason whatever for supposing this assumption to be true, and secondly, even if it were true, it would not do the work that is required of it. For what is being sought by those who demand to know the meaning of life is not an explanation of the facts of their existence, but a justification. Consequently a theory which informs them merely that the course of events is so arranged as to lead inevitably to a certain end does nothing to meet their need. For the end in question will not be the one that they themselves have chosen. As far as they are concerned it will be entirely arbitrary; and it will be a no less arbitrary fact that their existence is such as necessarily to lead to its fulfilment. In short, from the point of view of justifying one's existence, there is no essential difference between a teleological explanation of events and a mechanical explanation. In either case, it is a matter of brute fact that events succeed one another in the ways that they do and are explicable in the ways that they are. And indeed what is called an explanation is nothing other than a more general description. Thus, an attempt to answer the question why events are as they are must always resolve itself into saying only how they are. But what is required by those who seek the meaning of life is precisely an answer to their question 'Why?' that is something other than an answer to any question 'How?' And just because this is so they can never legitimately be satisfied.

But now, it may be objected, suppose that the world is designed by a superior being. In that case the purpose of our existence will be the purpose that it realizes for him; and the meaning of life will be found in our conscious adaptation of his purpose. But here again, the answer is, first, that there is no good reason whatsoever for believing that there is any such superior being; and, secondly, that even if there were, he could not accomplish what is here required of him. For let us assume, for the sake of argument, that everything happens as it does because a superior being has intended that it should. As far as we are concerned, the course of events still remains entirely arbitrary. True, it can now be said to fulfil a purpose; but the purpose is not ours. And just as, on the previous assumption, it merely happened to be the case that the course of events conduced to the end that it did, so, on this assumption, it merely happens to be the case that the deity has the purpose that he has, and not some other purpose, or no purpose at all. Nor does this unwarrantable assumption provide us even with a rule of life. For even those who believe most firmly that the world was designed by a superior being are not in a position to tell us what his purpose can have been. They may indeed claim that it has been mysteriously revealed to them, but how can it be proved that the revelation is genuine? And even if we waive this objection, even if we assume not only the world as we find it is working out the purpose of a superior being, but also that we are capable of discovering what this purpose is, we are still not provided with a rule of life. For either his purpose is sovereign or it is not. If it is sovereign, that is, if everything that happens is necessarily in accordance with it, then this is true also of our behaviour. Consequently, there is no point in our deciding to conform to it, for the simple reason that we cannot do otherwise. However we behave, we shall fulfil the purpose of this deity; and if we were to behave differently, we should still be fulfilling it; for if it were possible for us not to fulfil it it would not be sovereign in the requisite sense. But suppose that it is not sovereign, or, in other words, that not all events must necessarily bear it out. In that case, there is no reason why we should try to conform to it, unless we independently judge it to be good. But that means that the significance of our behaviour depends finally upon our own judgments of value; and the concurrence of a deity then becomes superfluous.

The point is, in short, that even the invocation of a deity does not enable us to answer the question why things are as they are. At the best it complicates the answer to the question how they are by pushing the level of explanation to a further stage. For even if the ways of the deity were clear to those who believed in him, which they apparently are not, it would still be, even to them, a matter of brute fact that he behaved as he did, just as to those who do not believe in him it is a matter of brute fact that the world is what it is. In either case the question 'Why?' remains unanswered, for the very good reason that it is unanswerable. That is to say, it may be answerable at any given level, but the answer is always a matter of describing at a higher level not why things are as they are, but simply how they are. And so, to whatever level our explanations may be carried, the final statement is never an answer to the question 'Why?' but necessarily only an answer to the question 'How?'

It follows, if my argument is correct, that there is no sense in asking what is the ultimate purpose of our existence, or what is the real meaning of life. For to ask this is to assume that there can be a reason for our living as we do which is somehow more profound than any mere explanation of the facts; and we have seen that this assumption is untenable. Moreover it is untenable in logic and not merely in fact. The position is not that our existence unfortunately lacks a purpose which, if the fates had been kinder, it might conceivably have had. It is rather that those who inquire, in this way, after the meaning of life are raising a question to which it is not logically possible that there should be an answer. Consequently, the fact that they are disappointed is not, as some romanticists would make it, an occasion for cynicism or despair. It is not an occasion for any emotional attitude at all. And the reason why it is not is just that it could not conceivably have been otherwise. If it were logically possible for our existence to have a purpose, in the sense required, then it might be sensible to lament the fact that it had none. But it is not sensible to cry for what is logically impossible. If a question is so framed as to be unanswerable, then it is not a matter for regret that it remains unanswered. It is, therefore, misleading to say that life has no meaning; for that suggests that the statement that life has a meaning is factually significant, but false; whereas the truth is that, in the sense in which it is taken in this context, it is not factually significant.

There is, however, a sense in which it can be said that life does have a meaning. It has for each of us whatever meaning we severally choose to give it. The purpose of a man's existence is constituted by the ends to which he, consciously or unconsciously, devotes himself. Some men have a single overriding purpose to which all their activities are subordinated. If they are at all successful in achieving it, they are probably the happiest, but they are the exceptions. Most men pass from one object to another; and at any one time they may pursue a number of different ends, which may or may not be capable of being harmonized. Philosophers, with a preference for tidiness, have sometimes tried to show that all these apparently diverse objects can really be reduced to one: but the fact is that there is no end that is common to all men, not even happiness. For setting aside the question whether men ought always to pursue happiness, it is not true even that they always do pursue it, unless the word 'happiness' is used merely as a description of any end that is in fact pursued. Thus the question what is the meaning of life proves, when it is taken empirically, to be incomplete. For there is no single thing of which it can truly be said that this is the meaning of life. All that can be said is that life has at various times a different meaning for different people, according as they pursue their several ends.

That different people have different purposes is an empirical matter of fact. But what is required by those who seek to know the purpose of their existence is not a factual description of the way that people actually do conduct themselves, but rather a decision as to how they should conduct themselves. Having been taught to believe that not all purposes are of equal value, they require to be guided in their choice. And thus the inquiry into the purpose of our existence dissolves into the question 'How ought men to live?'

IV

The question how ought men to live is one that would seem to fall within the province of moral philosophy; but it cannot be said of every moral philosopher that he makes a serious attempt to answer it. Moreover, those who do make a serious attempt to answer it are mostly pontiffs, who approach it wrongly. For having decided, on metaphysical grounds, that reality is of such and such a character they try to deduce from this the superiority of a certain rule of life. But, quite apart from the merits or demerits of their metaphysics, it is a mistake on their part to suppose that a mere description of reality is sufficient to establish any rule of life at all. A familiar instance of this mistake is the claim that men ought to live in such and such a way because such and such is their real nature. But if what is meant by their having such and such a real nature is that they really are of the nature in question, then all that can possibly be established is that they really do behave in the manner indicated. For if they behaved differently, they would thereby show that they had a different nature. Thus in telling men that they ought to live in accordance with their real nature you are telling them to do what they do; and your pretended rule of life dissolves into nothing, since it is equally consistent with any course of conduct whatsoever. If, on the other hand, what is meant by a man's real nature is not the nature that he actually displays but the nature that he ought to display, then the moral rule that the argument is supposed to justify is assumed at the outset, and assumed without proof. As a moral rule, it may be acceptable in itself; but the supposed deduction of it from a non-moral premiss turns out inevitably to be a fraud.

It is not only metaphysicians who commit this fallacy. There is, for example, a brand of 'scientific ethics' according to which the right rule of life is that which harmonizes with the course of human evolution. But here again the same ambiguity arises. For if 'the course of human evolution' is understood as an actually existent process, then there is no sense in telling people that they ought to adapt themselves to it, for the very good reason that they cannot possibly do otherwise. However they may behave they will be acting rightly, since it is just their behaving as they do that makes the course of evolution what it is. In short, if progress is defined in terms of merely historical development, all conduct is progressive; for every human action necessarily furthers the course of evolution, in the straightforward sense of adding to its history. If, on the other hand, it is only some among the many possible developments of human history that are considered to be progressive, then there is some sense in saying that we ought to strive to bring them about; but here again the moral rule which we are invited to adopt is not deduced but simply posited. It is neither itself a scientific statement of fact, nor a logical consequence of any such statement. By scientific methods we can indeed discover that certain events are more or less likely to occur; but the transition from this to deciding that some of these possible developments are more valuable than others carries us outside the domain of science altogether. In saying this, I do not wish to repudiate the humanistic values of those who put forward the claims of scientific ethics, or even to suggest that any other system of values is more securely founded. My objection to these moralists is simply that they fall into the logical error of confusing normative judgments of value with scientific statements of fact. They may have the advantage of the metaphysicians, in that their factual premisses are more deserving of belief, but the fundamental mistake of trying to extract normative rules from supposedly factual descriptions is common to them both.

In moral, as in natural, philosophy it is characteristic of the journeyman to have detected the flaw in the method of the pontiffs, but here also they have purchased their freedom from error at the price of a certain aridity. For not only do they not attempt to prove their judgments of value; for the most part they refrain from expressing them at all. What they do instead, apart from criticizing other moral philosophers, is to subject the terminology of ethics to logical analysis. Thus the questions that they discuss are whether the term 'good' or the term 'right' is to be taken as fundamental, and whether either is definable; whether it is a man's duty to do an action or merely to set himself to do it; whether his duty is to do what is objectively right or merely what he thinks to be right; whether the rightness of an action depends upon its actual consequences, or upon its probable consequences, or upon its consequences as foreseen by the agent, or not upon its consequences at all; whether it is possible to fulfil an obligation unintentionally; whether the moral goodness of an action depends upon its motive; and many other questions of a similar sort. Such questions can be interesting, though they are not always made so, and I do not wish to say that they are not important; but to the practical man they must appear somewhat academic. By taking a course in this kind of moral philosophy a man may learn how to make the expression of his moral judgments secure from formal criticism. What he will not learn is what, in any concrete situation, he actually ought to do.

I think, then, that it can fairly be made a reproach to the journeymen that they have overlooked the Aristotelian principle that the end of moral philosophy is 'not knowledge but action'.[7] But their excuse is that once the philosopher who wishes to be practical has said this, there is very little more that he can say. Like anyone else, he can make moral recommendations, but he cannot legitimately claim for them the sanction of philosophy. He cannot prove that his judgments

---

[7] See *Nicomachean Ethics*, Book 1, Section 3.

of value are correct, for the sufficient reason that no judgment of value is capable of proof. Or rather, if it is capable of proof, it is only by reference to some other judgment of value, which must itself be left unproved. The moral philosopher can sometimes affect men's conduct by drawing their attention to certain matters of fact; he may show, for example, that certain sorts of action have unsuspected consequences, or that the motives for which they are done are different from what they appear to be; and he may then hope that when his audience is fully aware of the circumstances it will assess the situation in the same way as he does himself. Nevertheless there may be some who differ from him not on any question of fact, but on a question of value, and in this case he has no way of demonstrating that his judgment is superior. He lays down one rule, and they lay down another; and the decision between them is a subject for persuasion and finally a matter of individual choice.

Since judgments of value are not reducible to statements of fact, they are strictly speaking neither true nor false; and it is tempting to infer from this that no course of conduct is better or worse than any other. But this would be a mistake. For the judgment that no course of conduct is better or worse than any other is itself a judgment of value and consequently neither true nor false. And while an attitude of moral indifference is legitimate in itself, it is not easily maintained. For since we are constantly faced with the practical necessity of action, it is natural for most of us to act in accordance with certain principles; and the choice of principles implies the adoption of a positive set of values. That these values should be consistent is a necessary condition of their being fully realized; for it is logically impossible to achieve the complete fulfilment of an inconsistent set of ends. But, once their consistency is established, they can be criticized only on practical grounds, and from the standpoint of the critic's own moral system, which his adversary may or may not accept. No doubt, in practice, many people are content to follow the model rules that are prescribed to them by others; but the decision to submit oneself to authority on such a point is itself a judgment of value. In the last resort, therefore, each individual has the responsibility of choice; and it is a responsibility that is not to be escaped.

V

The same considerations apply to the philosophy of politics. That moral and political philosophy are intimately connected is fairly widely recognized; but the nature of their connection is still a subject of dispute. Thus some philosophers believe that morals can be logically subordinated to politics. They think that if they can establish the proper forms of political association they will be able to deduce from this how men ought to live. But, as we shall see, it is the opposite that is true. A political system may take one form or another; and, in any actual case, there will usually be a historical explanation of its taking the form that it does. But even if its existence can be historically accounted for, there still remains the question whether it is worthy of allegiance. Political institutions are not sacrosanct. It may, in certain circumstances, be beyond the power of a given individual to change them, but it does not follow that he is bound to think them good. That they are what they are is an unmistakable fact, but it does not follow that they are what they ought to be. And the question what they ought to be is ultimately a moral question. It is for the individual to answer it in accordance with the values that he himself adopts.

The confusion of fact with value, which we have seen to be a feature of certain moral systems, is equally a pitfall to political philosophers. Thus Plato seems, in his *Republic*, to look upon his ideal city-state as the unique embodiment of the reality of 'justice'; and he seems even to suggest that in depicting the structure of this political community he has answered the moral question how men ought to live. But what he does not appear to have seen is that to assert that true, or real, justice is to be found in such and such a set of institutions is not to make a statement of fact at all, but rather to lay down a standard. It is not a way of describing the institutions in question, but of making a certain claim for them; and the claim is that they ought to be adopted. It may be objected that what is claimed is not merely that they ought to be adopted, but that they ought to be adopted because they are truly just. But the point is that to say that they are truly just is, in this usage, no more than another way of saying that they ought to be adopted: the one statement is not, as it is made to seem, a justification of the other, but simply a repetition of it. Thus, if anyone thinks, as he well may, that Plato's institutions are not the best possible, he may devise a different Utopia; and he too may seek to recommend it by saying that it alone fulfils the true conditions of justice. In saying this he will be disagreeing with Plato, but he will not be formally contradicting him: for neither party is making a statement of fact. What makes this easy to overlook is the occurrence in such a context of words like 'true' or 'real': for it is assumed that they are being given their ordinary descriptive use. But, in fact, their use in these contexts is not descriptive but persuasive. They serve only to put a little halo round the principles that the speaker wishes to recommend. Accordingly, the question whether one or other of two divergent political systems has the better claim to be considered just, is a question, not of truth or falsehood, in the ordinary sense, but of deciding where to give one's allegiance: and the answer to it will depend upon the system of values of the person who is called upon to judge. Thus, so far from its being the case, as Plato seems to have thought, that the choice of political institutions can determine how men ought to live, it is a previous conception of the way men ought to live that determines the value of the institutions themselves.

For Hegel, the perfect embodiment of justice was not an ideal republic but the contemporary Prussian State: and he based this illiberal view upon the principle that the real was the rational. But this convenient principle turned out to be two-edged. For while it was used by conservatives to prove that whatever happened to exist was best, it occurred to some followers of Hegel to argue that since the contemporary Prussian State was palpably irrational it was not wholly real; and they then conceived it to be their duty to try to put something more real in its place. In so doing they performed a political service, but they also unconsciously rendered a service to logic. For their inversion of Hegel's principle helps us to see how wretchedly ambiguous it is. Thus, if the word 'real' is used to mean 'existent' and the word 'rational' is used, as Hegel seems to have intended, to mean what is in accordance with logic, it will be necessarily true that everything that is real is rational; for what is logically impossible cannot exist. On the other hand, it will not be true that everything that is rational is real; for many states of affairs that do not exist are logically possible. The word 'rational', however, can also be used, and is indeed most commonly used, as a term of value. As applied to a political system, it serves to claim that the system is such as to bring about the ends of which the speaker approves; and it carries the implication that the ends in question are such as any reasonable man would share. But if the word 'rational' is used in this sense, the statement that the real is the rational is by no means necessarily true. For, whatever may be the set of values that is ascribed to the reasonable man, it is an open question whether they are satisfied. Assuredly much that exists will not come up to them, and very likely nothing exists that does. But, thirdly, the word 'real' may itself be used as a term of value; and in that case the principle that the real is the rational becomes entirely verbal. It merely expresses the speaker's intention to use the words 'real' and 'rational' as equivalent terms of approbation. Thus in the senses in which it is true the principle is trivial, and in the sense in which it is not trivial it is not necessarily true.

The merit of this example is that it again brings out the point that, in politics as in morals, the fact that something is what it is does not by any means entail that it is what it ought to be; nor does the fact that something is considered valuable by any means entail that it exists. Within the domain of fact, the study of politics can yield us fruitful hypotheses about the ways in which political institutions develop. It can enable us to assess the probability that from a given set of circumstances a given situation will result. But over and above this, there remains the question what it is that we desire to bring about. Thus, when Marx said 'Philosophers have previously offered various interpretations of the world. Our business is to change it,'[8] he was making a judgment of value. He was implying that the existing state of affairs was not what it ought to be, and consequently that it ought to be changed. He himself, indeed, might not have admitted this, because of his historical determinism. He might have replied that in saying it was 'our business' to change the world, he was merely calling upon his contemporaries to fulfil their necessary historical role. But if their role was really determined for them, then they were bound to fulfil it, and there was no sense in urging them to do so. The call to arms was needed to bring about something that Marx wished to happen; it was designed to influence events, not merely to encumber fate with help. That the future will be what it will be is indeed an analytic truth: but it does not prevent it also being true that the future will be what we make it. What changes are possible at any given moment is a subject for scientific inquiry; but the decision, which we then have to make, that one or other of these changes is the most desirable is not itself a scientific hypothesis but a judgment of value. It represents a moral choice.

No more than the scientist is the philosopher specially privileged to lay down the rules of conduct, or to prescribe an ideal form of life. If he has strong opinions on these points, and wishes to convert others to them, his philosophical training may give him a certain advantage in putting them persuasively: but, whether or not the values that he recommends are found to be acceptable, it is not from his philosophy that they can derive their title to acceptance. His professional task is done when he has made the issues clear. For in morals and in politics,

[8] See his 'Eleven Theses on Feuerbach'.

at the stage where politics become a matter of morals, there is no repository of truth to which only the learned few have access. The question how men ought to live is one to which there is no authoritative answer. It has to be decided by each man for himself.

TWO

Logical Positivism – A Debate[1]

Metaphysics, Analytic Philosophy and Science

AYER: Well, Father Copleston, you've asked me to summarize Logical Positivism for you and it's not very easy. For one thing, as I understand it, Logical Positivism is not a system of philosophy. It consists rather in a certain technique – a certain kind of attitude towards philosophic problems. Thus, one thing which those of us who are called logical positivists tend to have in common is that we deny the possibility of philosophy as a speculative discipline. We should say that if philosophy was to be a branch of knowledge, as distinct from the sciences, it would have to consist in logic or in some form of analysis, and our reason for this would be somewhat as follows. We maintain that you can divide propositions into two classes, formal and empirical. Formal propositions, like those of logic and mathematics, depend for their validity on the conventions of a symbol system. Empirical propositions, on the other hand, are statements of actual or possible observation, or hypotheses, from which such statements can be logically derived; and it is they that constitute science in so far as science isn't purely mathematical. Now our contention is that this exhausts the field of what may be called speculative knowledge. Consequently we reject metaphysics, if this be understood, as I think it commonly has been, as an attempt to gain knowledge about the world by nonscientific means. In as much as metaphysical statements are not testable by observation, we hold they are not descriptive of anything. And from this we should conclude that if philosophy is to be a cognitive activity it must be purely critical. It would take the form of trying to elucidate the concepts that were used in science or mathematics or in everyday language.

[1] 'Logical Positivism' was originally a debate between A. J. Ayer and F. C. Copleston on the Third Programme of the BBC on 13 June 1949. It was included in A. J. Ayer (ed.), *Logical Positivism* (Glencoe, Illinois, Free Press; London, George Allen & Unwin, 1959).

COPLESTON: Well, Professor Ayer, I can quite understand, of course, philosophers confining themselves to logical analysis if they wish to do so, and I shouldn't dream of denying or of belittling in any way its utility: I think it's obviously an extremely useful thing to do to analyze and clarify the concepts used in science. In everyday life, too, there are many terms used that practically have taken on an emotional connotation – 'progressive' or 'reactionary' or 'freedom' or 'the modern mind' – to make clear to people what's meant or what they mean by those terms, or the various possible meanings, is a very useful thing. But if the logical positivist means that logical analysis is the *only* function of philosophy – that's the point at which I should disagree with him. And so would many other philosophers disagree – especially on the Continent. Don't you think that by saying what philosophy is, one presupposes a philosophy, or takes up a position as a philosopher? For example, if one divides significant propositions into two classes, namely, purely formal propositions and statements of observation, one is adopting a philosophical position: one is claiming that there are no necessary propositions which are not purely formal. Moreover, to claim that metaphysical propositions, to be significant, should be verifiable as scientific hypotheses are verifiable is to claim that metaphysics, to be significant, should not be metaphysics.

AYER: Yes, I agree that my position is philosophical, but not that it is metaphysical, as I hope to show later. To say what philosophy is, is certainly a philosophical act, but by this I mean that it is itself a question of philosophical analysis. We have to decide, among other things, what it is that we are going to call 'philosophy' and I have given you my answer. It is not, perhaps, an obvious answer but it at least has the merit that it rescues philosophical statements from becoming either meaningless or trivial. But I don't suppose that we want to quarrel about how we're going to use a word, so much as to discuss the points underlying what you've said. You would hold, I gather, that in the account I gave of the possible fields of knowledge something was left out.

COPLESTON: Yes.

AYER: And that which is left out is what people called philosophers might well be expected to study?

COPLESTON: Yes, I should hold that philosophy, at any rate metaphysical philosophy, begins, in a sense, where science leaves off. In my personal opinion, one of the chief functions of metaphysics is to open the mind to the transcendent – to remove the ceiling of the room, as it were, the room being the world as amenable to scientific handling and investigation. But this is not to say that the metaphysician is simply concerned with the transcendent. Phenomena themselves (objects of what you would probably call 'experience') can be considered from the metaphysical angle. The problem of universals, for instance, is a metaphysical problem. I say that metaphysical philosophy begins, *in a sense*, where science leaves off, because I do not mean to imply that the metaphysician cannot begin until science has finished its work. If this were so, the metaphysician would be quite unable to start. I mean that he asks other questions than those asked by the scientist and pursues a different method.

AYER: To say that philosophy begins where science leaves off is perfectly all right if you mean that the philosopher takes the results of the scientist, analyzes them, shows the logical connection of one proposition with another, and so on. But if you say that it leaps into a quite different realm – the realm which you describe as the 'transcendent' – then I think I cease to follow you. And I think I can explain why I cease to follow you. I hold a principle, known as the principle of verification, according to which a statement intended to be a statement of fact is meaningful only if it's either formally valid, or some kind of observation is relevant to its truth or falsehood. My difficulty with your so-called transcendent statements is that their truth or falsehood doesn't, it seems to me, make the slightest difference to anything that anyone experiences.

COPLESTON: I don't care for the phrase 'transcendent statement'. I think myself that some positive descriptive statements about the transcendent are possible; but, leaving that out of account, I think that one of the possible functions of the philosopher (a function which you presumably exclude) is to reveal the limits of science as a complete and exhaustive description and analysis of reality.

AYER: Limits of science? You see I can quite well understand your saying that science is limited if you mean only that many more things may be discovered. You may say, for example, that the physics of the seventeenth century was limited in so far as physicists of the eighteenth, nineteenth and twentieth centuries have gone very much further.

COPLESTON: No, I didn't mean that at all. Perhaps I can illustrate what I mean in reference to anthropology. The biochemist can describe man within his own terms of reference and up to a certain extent. But, although biochemistry may doubtless continue to advance, I see no reason to suppose that the biochemist will be able to give an exhaustive analysis of man. The psychologist certainly would not think so. Now, one of the possible functions of a philosopher is to show how all these scientific analyses of man – the analyses of the biochemist, the empirical psychologist and so on – are unable to achieve the exhaustive analysis of the individual human being. Karl Jaspers, for example, would maintain that man as free, i.e. precisely as free, cannot be adequately handled by any scientist who presupposes the applicability of the principle of deterministic causality and conducts his investigations with that presupposition in mind. I am not a follower of Karl Jaspers; but I think that to call attention to what he calls *Existenz* is a legitimate philosophical procedure.

Metaphysical and Scientific Explanation

AYER: I do not see that you can know *a priori* that human behaviour is inexplicable. The most you can say is that our present stock of psychological hypotheses isn't adequate to explain certain features of it: and you may very well be right. But what more is required is better psychological investigation. We need to form new theories and test the theories by further observation, which is again the method of science. It seems to me that all you've said, when you've talked of the limits of science, is simply that a given science may not explain things, or explain as much as you would like to see explained. But that, which to me seems to be perfectly acceptable, is only a historical statement about a point which science has reached at a given stage. It doesn't show that there's room for a quite different kind of discipline, and you haven't made clear to me what that different kind of discipline which you reserve for the philosopher is supposed to be.

COPLESTON: Well, I think that one of the possible functions of the philosopher is to consider what is sometimes called the non-empirical or intelligible self. There is an obvious objection, from your point of view, against the phrase 'non-empirical self'; but I would like to turn to metaphysics in general. The scientists can describe various particular aspects of things, and all the sciences together can give, it is true, a very general description of reality. But the scientist, precisely as scientist, does not raise, for example, the question why anything is there at all. To raise this question is, in my opinion, one of the functions of the philosopher. You may say that the question cannot be answered. I think that it can; but, even if it could not be answered, I consider that it is one of the functions of the philosopher to show that there is such a problem. Some philosophers would say that metaphysics consists in raising problems rather than in answering them definitively; and, though I do not myself agree with the sheerly agnostic position, I think that there is value in raising the metaphysical problems, quite apart from the question whether one can or cannot answer them definitively. That is why I said earlier on that one of the functions of the philosopher is to open the mind to the transcendent, to take the ceiling off the room – to use again a rather crude metaphor.

AYER: Yes, but there's a peculiarity about these 'why' questions. Supposing someone asks you 'Why did the light go out?' You may tell him the light went out because there was a fuse. And he then says 'Why does the light go out when it is fused?' Then perhaps you tell him a story about electrical connections, wires, and so on. That is the 'how' story. Then, if he's not satisfied with that, you may give him the general theory of electricity which is again a 'how' story. And then if he's not satisfied with that, you give him the general theory of electromagnetics, which is again a 'how' story. You tell him that things function in this way at this level, and then your 'why' answers are deductions from that. So that in the ordinary sense of a 'why' question, putting a 'why' question is asking for a 'how' answer at a higher logical level – a more general 'how' answer. Well now if you raise this question with regard to the world as a whole, you're asking for what? The most general possible theory?

COPLESTON: No, the metaphysical question I have in mind is a different sort of question. If I ask, for example, how the earth comes to be in its present condition, I expect an answer which refers to empirical causes and conditions. There I quite agree with you. I go to the astronomer for an answer. And if one persists in asking such questions, I dare say one could, in theory, go back indefinitely. At least, I am prepared to admit the possibility. But if I ask why there are phenomena at all, why there is something rather than nothing, I am not asking for an answer in terms of empirical causes and conditions. Even if the series of phenomena did go back indefinitely, without beginning, I could still raise the question as to why the infinite series of phenomena exists, how it comes to be there. Whether such a question can be answered or not is obviously another matter. But if I ask whether anything lies behind phenomena, whether anything is responsible for the series, finite or infinite, of phenomena, the answer – supposing that there is an answer – must, in my opinion, refer to a reality beyond or behind phenomena. But in any case to ask why any finite phenomena exist, why there is something rather than nothing, is to ask a different sort of question from the question why water tends to flow downhill rather than uphill.

AYER: But my objection is that your very notion of an explanation of all phenomena is self-contradictory.

COPLESTON: What is the contradiction?

AYER: The contradiction is, I think, that if you accept my interpretation of what 'why' questions are, then asking a 'why' question is always asking for a more general description; and asking for the 'why' of that is asking for a more general description still. And then you say, 'Give me an answer to a "why" which doesn't take the form of a description', and that's a contradiction. It's like saying 'Give me a description more general than any description, which itself is not a description.' And clearly nobody can do that.

COPLESTON: That is not the question I am asking. There would be a contradiction if I did not distinguish between a scientific question and a metaphysical question, but a metaphysical question concerns the intelligible structure of reality in so far as it is *not* amenable to the investigation by the methods of empirical science. It seems to me that when I propose a metaphysical question you ask me to restate the question as though it were a scientific question. But, if I could do that, the question would not be a metaphysical question, would it?

AYER: Well, what form would your metaphysical question take?

COPLESTON: Well, in my opinion, the existence of phenomena in general requires some explanation, and I should say explanation in terms of a transcendent reality. I maintain that this is a possible philosophical question. Whatever the answer may be, it obviously cannot consist in a further description of phenomena. Aristotle asserted that philosophy begins with wonder. If someone feels no wonder at the existence of the physical world, he is unlikely to ask any questions about its existence as such.

AYER: If you ask anything of that kind, it still means that you're treating your transcendent reality, or rather the statements about your transcendent reality, in the same way as a scientific hypothesis. It becomes a very, very general scientific hypothesis. Only you want to say it's not like a scientific hypothesis. Why not? I suppose it's because you can't test it in any way. But if you can't test it in any way, then you've not got an explanation and you haven't answered my question.

COPLESTON: Well, at this point I should like to remark that you're presupposing that one must be able to test every hypothesis in a certain way. I do not mean to allow that every metaphysical statement is a hypothesis; but even if it were, it would not be scientifically testable without ceasing to be a metaphysical statement. You seem to me to reject from the beginning the reflective work of the intellect on which rational metaphysics depends. Neither Spinoza nor Fichte nor Hegel nor St Thomas Acquinas supposed that one could investigate scientifically what they respectively believed to be the metaphenomenal reality. But each of them thought that intellectual reflection can lead the mind to postulate that reality.

AYER: Well in one sense of the word, of course it can. You can penetrate disguises. If something's heavily camouflaged you can understand that it's there even if you can't see it. That's because you know what it would be like to see it independently of seeing it in disguise. Now your kind of penetration is a very queer one, because you say you can discern things lying behind other things with simply no experience of stripping off the disguise and coming across the thing undisguised.

COPLESTON: It's not exactly a question of a disguise. I can strip off camouflage and see the camouflaged thing with my eyes. But no metaphysician would pretend that one could see a metaphenomenal reality with the eyes: it can be apprehended only by an intellectual activity, though that activity must, of necessity, begin with the objects of sense experience and introspection. After all, you yourself *reflect on* the data of experience: your philosophy does not consist in stating atomic experiences.

AYER: No indeed it doesn't. Since I hold that philosophy consists in logical analysis, it isn't in my view a matter of stating experiences at all: if by stating experiences you mean just describing them.

COPLESTON: It seems to me that we are discussing my particular brand of metaphysics rather than Logical Positivism. However, I should maintain that the very ability to raise the question of the existence of the world (or of the series of phenomena, if you like) implies a dim awareness of the non-self-sufficiency of the world. When this awareness becomes articulate and finds expression, it may lead to a metaphysical speculation, to a conscious thinking of contingent existence *as such*. And I should maintain that an intellectual apprehension of the nature of what I call contingent being as such involves an apprehension of its relatedness to self-grounded being. Some philosophers (Hegel among them, I think) would hold that one cannot think finite being *as such* without implicitly thinking the infinite. The words 'as such' are, I should say, important. I can perfectly well think of a cow, for example, without thinking of any metaphysical reality; but if I abstract from its characteristics as a cow and think of it merely as contingent being, I pass into the sphere of metaphysics.

AYER: But it's precisely questions like this question about the world as a whole that I think we should rule out. Supposing you asked a question like 'Where do all things come from?' Now that's a perfectly meaningful question as regards any given event. Asking where it came from is asking for a description of some event prior to it. But if you generalize that question, it becomes meaningless. You're then asking what event is prior to all events. Clearly no event can be prior to all events, because if it's a member of the class of all events it must be included in it and therefore can't be prior to it. Let me give another instance which illustrates the same point. One can say of any one perception that it's a hallucination, meaning by this that it isn't corroborated by one's own further perceptions or by those of other people, and that makes sense. Now, some people, and philosophers too, I'm afraid, want to generalize this and say with a profound air: 'Perhaps all our experiences are hallucinatory.' Well, that of course becomes meaningless. In exactly the same way I should say that this question of where does it all come from isn't meaningful.

COPLESTON: It isn't meaningful if the only meaningful questions are those which can be answered by the methods of empirical science, as you presuppose. In my opinion, you are unduly limiting 'meaningfulness' to a certain restricted kind of meaningfulness. Now, the possibility of raising the question of the absolute seems to depend largely on the nature of relations. If one denies that one can discern any implication or internal relation in the existing phenomena considered as such, then a metaphysic of the absolute becomes an impossible thing. If the mind can discern such a relation, then I think a metaphysic of the absolute is possible.

AYER: Metaphysic of the absolute? I am afraid my problem still is, What questions are being asked? Now supposing one were to ask, Is the world dependent on something outside itself? Would you regard that as a possible question?

COPLESTON: Yes I think it's a possible question.

AYER: Well then you're using a very queer sense of causation, aren't you? Because in the normal sense in which you talk of one event being dependent or consequent on another, you'd be meaning that they had some kind of temporal relation to each other. In fact, normally if one uses the word causation one is saying that the later event is dependent on the earlier, in the sense that all cases of the earlier are also cases of the later. But now you can't be meaning that, because if you were you'd be putting your cause in the world.

COPLESTON: Well now, aren't you presupposing the validity of a certain philosophical interpretation of causality? It may be true or false; but it is a philosophical view, and it is not one which I accept.

AYER: But surely on any view of causality, the causal relation holds between things that happen, and presumably anything that happens is in the world. I don't know what you mean by your other-worldly reality, but if you make it a cause you automatically bring this supposed reality into the world.

COPLESTON: It would bring the world into relation with the reality; and personally I should not dream of adopting any metaphysic which did not start with experience of this world. But the relating of the world to a being outside the world would not bring that being into the world. Incidentally, I have just used the word 'outside'. This illustrates admirably the inadequacy of language for expressing metaphysical ideas. 'Outside' suggests distance in space, 'independent' would be better. But I should like to make some remarks about this use of the word 'cause'. I am very glad you brought the question up. First of all, as far as I understand the use of the term by scientists, causal laws would mean for them, I suppose, statistical generalizations from observed phenomena. At least this would be one of the meanings, I think.

AYER: That makes it rather more genetic than it need be. I mean the question is not really where these scientific expressions have come from, but what use they're put to. Let us say that they are generalizations which refer to observable events or phenomena, if you will.

COPLESTON: I agree, of course, that one cannot use the principle of causality, if understood in a sense which involves references to phenomena exclusively, in order to transcend phenomena. Supposing, for example, that I understood by the principle of causality the proposition that the initial state of every phenomenon is determined by a preceding phenomenon or by preceding phenomena, quite apart from the fact that it may not apply even to all phenomena. But what I understand by the philosophic principle of causality is the general proposition that every being which has not in itself its reason of existence depends for its existence on an extrinsic reality which I call, in this connection, cause. This principle says nothing as to the character of the cause. It may be free or not free. Therefore it cannot be refuted by infra-atomic indeterminism, if there is such a thing, any more than it is refuted by the free acts of men. Some philosophers would probably say that this principle has only subjective necessity; but I don't hold this view myself, nor do I see any very cogent reason for holding it. Moreover, though the principle is, in a sense, presupposed by the scientist when he traces the connection between a phenomenal effect and a phenomenal cause, the principle mentions not phenomenal causes, but an extrinsic reality. If one is speaking of all beings which have not in themselves the reason for their existence, the extrinsic reality in question must transcend them. To my way of thinking the philosophic principle of causality is simply an implication of the intelligibility of phenomena, if these are regarded as contingent events.

AYER: Well then, again I think I should accuse you of the fallacy of misplaced generalization. You see, what is the intelligibility of phenomena? You can understand sentences; you can understand an argument; they can be intelligible or not. But what is the understanding of phenomena? Even a particular one, let alone all phenomena? Well I think you could give a sense to understanding a particular phenomenon. You would recognize some description of it as an accurate description, and then understanding the phenomenon would be a matter of explaining this description, that is, of deducing it from some theory. Now, you say, are all phenomena intelligible? Does that mean that you are looking for a single theory from which every true proposition can be deduced? I doubt if you could find one, but even if you did, you'd want that theory again, wouldn't you, to be explained in its turn, which gives you an infinite regress? You see, phenomena just happen, don't they? Is there a question of their being intelligible or not intelligible?

COPLESTON: No, phenomena don't 'just happen'. I didn't 'just happen'. If I did, my existence would be unintelligible. And I am not prepared to acquiesce in the idea that the series of phenomena, even if infinite, just happens, unless you can give me a good reason for doing so. I think you can legitimately raise the question why there is finite existence as such. Whether it's answerable or not is another pair of shoes.

AYER: Well, I quite agree that many metaphysicians have supposed themselves to be asking and answering questions of this kind. But I still want to say that I don't regard these as genuine questions, nor do I regard the answers as intelligible. For example, let us take the case of someone who says that the answer is that reality is the absolute expressing itself. I say such an answer explains nothing because I can do nothing with it, and I don't know what it would be like for such a proposition to be true. I should say the same about all statements of this kind.

COPLESTON: And why should it be necessary to do anything with a proposition?

AYER: Because you put this up as a hypothesis, and a hypothesis is supposed to explain.

COPLESTON: An explanation is meant to explain, certainly. What I meant was that there is no reason why we should be able to deduce 'practical' consequences from it.

AYER: Well, if you don't get practical answers what kind of answers do you get?

COPLESTON: Theoretical answers, of course. I should have thought, as a simple-minded historian of philosophy, that one has been given a good many metaphysical answers. They cannot all be true; but the answers are forthcoming all the same.

AYER: Yes, but the trouble still is that these answers are given not as explanations of any particular event, but of all events. And I wonder if this notion of an explanation of all events isn't itself faulty. When I explain something by telling you that *this* is the way it works, I thereby exclude other possibilities. So that any genuine explanation is compatible with one course of events, and incompatible with another. That, of course, is what distinguishes one explanation from another. But something which purported to explain all events, not merely all events that did occur, but any event that could occur, would be empty as an explanation because nothing would disagree with it. You might explain all events as they do occur, provided you allowed the possibility that if they occurred differently your explanation would be falsified. But the trouble with these so-called metaphysical explanations is that they don't merely purport to explain what does happen, but to serve equally for anything that could conceivably happen. However you changed your data, the same explanation would still hold, but that makes it as an explanation absolutely vacuous.

COPLESTON: I think that what you are demanding is that any explanation of the existence of phenomena should be a scientific hypothesis. Otherwise you will not recognize it as an explanation. This is to say, 'All explanations of facts are of the type of scientific hypotheses or they are not explanations at all.' But the explanation of all finite beings cannot be a scientific explanation, i.e. in the technical use of the word 'scientific'. But it can be a rational explanation all the same. 'Rational' and 'scientific' are not equivalent terms, and it is a prejudice to think that they are equivalent.

AYER: But does a nonscientific explanation explain anything? Let me take an example. Suppose someone said that the explanation for things happening as they did was that it answered the purposes of the deity. Now I should say that would only be meaningful if you could show that events going this way rather than that way answered his purpose. But if you're going to say that whatever happens is going to answer his purpose, then it becomes useless as an explanation. In fact it's not an explanation at all. It becomes empty of significance because it's consistent with everything.

COPLESTON: If I seek the explanation of the world, I am considering an ontological question, and what I am looking for is an ontological explanation and not simply a logical explanation.

Necessary and Contingent Propositions

AYER: Now I think I get more of what you're saying. But aren't you asking for something contradictory? You see, so long as an explanation is contingent, that is something that might be otherwise logically, you're going to say it's not a sufficient explanation. So that you want for your proposition something that is logically necessary. But of course once your proposition becomes logically necessary it is a purely formal one, and so doesn't explain anything. So what you want is to have a proposition that is both contingent and necessary, contingent in so far as it's got to describe the world, necessary in so far as it's not just something happening to be, but something that must be. But that's a contradiction in terms.

COPLESTON: There is a contradiction only if one grants an assumption of yours which I deny. A proposition which is applicable to a contingent thing or event is not necessarily a contingent proposition. Nor is the proposition that it is contingent an analytic or self-evident proposition. In any case I'm not seeking the ontological explanation of the world in a proposition.

AYER: But shouldn't you be?

COPLESTON: Why should one be?

AYER: Well, what is explanation except a matter of deriving one proposition from another? But perhaps you prefer to call your ontological principle a fact. Then what you're asking for is a fact that is at one and the same time contingent and necessary, and you can't have it.

COPLESTON: Why should it at one and the same time be contingent and necessary?

AYER: It's got to be contingent in order to do for an explanation. It's got to be necessary because you're not satisfied with anything contingent.

COPLESTON: I shouldn't admit that it's got to be contingent in order to do its work of explanation. I'd say that it didn't do its work of explanation if it was contingent.

AYER: But how possibly could you derive anything empirical from a necessary proposition?

COPLESTON: I am not attempting to derive an empirical thing from a necessary proposition. I do attempt, however, to render empirical things intelligible by reference to an absolute or necessary being.

AYER: But surely a necessary being can only be one concerning which the proposition that it exists is necessary?

COPLESTON: The proposition would be necessary, yes. But it doesn't follow that one can discern its necessity. I'm not holding, for instance, the ontological argument for the existence of God, though I do believe that God's existence is the ultimate ontological explanation of phenomena.

AYER: Well now, ultimate in what sense? In the sense that you can't find a more general proposition from which it can be deduced?

COPLESTON: An ultimate principle or proposition is obviously not deducible – if you must speak of propositions instead of beings.

AYER: Well, it is better so.

COPLESTON: The world doesn't consist of contingent propositions, though things may be expressed in contingent propositions. Nor should I say that a necessary being consists of necessary propositions.

AYER: No, of course I shouldn't say that the world consists of propositions: it's very bad grammar, bad logical grammar. But the words necessary and contingent, which you introduced, do apply to propositions in their ordinary logical acceptance.

COPLESTON: Yes, they do apply to propositions, but I do not accept the position that all necessary or certain propositions are tautologies. I think that there are necessary or certain propositions which also apply to things.

AYER: Yes, but not in any different sense. A statement to the effect that a being is necessary could be translated into a statement that a proposition referring to that being was necessary. Now you've got into the difficulty that from a logically necessary proposition, which I should say meant a *formally* valid proposition, and therefore a materially empty proposition, you want to derive a proposition with material content. You do want to have it both ways, you want to have statements, facts if you like, which are both contingent and necessary, and that, of course, you can't have. And a metaphysician can't have it either.

COPLESTON: But, you see, I do not believe that all certain propositions are only formally valid, in the sense of being tautologies. I am not saying that there are propositions which are both necessary and contingent: what I am saying is that there are, in my opinion, propositions which are certain and which are yet applicable to reality. If the reality in question happens to be contingent, that doesn't make the proposition contingent, if by contingent you mean an uncertain empirical hypothesis.

AYER: Well, then I must protest I *don't* understand your use of the word 'necessary'. You see, it seems to me we've got a fairly clear meaning for 'logically necessary', propositions that are formally valid, I should call logically necessary; and I can understand 'causally necessary'. I should say that events are linked by causal necessity when there is some hypothesis, not itself logically necessary, from which their connection is deducible. Now you want to introduce a third sense of necessity, which is the crucial sense for you, which isn't either of those, but is – what?

The Nature of Logical Necessity

COPLESTON: By a necessary proposition I mean a *certain* proposition. You may say that there are no certain propositions which are applicable to reality; but that is another matter. Earlier in our discussion I distinguished at least two senses of the principle of causality. I regard the philosophic version as certain. In other words, besides purely logical propositions and what you would, I think, call empirical hypotheses, I believe that there are metaphysical propositions which are certain. Now take the principle of contradiction. I think that there is a metaphysical version of the principle which is not simply what is sometimes called 'a law of thought', but is rather imposed on the mind by its experience of being, or, better, by its reflection on its experience of being. But I presume that you would say that the principle is only formal. Well, it seems to me that if it's purely formal, then I ought to admit there's a possibility of this piece of paper being white and not white at the same time. I can't think it, but I ought, I think, on your assumption, to admit the abstract possibility of it. But I can't think it, I can't admit its abstract possibility.

AYER: Well, if you tell me that the paper is both white and not-white, of course you don't tell me anything about fact, do you?

COPLESTON: Well, no, I should say that is because one can't admit the possibility of its being both white and not-white at the same time.

AYER: You can't admit that possibility, given existing conventions, about the use of the word 'not', but of course you could perfectly well introduce a convention by which it would be meaningful. Supposing you chose, when the paper was grey, to say it was white and not-white. Then you would have altered your logic. But given that you're using a logic in which you exclude 'p and not-p', then of course you exclude the paper's being white and not-white.

COPLESTON: A logic in which you don't exclude 'p and not-p' may have uses; but I do not see that any significant statement can be made about this piece of paper in such a logic. It seems to me that if the principle of contradiction is purely formal and tautological, that I ought to admit the possibility of its being white – what I *call* white – of its being white and not-white at the same time; but I can't think that.

AYER: No, of course you can't. You shouldn't be expected to, because to think that would be to use symbols in a way not in accordance with the conventions under which that particular group of symbols is to be used. But of course you could describe the same experience in a different sort of logic; you could introduce a different grammar of colour-classification which allowed you to say that the paper was and was not a certain colour, for example in the case where the colour is changing. Certain Hegelians want to do that, and we have no call to stop them. There's no particular advantage in doing it, because you can equally well describe the phenomenon in Aristotelian logic; but if, in the case where it's changing its colour, you like to say that it's both white and not-white, that's all right, so long as it's understood how your terms are being used.

COPLESTON: It seems to me that it would be the nature of the thing itself that forced me to speak in a certain way. If I have before me Smith and Jackson, I can't think of Smith being Smith-and-Jackson at the same time. I should say that it's not merely a law of thought or an analytic tautology that forces me to say that, but the nature of the things themselves.

AYER: I agree that such conventions are based on empirical facts, the nature of your experiences, and adapted to meet them; but you can again quite easily imagine circumstances in which you would be inclined to change your logic in that respect. Certain neurotic phenomena might very well incline one to say that Smith had acquired some of Jackson's personality, and then if such things were very common, you might get a new usage of 'person', according to which you could have two different persons inhabiting one body, or one person inhabiting different bodies.

COPLESTON: Well, I can agree to speak about things using any terms I like, I suppose: I can agree to call this paper red, when I know that it's white, but that in no way alters the nature of the paper.

AYER: No. No one is claiming that it does. The fact is that the paper looks as it does. If you have a symbol system which you use to describe those facts, then that symbol system will itself have certain conventions, governing the use of certain symbols in it. Now I think in any given symbol system I could separate what I call the logical expressions, and the descriptive expressions. Words like 'not', I should say, were logical expressions.

COPLESTON: Supposing one had another logical system. Is there any rule of speaking within that system? And suppose now you are using a three-valued logic. You could perfectly well use that to describe what you now describe, could you?

AYER: Yes, the difference would be that you couldn't make certain inferences that you now make. Thus, from the fact that the paper was *not* not-white you couldn't then infer that it was white: you could only infer that it was either white or the intermediate state, which you would choose to describe, not by a separate word, which brings you back to your two-valued system, but by saying both white and not-white.

COPLESTON: My point is that there are, in my opinion, certain propositions which are founded on an experience of reality and which are not, therefore, simply formal propositions or tautologies. If one wishes to keep within the sphere of purely formal logic one can, on this understanding, employ a three-valued logic. But purely formal propositions are not likely to help one in metaphysics. No doubt you would say 'Hear, hear.' But I admit, and you do not, propositions which are certain and yet not purely formal. Some people would call such propositions 'synthetic *a priori* propositions', but I do not care for the phrase myself, on account of its associations with the philosophy of Kant. However, the issue between us is in any case whether or not there are propositions which are certain and which yet apply to reality; and I do not think that the introduction of the three-valued logic really affects the point. I have no wish to deny that there may be propositions which *are* purely formal. But I am convinced of the existence of valid metaphysical propositions. However, I should like to raise another question, in order to get your views on it. Perhaps you would help me to attain clarity in the matter. My question is this. Within a three-valued system of logic is there any rule of consistency at all?

AYER: Yes. Otherwise it wouldn't be a system of logic.

COPLESTON: Then does it not seem that there is at least one proto-proposition which governs all possible systems of logic?

AYER: No, that doesn't follow.

COPLESTON: Well, supposing in a system without the principle of contradiction one simply disregarded the principles of consistency within the system. Would you say then that one was contradicting oneself?

AYER: No, because in that sense the notion of contradiction as you understand it wouldn't apply.

COPLESTON: Well, would you say one was at variance with the rules of the game?

AYER: Yes, you wouldn't be playing that game.

COPLESTON: Then there *are* some laws, if one likes to speak in that way, that govern all games?

AYER: No, there are no laws that govern all games, but each game has a certain set of laws governing it.

COPLESTON: Well, consistency, or observation of law, within a game, whatever these laws may be, is itself, it seems to me, a kind of proto-principle.

AYER: What's common to all of them is that if the game is conducted in accordance with certain rules, then if you don't observe those rules, you're not playing that game, though possibly some other.

COPLESTON: And are you producing unintelligible statements?

AYER: Whether the statements were intelligible or not, of course, would depend on whether they could be interpreted as counters in some other game.

COPLESTON: Ah, but within the game itself . . .

AYER: No, they would not be.

COPLESTON: Well then, it does seem to me that there is, at any rate, a principle of consistency, which seems to me to be a kind of proto-proposition governing all reasoning.

AYER: Well, take it this way. Take it in the case of chess, or bridge. Now you might play bridge, and revoke.

COPLESTON: Yes.

AYER: And if it's done once, occasionally, that's considered to be a slip, and you haven't stopped playing bridge. But supposing now you make revoking a general habit, and nobody worries, you're allowed to revoke when you please, then you're playing some different game. Now possibly you might be able to determine the rules of that game too.

COPLESTON: Yes.

AYER: Well now, exactly the same with logic, you see: in an ordinary, say Aristotelian, logic, certain moves are allowed.

COPLESTON: Necessitated, I should say. Yes.

AYER: And certain moves, including not admitting contradictories, are disallowed.

COPLESTON: Well?

AYER: Now supposing you have a game which breaks those rules, then you have a different game.

COPLESTON: Granted. But I don't admit that all logics are games, in the sense that no logic applies to reality or that all possible logics apply equally well. I see no *reason* to say this. If one did say it, the statement would be a philosophical, even a metaphysical, statement, and therefore, I suppose, according to your view, technically meaningless. However, supposing that they are games, there is a certain architectonic governing the playing of those games.

AYER: No. All you can say is, not that there's any given rule that must be observed in every game, because there isn't, but that in any game there must be some rule. And it is an empirical question which logic is the most useful. Compare the case of alternative geometries.

COPLESTON: Observance of consistency seems to me to mean something more than 'Unless you observe the rules of the game you do not observe the rules of the game.' It means, 'If you contradict yourself, that is, if you contradict your premises and definitions, you do not reason significantly.' That is not an arbitrary or conventional principle, I should suggest.

AYER: But surely all that you are saying is that in a language, namely the one we are now using, where one of the principles of correct reasoning is the observance of the law of non-contradiction, anyone who violates this law isn't reasoning correctly. That is certainly a valid statement, but it *is* conventional.

The Relation of Language to Philosophy

COPLESTON: I should like to know what you, as a logical positivist, think about the relation of language to philosophy. Would you say that philosophy depends on language, in the sense that philosophical ideas depend on grammatical and syntactical structure?

AYER: Not quite in that sense, but I think that philosophy can be said to be about language.

COPLESTON: And you think that to some extent it depends on the language you use to do it in?

AYER: What you can imagine to be possible depends very much upon what kind of symbol system you're using. Yes.

COPLESTON: Can you give me an illustration of the way in which philosophy depends on language?

AYER: Well, I should say, for example, that the belief of Western philosophers in substance was very much bound up with the subject-predicate form of most sentences in Western languages.

COPLESTON: In that case it's a question of empirical investigation, isn't it? I mean as to whether that is the case or not. And we should find, if the theory is true, that if the grammatical and syntactical structure of different languages is different, philosophical problems raised in those languages are different. Surely you can translate the Western philosophical problems into some quite primitive non-European languages. And where difficulty in doing so arises, this is not owing to the grammatical and syntactical structure of the language in question, but owing to the absence of the abstract expression which will correspond to the Western idea. It seems to me that the ideas come before the expression. To say that the expression governs the ideas and the formation of the ideas, is to put the cart before the horse.

AYER: The idea comes before the expression? As an image, or something of that sort?

COPLESTON: Sometimes, of course, it will be an image, but I'm a little doubtful whether all ideas are accompanied by images. But let us take your concrete example, substance. Presumably the Greeks got the idea of substance before they applied the word 'ousia' to it. Let's take a test case. Aristotle wrote in Greek, Avicenna and Averroes in Arabic, and Maimonides, partly at least, in Hebrew. Well, if the theory of the dependence of philosophy on language is true, it ought, I think, to be empirically provable that the difference between the philosophies of

Aristotle, Avicenna, Averroes and Maimonides were due to differences in the grammatical and syntactical structures of the languages they respectively employed. As far as I know that's never been shown. It seems to me that the differences are due to quite other causes, partly theological.

AYER: Maybe. But I still maintain that philosophers have been influenced by language. Of course the interesting thing now is not to find out why they said what they did, but evaluate what it is they were saying, and how far it was significant or true. Now I do think it rather queer that people have been so inclined to believe in substance with no empirical evidence about it whatsoever. I think the grammatical distinction of subject and predicate may be one cause, but I admit that I haven't made the empirical investigation. This is only a conjecture. Similarly I should expect people with ideographic languages to be less concerned about the problem of universals, for example, not being easily able to isolate abstract words.

COPLESTON: Yes, in some cases I should think it would be due not to deficiency of language so much as to direction of interest.

AYER: And then you get things like the tendency to treat all words as names.

COPLESTON: Yes, I know. I mean, I'm not trying to adopt an extreme position. I should question any such extreme position, which I understand you don't hold, as that philosophical problems are simply due to the form of the language which the philosophers who raised those problems used. But I don't wish to deny that some philosophers have been misled by language. For example, if one supposes that to every word there is a corresponding thing, that to redness, for example, there corresponds a redness which is different from the redness of a rose, or any particular red thing; then I should say that the philosopher was misled by language. What I would emphasize would be that this question of the influence of language on philosophy is simply a question of empirical investigation in any given case. The dogmatic *a priori* statement concerning the influence of a language on philosophy should be studiously avoided.

AYER: I agree that it's an empirical question how our own philosophical problems have grown up. But that doesn't affect my contention that the method of solving these problems is that of linguistic analysis.

The Principle of Verifiability

COPLESTON: Well, perhaps we'd better attend to your principle of verifiability. You mentioned the principle of verification earlier. I thought possibly you'd state it, Professor, would you?

AYER: Yes. I'll state it in a fairly loose form, namely that to be significant a statement must be either, on the one hand, a formal statement, one that I should call analytic, or on the other hand empirically testable, and I should try to derive this principle from an analysis of understanding. I should say that understanding a statement meant knowing what would be the case if it were true. Knowing what would be the case if it were true means knowing what observations would verify it, and that in turn means being disposed to accept certain situations as warranting the acceptance or rejection of the statement in question. From which there are two corollaries: one, which we've been talking about to some extent, that statements to which no situations are relevant one way or the other are ruled out as non-factual; and, secondly, that the content of the statement, the cash value, to use James's term, consists of a range of situations, experiences, that would substantiate or refute it.

COPLESTON: Thank you. Now I don't want to misinterpret your position, but it does seem to me that you are presupposing a certain philosophical position. What I mean is this. If you say that any factual statement, in order to be meaningful, must be verifiable, and if you mean by 'verifiable' verifiable by sense experience, then surely you are presupposing that all reality is given in sense experience. If you are presupposing this, you are presupposing that there can be no such thing as a metaphysical reality. And if you presuppose this, you are presupposing a philosophical position which cannot be demonstrated by the principle of verification. It seems to me that logical positivism claims to be what I might call a 'neutral' technique, whereas in reality it presupposes the truth of positivism. Please pardon my saying so, but it looks to me as though the principle of verifiability were excogitated partly *in order to* exclude metaphysical propositions from the range of meaningful propositions.

AYER: Even if that were so, it doesn't prove it invalid. But, to go back, I certainly should not make any statement about *all* reality. That is precisely the kind of statement that I use my principle in order not to make. Nor do I wish to restrict experience to sense experience: I should not at all mind counting what might be called introspectible experiences, or feelings, mystical experiences if you like. It would be true, then, that people who haven't had certain experiences won't understand propositions which refer to them; but that I don't mind either. I can quite well believe that you have experiences different from mine. Let us assume (which after all is an empirical assumption) that you have even a sense different from mine. I should be in the position of the blind man, and then I should admit that statements which are unintelligible to me might be meaningful for you. But I should then go on to say that the factual content of your statements *was* determined by the experiences which counted as their verifiers or falsifiers.

COPLESTON: Yes, you include introspection, just as Hume did. But my point is that you assume that a factually informative statement is significant only if it is verifiable, at least in principle, by direct observation. Now obviously the existence of a metaphysical reality is not verifiable by direct observation, unless you are willing to recognize a purely intellectual intuition as observation. I am not keen on appealing to intuition, though I see no compelling reason to rule it out from the beginning. However, if you mean by 'verifiable' verifiable by direct sense observation and/or introspection, you seem to me to be ruling out metaphysics from the start. In other words, I suggest that acceptance of the principle of verifiability, as you appear to understand it, implies the acceptance of philosophical positivism. I should probably be prepared to accept the principle if it were understood in a very wide sense, that is, if 'verifiable by experience' is understood as including intellectual intuition and also as meaning simply that some experience, actual or conceivable, is relevant to the truth or falsity of the proposition concerned. What I object to is any statement of the principle of verifiability which tacitly assumes the validity of a definite philosophical position.

Now, you'd make a distinction, I think, between analytic statements on the one hand, and empirical statements, and metaphysical and ethical statements on the other. Or at any rate metaphysical statements; leave ethical out of it. You'd call the first group cognitive, and the second emotive. Is that so?

AYER: I think the use of the word emotive is not very happy, although I have used it in the past, because it suggests that they're made with emotion, which isn't necessarily the case; but I accept what you say, if you mean by 'emotive' simply 'non-cognitive'.

COPLESTON: Very well. I accept, of course, your substitution of 'non-cognitive' for 'emotive'. But my objection still remains. By cognitive statements I presume that you mean statements which satisfy the criterion of meaning, that is to say, the principle of verifiability: and by non-cognitive statements I presume you mean statements which do not satisfy that criterion. If this is so, it seems to me that when you say that metaphysical statements are non-cognitive you are not saying much more than that statements which do not satisfy the principle of verifiability do not satisfy the principle of verifiability. In this case, however, no conclusion follows as to the significance or nonsignificance of metaphysical propositions. Unless, indeed, one has previously accepted your philosophical position; that is to say, unless one has first assumed that they are nonsignificant.

AYER: No, it's not as simple as that. My procedure is this: I should claim that the account I've given you of what understanding a statement is, is the account that does apply to ordinary common-sense statements, and to scientific statements, and then I would give a different account of how mathematical statements functioned, and a different account again of value judgments.

COPLESTON: Yes.

AYER: I then say that statements which don't satisfy these conditions are not significant, not to be understood; and I think you can quite correctly object that by putting my definitions together, all I come down to saying is that statements that are not scientific or common-sense statements are not scientific or common-sense statements. But then I want to go further and say that I totally fail to understand – again, I'm afraid, using my own use of understanding: what else can I do? – I fail to understand what these other nonscientific statements and non-common-sense statements, which don't satisfy these criteria, are supposed to be. Someone may say he understands them, in some sense of understanding other than the one I've defined. I reply, It's not clear to me what this sense of understanding is, nor *a fortiori* of course, what it is he understands, nor how these statements function. But of course you may say that in making it a question of how these statements function, I'm presupposing my own criterion.

COPLESTON: Well, then, in your treatment of metaphysical propositions you are either applying the criterion of verifiability or you are not. If you are, then the significance of metaphysical propositions is ruled out of court *a priori*, since the truth of the principle of verifiability, as it seems to be understood by you, inevitably involves the nonsignificance of such propositions. In this case the application of the criterion to concrete metaphysical propositions constitutes a proof neither of the nonsignificance of these propositions nor of the truth of the principle. All that is shown, it seems to me, is that metaphysical propositions do not satisfy a definite assumed criterion of meaning. But it does not follow that one must accept that criterion of meaning. You may legitimately say, if you like, 'I will accept as significant factual statements only those statements which satisfy these particular demands'; but it does not follow that I, or anyone else, has to make those particular demands before we are prepared to accept a statement as meaningful.

AYER: What I do is to give a definition of certain related terms: understanding, meaningful, and so on. I can't force you to accept them, but I can perhaps make you unhappy about the consequences of not accepting them. What I should do is this. I should take any given proposition, and show how it functioned. In the case of a scientific hypothesis, I would show that it had a certain function, namely that, with other premisses, you could deduce certain observational consequences from it. I should then say, this is how this proposition works, this is what it does, this is what it amounts to. I then take a mathematical proposition and play a slightly different game with that, and show that it functions in a certain way, in a calculus, in a symbolic system. You then present me with these other statements, and I then say: On the one hand, they have no observational consequences; on the other hand, they aren't statements of logic. All right. So you understand them. I have given a definition of understanding according to which they're not, in my usage of the term, capable of being understood. Nevertheless you reject my definition. You're perfectly entitled to, because you can give understanding a different meaning if you like. I can't stop you. But now I say, tell me more about them. In what sense are they understood? They are not understood in my sense. They aren't parts of a symbolic system. You can't do anything with them, in the sense of deriving any observational consequences from them. What *do* you want to say about them? Well, you may just want to say, 'They're facts', or something of that sort. Then again I press you on your use of the word 'facts'.

COPLESTON: You seem to me to be demanding that in order for a factual statement to be significant one must be able to deduce observational consequences from it. But I do not see why this should be so. If you mean directly observable consequences, you appear to me to be demanding too much. In any case are there not some propositions which are not verifiable, even in principle, but which would yet be considered by most people to have meaning and to be either true or false? Let me give an example. I don't want to assume the mantle of a prophet, and I hope that the statement is false; but it is this: 'Atomic warfare will take place, and it will blot out the entire human race.' Now, most people would think that this statement has meaning; it means what it says. But how could it possibly be verified empirically? Supposing it were fulfilled, the last man could not say with his last breath, 'Copleston's prediction has been verified', because he would not be entitled to say this until he was dead, that is, until he was no longer in a position to verify the statement.

AYER: It's certainly practically unverifiable. You can't be man, surviving all men. On the other hand, there's no doubt it describes a possible situation. Putting the observer outside the story, one knows quite well what it would be like to observe devastation, and fail to observe any men. Now it wouldn't necessarily be the case that, in order to do that, one had to observe oneself. Just as, to take the case of the past, there were dinosaurs before there were men. Clearly, no man saw that, and clearly I, if I am the speaker, can't myself verify it: but one knows what it would be like to have observed animals and not to have observed men.

COPLESTON: The two cases are different. In regard to the past we have empirical evidence. For example, we have fossils of dinosaurs. But in the case of the prediction I mentioned there would be nobody to observe the evidence and so to verify the proposition.

AYER: In terms of the evidence, of course, it becomes very much easier for me. That would be too easy a way of getting out of our difficulty, because there is also evidence for the atomic thing.

COPLESTON: Yes, but there would be no evidence for the prediction that it will blot out the human race, even if one can imagine the state of affairs that would verify it. Thus by imagining it, one's imagining oneself into the picture.

AYER: No, no.

COPLESTON: Yes, yes. One can imagine the evidence and one can imagine oneself verifying it; but, in point of fact, if the prediction were fulfilled there would be no one there to verify. By importing yourself imaginatively into the picture, you are cancelling out the condition of the fulfillment of the prediction. But let us drop the prediction. You have mentioned imagination. Now, what I should prefer to regard as the criterion of the truth or falsity of an existential proposition is simply the presence or absence of the asserted fact or facts, quite irrespective of whether I can know whether there are corresponding facts or not. If I can at least imagine or conceive the facts, the existence of which would verify the proposition, the proposition has significance for me. Whether I can or cannot know that the facts correspond is another matter.

AYER: I don't at all object to your use of the word 'facts' so long as you allow them to be observable facts. But take the contrary case. Suppose I say 'There's a "drogulus" over there', and you say 'What?' and I say 'Drogulus', and you say 'What's a drogulus?' Well, I say 'I can't describe what a drogulus is, because it's not the sort of thing you can see or touch, it has no physical effects of any kind, but it's a disembodied being.' And you say, 'Well how am I to tell if it's there or not?' and I say 'There's no way of telling. Everything's just the same if it's there or it's not there. But the fact is it's there. There's a drogulus there standing just behind you, spiritually behind you.' Does that make sense?

COPLESTON: It seems to me to do so. I should say that to state that there is a drogulus in the room or not is true or false, provided that you can – that you, at any rate, have some idea of what is meant by a drogulus; and if you can say to me it's a disembodied spirit, then I should say the proposition is either true or false whether one can verify it or not. If you said to me 'By drogulus I merely mean the word "drogulus", and I attach no other significance to it whatsoever.' then I should say that it isn't a proposition any more than if I said 'piffle' was in the room.

AYER: That's right. But what is 'having some idea' of something? I want to say that having an idea of something is a matter of knowing how to recognize it. And you want to say that you can have ideas of things even though there's no possible situation in which you could recognize them, because nothing would count as finding them. I would say that I understand the words 'angel', 'table', 'cloth', 'drogulus', if I'm disposed to accept certain situations as verifying the presence or absence of what the word is supposed to stand for. But you want to admit these words without any reference to experience. Whether the thing they are supposed to stand for exists or not, everything is to go on just the same.

COPLESTON: No. I should say that you can have an idea of something if there's some experience that's relevant to the formation of the idea, not so much to its verification. I should say that I can form the idea of a drogulus or a disembodied spirit from the idea of body and the idea of mind. You may say that there's no mind and there's no spirit, but at any rate there are, as you'll admit, certain internal experiences of thinking and so on which at any rate account for the formation of the idea. Therefore I can say that I have an idea of a drogulus or whatever it is, even though I'm quite unable to know whether such a thing actually exists or not.

AYER: You would certainly not have to know that it exists, but you would have to know what would count as existing.

COPLESTON: Yes. Well, if you mean by 'count as its existing' that there must be some experience relevant to the formation of the idea, then I should agree.

AYER: Not to the formation of the idea, but to the truth or falsity of the propositions in which it is contained.

Are Statements about God Meaningful?

COPLESTON: The word 'metaphysics' and the phrase 'metaphysical reality' can have more than one meaning: but when I refer to a metaphysical reality in our present discussion, I mean a being which in principle, and not merely in fact, transcends the sphere of what can be sensibly experienced. Thus God is a metaphysical reality. Since God is *ex hypothesi* immaterial, He cannot *in principle* be apprehended by the senses. May I add two remarks? My first remark is that I do not mean to imply that no sense experience is in any way relevant to establishing or discovering the existence of a metaphysical reality. I certainly do believe that metaphysics must be based on experiences of some sort. But metaphysics involves intellectual reflection on experience: no amount of immediate sense experience will disclose the existence of a metaphysical reality. In other words, there is a halfway house between admitting only the immediate data of experience and on the other hand leaping to the affirmation of a metaphysical reality without any reference to experience at all. You yourself reflect on the data of experience. The metaphysician carries that reflection a stage further. My second remark is this: because one cannot have a sense experience of a metaphysical reality, it does not follow that one could not have another type of experience of it. And if anyone has such an experience, it does not mean that the metaphysical reality is deprived, as it were, of its metaphysical character and becomes non-metaphysical. I think that this is an important point.

AYER: Yes, but asking are there metaphysical realities isn't like asking are there still wolves in Asia, is it? It looks as if you've got a clear usage for metaphysical reality, and are then asking 'Does it occur or not? Does it exist or not?' and as if I'm arbitrarily denying that it exists. My difficulty is not in answering the question 'Are there, or are there not, metaphysical realities?' but in understanding what usage is being given to the expression 'metaphysical reality'. When am I to count a reality as metaphysical? What would it be like to come upon a metaphysical reality? That's my problem. It isn't that I arbitrarily say there can't be such things, already admitting the use of the term, but that I'm puzzled about the use of the term. I don't know what people who say there are metaphysical realities *mean* by it.

COPLESTON: Well, that brings us back to the beginning, to the function of philosophy. I should say that one can't simply raise in the abstract the question 'Are there metaphysical realities?' Rather one asks, 'Is the character of observable reality of such a kind that it leads one to postulate a metaphysical reality, a reality beyond the physical sphere?' If one grants that it is, even then one can only speak about that metaphysical reality within the framework of human language. And language is after all primarily developed to express our immediate experience of surrounding things, and therefore there's bound to be a radical inadequacy in any statements about a metaphysical reality.

AYER: But you're trying to have it both ways, you see. If it's something that you say doesn't have a meaning in my language, then I don't understand it. It's no good saying 'Oh well, of course it really has a meaning', because what meaning could it have except in the language in which it's used?

COPLESTON: Let's take a concrete example. If I say, for example, 'God is intelligent', well, you may very well say to me 'What meaning can you give to the word "intelligent", because the only intelligence you have experienced is the human intelligence, and are you attributing that to God?' And I should have to say no, because I'm not. Therefore, if we agreed to use the word intelligent simply to mean human intelligence, I should have to say 'God is not intelligent'; but when I said that a stone is not intelligent, I should mean that a stone was, speaking qualitatively, less than intelligent. And when I said that God was intelligent, I should mean that God was more than intelligent, even though I could give no adequate account of what that intelligence was in itself.

AYER: Do you mean simply that he knows more than any given man knows? But to what are you ascribing this property? You haven't begun to make that clear.

COPLESTON: I quite see your point, of course. But what you are inviting me to do is to describe God in terms which will be as clear to you as the terms in which one might describe a familiar object of experience, or an unfamiliar object which is yet so like to familiar objects that it can be adequately described in terms of things which are already familiar to you. But God is *ex hypothesi* unique; and it is quite impossible to describe him adequately by using concepts which normally apply to ordinary objects of experience. If it were possible, he would not be God. So you are really asking me to describe God in a manner which would be possible only if he were not God. I not only freely admit that human ideas of God are inadequate, but also affirm that this must be so, owing to the finitude of the human intellect and to the fact that we can come to a philosophical knowledge of God only through reflection on the things we experience. But it does not follow that we can have *no* knowledge of God, though it does follow that our philosophical knowledge of God cannot be more than analogical.

AYER: Yes, but in the case of an ordinary analogy, when you say that something is like something else you understand what both things are. But in this case if you say something is analogical, I say 'analogical of what?' And then you don't tell me of what. You merely repeat the first term of analogy. Well, I *got* no analogy. It's like saying that something is 'taller than', and I say 'taller than?' and you repeat the first thing you say. Then I understand it's taller than itself, which is nonsense.

COPLESTON: I think that one must distinguish physical analogy and metaphysical analogy. If I say that God is intelligent, I do not say so simply because I want to call God intelligent, but either because I think that the world is such that it must be ascribed in certain aspects at least to a being which can be described in human terms only as intelligent, or because I am satisfied by some argument that there exists an absolute being and then deduce that that being must be described as intelligent. I am perfectly aware that I have no adequate idea of what that intelligence is in itself. I am ascribing to God an attribute which, translated into human terms, must be called intelligence. After all, if you speak of your dog as intelligent, you are using the word in an analogous sense, and it has some meaning for you, even though you do not observe the dog's physical operations. Mathematicians who speak of multi-dimensional space have never observed such a space; but presumably they attach some meaning to the term. When we speak of 'extrasensory perception' we are using the word 'perception' analogously.

AYER: Yes, but mathematical physicists do test their statements by observation, and I know what counts as a case of extrasensory perception. But in the case of your statements I don't know what counts. Of course you *might* give them an empirical meaning, you might say that by 'God is intelligent' you meant that the world had certain features. Then we'd inspect it to see if it had these features or not.

COPLESTON: Well of course I should prefer to start from the features of the world before going to God. I shouldn't wish to argue from God to the features of the world. But to keep within your terms of reference of empiricism, well then I'd say that if God is personal, then he's capable, for example, of entering into relationship with human beings. And it's possible to find human beings who claim to have a personal intercourse with God.

AYER: Then you've given your statement a perfectly good empirical meaning. But it would then be like a scientific theory, and you would be using this in exactly the same way as you might use a concept like electron to account for, explain, predict, a certain range of human experience, namely, that certain people did have these experiences which they described as 'entering into communion with God'. Then one would try to analyze it scientifically, find out in what conditions these things happened, and then you might put it up as a theory. What you'd have done would be psychology.

COPLESTON: Well, as I said, I was entering into your terms of reference. I wouldn't admit that when I say God is personal I merely mean that God can enter into intercourse with human beings. I should be prepared to say that he was personal even if I had no reason for supposing that he entered into intercourse with human beings.

AYER: No, but it's only in that case that one has anything one can control. The facts are that these human beings have these experiences. They describe these experiences in a way which implies more than that they're having these experiences. But if one asks what more, then what answer does one get? Only, I'm afraid, a repetition of the statement that was questioned in the first place.

COPLESTON: Let's come back to this religious experience. However you subsequently interpret the religious experience, you'd admit that it was relevant to the truth or falsity of the proposition that, say, God existed.

AYER: Relevant in so far as the proposition that God existed is taken as a description or prediction of the occurrence of these experiences. But not, of course, relevant to any inference you might want to draw, such as that the world was created, or anything of that kind.

COPLESTON: No, we'll leave that out. All I'm trying to get at is that you'd admit that the proposition 'God exists' could be a meaningful form of metaphysical proposition.

AYER: No, it wouldn't then be a metaphysical proposition. It'd be a perfectly good empirical proposition like the proposition that the unconscious mind exists.

COPLESTON: The proposition that people have religious experiences would be an empirical proposition; and the proposition that God exists would also be an empirical proposition, provided that all I meant by saying that God exists was that some people have a certain type of experience. But it is *not* all I mean by it. All I originally said was that if God is personal, then one of the consequences would be that he could enter into communication with human beings. If he does so, that does not make God an empirical reality, in the sense of not being a metaphysical reality. God can perfectly well be a metaphysical reality, that is, independent of *physis* or nature, even if intelligent creatures have a non-sensible experience of him. However, if you wish to call metaphysical propositions empirical propositions, by all means do so. It then becomes a question of terminology.

AYER: No. I suggest that you're trying to have it both ways. You see, you allow me to give these words, these shapes or noises, an empirical meaning. You allow me to say that the test whereby what you call God exists or not is to be that certain people have experiences, just as the test for whether the table exists or not is that certain people have experiences, only the experiences are of a different sort. Having got that admission you then shift the meaning of the words 'God exists.' You no longer make them refer simply to the possibility of having these experiences, and so argue that I have admitted a metaphysical proposition, but of course I haven't. All I've admitted is an empirical proposition, which you've chosen to express in the same words as you also want to use to express your metaphysical proposition.

COPLESTON: Pardon me, but I did not say that the test whereby what I call God exists or not is that certain people have certain experiences. I said that if God exists, one consequence would be that people could have certain experiences. However, even if I accept your requirements, it follows that in one case at least you are prepared to recognize the word 'God' as meaningful.

AYER: Of course I recognize it as meaningful if you give it an empirical meaning, but it doesn't follow there's any empirical evidence for the truth of your metaphysical proposition.

Again: Are There Metaphysical Explanations?

COPLESTON: But then I don't claim that metaphysical propositions are not in some way founded on reflection on experience. In a certain sense I should call myself an empiricist, but I think that your empiricism is too narrow. Another point. You will not allow a factual statement to be significant unless it is verifiable. Now, suppose I say that we both have immortal souls. If we have, then the proposition will be empirically verified in due course. Are you then prepared to admit that my statement that we both have immortal souls is a significant statement? If you are not prepared, is this because you demand a particular kind of verification and reject any other type? Such an attitude would not seem to me to be warranted. And I don't see that thereby any statement about reality to which one concludes via the experience is deprived of its metaphysical character, and introduced into the empirical sphere.

AYER: Oh, surely. Let us take a case of a common-sense proposition, such as that there is a glass of water in front of us. The evidence of that is my seeing it, touching it. But of course the meaning of that proposition, the factual content of that proposition, isn't exhausted by any one particular piece of evidence of that sort. I may be having a hallucination. What my proposition predicts is more evidence of the same kind. It isn't that my seeing what I do is evidence for the existence of something totally unobservable. I go beyond the immediate evidence only in so far as I take this experience to be one of an indefinite series of experiences of seeing, touching it, etc., which my statement covers. Equally, in the case of your statement I should want to say that if you want to treat it empirically, you must then treat it as predicting, in exactly the same way, in certain conditions, religious experiences. What it will mean will be the possibility of further religious experiences.

COPLESTON: It's this predicting that I don't like, because it doesn't seem to me that even a scientific proposition necessarily consists in a prediction. Surely it's explicative, and also can be simply explicative, not necessarily a prediction.

AYER: But isn't it explicative in the sense that it links up with a particular phenomenon, or with lots and lots of other ones that either will occur, have occurred, or would occur in certain circumstances? Take the case of physics. Do you want a world of electrons somehow behind the perceptual world? Is that what you're after?

COPLESTON: No. We'll take the electronic theory. I should have thought that its function was to explain certain phenomena; that it originated in an endeavour to explain certain phenomena or, more generally, that it is part of the attempt to discover the constitution of matter. I should not describe it as an attempt to predict events, except secondarily perhaps.

AYER: Oh, I don't want to make the prediction a practical question, but I do want to say that understanding phenomena is a matter of lining them, of grouping them, and that the test of an explanation is that it applies to the hitherto unobserved cases. Suppose I am describing the path of a body and I draw a graph. Then the test of my having explained the observations is that hitherto unobserved points fall on the line I draw.

COPLESTON: Then my idea of metaphysics would be that of explaining, as I said at the beginning, the series of phenomena, so that the reasoning would rise out of the phenomena themselves, or out of things themselves. In that sense it would be based on experience, even though the term of the reasoning might not itself be an object of experience. I can understand your ruling out all that reflective inquiry and reasoning that constitutes metaphysics, but if you rule it out it would seem to me to be in virtue of a presupposed philosophy.

AYER: No, I want to say that I rule out nothing as an explanation so long as it explains. I make no statements about what is real and what is not real. That seems to me again an empirical question.

My objection to the kind of statements that we've agreed to call metaphysical is that they don't explain.

COPLESTON: That's a matter for detailed argument and detailed discussion of some particular argument. It's distinct, it seems to me, from the question of meaning. I can quite imagine somebody saying, 'Your argument for, say, the existence of God is false. Your principles on which you're arguing are quite false.' And if so, there's a conclusion.

AYER: No, I don't want to say it isn't an accurate explanation. What I want to say is that it isn't an explanation at all. That's to say it doesn't even purport to do the work that an explanation does, simply because any given observation or situation is compatible with it. Now if you want to say that you are using the word in some peculiar sense, of course I can't stop you, but equally I should say that (a) it isn't the ordinary sense, and (b) that this peculiar sense hasn't been made clear to me.

COPLESTON: But you see I consider that the existence of what we call the world not only is compatible with God's existence, but demands the conclusion that God exists. I may have misunderstood you: but you seem to me to be saying that if the proposition that God exists means anything, one should be able to deduce some observation statement from it. If you mean by deducing an observation statement deducing a thing, I certainly do not think that one can do this. I believe that the existence of God can be inferred from the existence of the world, but I do not think that the world can be deduced from God. Spinoza might think otherwise, of course. If you are demanding that I should deduce the world from God, if I am to make the proposition 'God exists' significant, you are demanding that I should adopt a particular idea of God and of creation. For, if one could deduce the world from God, creation would be necessary, and God would create necessarily. If I say that I cannot deduce observation statements from the existence of God, it is not because I have no idea of God, but because my idea of God will not permit me to say this.

AYER: You said that the existence of the world demands the conclusion that God exists. Do you mean that this conclusion follows logically, or follows causally?

COPLESTON: I should say causally. I'm certainly not going to say that God exists means that a world exists, if by that you mean that the world follows necessarily from God, but given the world then I should say that there is a necessary relationship.

AYER: Logical or causal?

COPLESTON: Causal.

AYER: Well, then we're back on the point we've already been over, aren't we? – this difficulty of a notion of causation that isn't the ordinary notion of causation, a notion that's still totally unexplained.

COPLESTON: On the contrary, I mentioned earlier on that what I mean by the principle of causality is that anything which comes into existence owes that existence to an extrinsic reality, which I term 'cause'. Incidentally, this notion of causality is much more like the ordinary notion of causation than the phenomenalistic notion which you would regard as the scientific notion. However, I agree that we are back where we were, namely at the question whether there are any principles which can be called certain metaphysical principles. That seems to me one of the chief issues between logical positivist and the metaphysician.

Summary of the Major Disagreements

AYER: It seems to me, indeed, that this has been my quarrel with you all along, that you fail to supply any rules for the use of your expressions. I am not asking for explicit definitions. All that I require is that some indication be given of the way in which the expression relates to some possible experience. It is only when a statement fails to refer, even indirectly, to anything observable that I wish to dismiss it as metaphysical. It is not necessary that the observations should actually be made. There are cases, as you have pointed out, where for practical, or even for theoretical, reasons, the observations could not in fact be made. But one knows what it would be like to make them. The statements which refer to them may be said to be verifiable in principle, if not in fact. To put the point more simply, I understand a statement of fact if I know what to look for on the supposition that it is true. And my knowing what to look for is itself a matter of my being able to interpret the statement as referring at least to some possible experience.

Now, you may say, indeed you have said, that this is all entirely arbitrary. The principle of verifiability is not itself a descriptive statement. Its status is that of a persuasive definition. I am persuaded by it, but why should you be? Can I prove it? Yes, on the basis of other definitions. I have, in fact, tried to show you how it can be derived from an analysis of understanding. But if you are really obstinate, you will reject these other definitions too. So it looks as if we reach a deadlock. But let us then see in what positions we are left. I claim for my method that it does yield valuable results in the way of analysis, and with this you seem disposed to agree. You do not deny the importance of the analytic method in philosophy, nor do you reject all the uses to which I put it. Thus you accept in the main the account that I give of empirical propositions. You have indeed objected to my treatment of the propositions of logic, but there I think that I am in the right. At least I am able to account for their validity: whereas on your view it is utterly mysterious. The main difference between us is that you want to leave room for metaphysics. But now look at the results you get. You put forward your metaphysical statements as ultimate explanations of fact, but you admit that they are not explanations, in any accepted sense of the term, and you cannot say in what sense they are explanations. You cannot show me how they are to be tested, and you seem to have no criterion for deciding whether they are true or false. This being so, I say they are unintelligible. You say, no, you understand them; but for all the good they do you (I mean cognitively, not emotionally) you might just as well abandon them. This is my case against your metaphysical statements. You may decline to be persuaded by it, but what sort of a case can you make for them? I leave the last word to you.

COPLESTON: I have enjoyed our discussion very much. I have contended that a metaphysical idea has meaning if some experience is relevant to the formation of that idea, and that a rational metaphysic is possible if there are, as I think there are, principles which express an intellectual apprehension of the nature of being. I think that one *can* have an intellectual experience – or intuition if you like – of being. A metaphysical proposition is testable by rational discussion, but not by purely empirical means. When you say that metaphysical propositions are meaningless because they are unverifiable in your sense, I do not think that this amounts to more than saying that metaphysics are not the same thing as empirical science. In short, I consider that logical positivism, apart from its theory of analytic propositions, simply embodies the notion of nineteenth-century positivism that the terms 'rational' and 'scientific' have the same extension. This notion may correspond to a popular prejudice, but I see no adequate reason for accepting it.

I still find it difficult to understand the status of the principle of verification. It is either a proposition or no proposition. If it is, it must be, on your premises, either a tautology or an empirical hypothesis. If the former, no conclusion follows as to metaphysics. If the latter, the principle itself would require verification. But the principle of verification cannot itself be verified. If, however, the principle is not a proposition, it must, on your premises, be meaningless. In any case, if the meaning of an existential proposition consists, according to the principle, in its verifiability, it is impossible, I think, to escape an infinite regress, since the verification will itself need verification, and so on indefinitely. If this is so, then all propositions, including scientific ones, are meaningless.

THREE

Philosophy[1]

Philosophy must be of some use and we must take it seriously; it must clear our thoughts and so our actions. Or else it is a disposition we have to check, and an inquiry to see that this is so; i.e., the chief proposition of philosophy is that philosophy is nonsense. And again we must then take seriously that it is nonsense, and not pretend, as Wittgenstein does, that it is important nonsense.

In philosophy we take the propositions we make in science and in everyday life, and try to exhibit them in a logical system with primitive terms and definitions, etc. Essentially a philosophy is a system of definitions or, only too often, a system of descriptions of how definitions might be given.[2]

This quotation is taken from a paper of F. P. Ramsey's which was written in 1929, the year in which I came up to Oxford and began the systematic study of philosophy. It represents a view of the subject which was then coming into fashion and one that I adopted wholeheartedly. Of the alternatives that Ramsey offered I chose the one in which philosophy is required to furnish definitions. Though it was pleasant to fasten the charge of uttering nonsense onto other would-be philosophers, the idea that the chief proposition of philosophy is that philosophy is nonsense appeared to devalue the subject more than it deserved. It might well have been thought that to represent philosophy as a system of definitions was also to devalue it unduly, but that was not how it seemed to many of us then. We realized that a great deal of what had passed for philosophy would have to be sacrificed – in a rather insensitive fashion we offered it the consolation prize of being

---

[1] 'Philosophy' was a contribution to Charles J. Bontemps and S. Jack Odell (eds.), *The Owl of Minerva: Philosophers on Philosophy* (USA, McGraw-Hill, 1975).
[2] F. P. Ramsey, *The Foundations of Mathematics*, Totawa, N. J., Littlefield Adams, 1960), p. 263.

reclassified as poetry – but we thought that enough remained to justify our claim to the goodwill of the former establishment. There was after all a Socratic tradition of which we could claim to be the heirs, and had not Locke declared himself content 'to be employed as an under-labourer in clearing the ground a little, and removing some of the rubbish that lies in the way of knowledge'?

We were wrong. Socratic questions like 'What is justice?' or 'What is knowledge?' are not requests for definitions, at least in a straightfor-ward sense, and even if they were, our conception of philosophy would still have been unduly narrow. The interesting point is how we came to adopt it.

I think that the main reason lay in the grant of autonomy which we thought ourselves obliged to accord both to science and to common sense. For this G. E. Moore was largely responsible, not just through his defence of common sense, which we accepted, but because of what lay behind it. For if one could know, independently of any philosophical argument, the truth of propositions of the sorts that Moore listed, propositions about physical objects as common sense conceives of them, propositions about the past, propositions about one's own and other people's mental life, it followed that the evidence which we had in favour of such propositions was sufficient to establish them without their needing any licence from philosophy. And plainly this point could be generalized. If there were adequate criteria for the truth of propositions belonging to the formal or the natural sciences, to literary scholarship, to history, or to law. Perhaps inconsistently, we drew the line at morals, aesthetics, and politics. Partly our reason was that there was not enough general agreement on these topics to support the assumption that we were supplied with adequate criteria; partly, that with metaphysics and theology in the offing we did not want to run any risks of legitimizing appeals to intuition. So we did not go all the way along the road which ends in admitting everything on its own terms. But to the very considerable extent that we did go along it, we drew the obvious conclusion that whether the appropriate criteria were satisfied was a matter of empirical or formal fact. The philosopher had nothing to say to it.

Not only did this put the sceptic out of court – for if we knew for certain the truth of what he professed to doubt, he could not possibly win, though there might be some sport in seeing how he lost – but it left the philosopher with nothing to justify and no occasion even to speculate. For what could he have to speculate about? All the places were already taken. In what way then could he advance knowledge except by sifting out nonsense? He could tell us what was meant by various types of statement. He could not criticize, but he could clarify.

But did we not already know what was meant? Was there any problem about the meaning of such statements as 'This is an inkstand' or 'Hens lay eggs', to take two of Moore's examples? And in the cases where there might be a problem for many people, those of technical statements in the sciences or in other fields, would not the relevant specialist be the man to ask? Surely it would be a lawyer's rather than a philosopher's business to say what was meant by 'barratry', a physicist's rather than a philosopher's business to construe statements about mesons or neutrinos.

The official answer was that in a way we did know what was meant and in another way did not. And to the extent that we did not, it was not because the terms in question were obscure or technical. They could just as easily be terms in everyday use. 'I know what time it is', said St Augustine, 'so long as you do not ask me.' But what was he hesitating about when they did ask him? What definition to give? Perhaps. But if we look at what philosophers like Kant or McTaggart or Bergson, who have concerned themselves with time, have said about it, they seem to be offering us theories rather than definitions. And to go back to Moore's examples, surely there is no difficulty about defining 'inkstand' or 'hens' or 'eggs' or the verb 'to lay'. The dictionary does it quite adequately. It is not in that sense that we do not know what is meant by the sentences in which these words occur.

But in what sense then? We do not know how to analyze these sentences. We know what is meant by the English sentence 'This is an inkstand', but we do not know what its correct analysis is. But how does 'knowing the analysis' differ from 'knowing the meaning'? The distinction is due to Moore, but he never properly explains it. In some cases there would seem to be no difference. Thus one example which is sometimes offered of a successful analysis is the proposition that brothers are male siblings, which one can certainly learn from a dictionary. It is, however, not a very good example, since the question what brothers are is not of any philosophical interest. What is of philosophical interest is the more general question how to interpret statements of identity, and how it comes about that they are not trivial. And here consulting the dictionary would not be helpful.

Neither would it be helpful when it comes to analyzing sentences like 'This is an inkstand', and this not only because the inkstand is not appearing in its own right but merely as a specimen of a physical object. For looking up the dictionary definition of a physical object would not be of any use either. The question which Moore raised when he asked for the analysis of sentences like 'This is an inkstand' was, in general terms, the question how physical objects are related to the sense data which he thought that the demonstratives in such sentences were used to designate.

But now we see that a gulf has opened up between knowing the meaning of the sentence and knowing its analysis. For how could reflection on the meaning of sentences like 'This is an inkstand' ever lead one to formulate Moore's question? How do sense data get into the picture?

The answer lies in there being another chink in the armour of Moore's position. Not only did he not know *what* he knew, in the sense of not knowing its analysis, but he also did not know *how* he knew it. And the answer to the first question was supposed to yield the answer to the second. What was going to count as a satisfactory analysis of sentences expressing perceptual judgments was a way of re-formulating them which would show how these judgments could be known to be true. Thus sense data were brought in because of Moore's assumption that it was only through being presented with some sense datum that one could ever know of the existence of a physical object. And if one asks how he and Russell and so many other philosophers before them came by this assumption, the answer is that they were persuaded by a set of arguments, not about the meaning of words like 'see' and 'touch', but about the possibility of hallucinations, the variations of appearances under different condi-tions, the causal dependence of the way things look to us on the state of our nervous systems. These arguments bear on the meaning of sentences like 'This is an inkstand' only in so far as they provide a motive for redescribing the situations which we take as warranting our acceptance of such sentences. The introduction of a term like 'sense datum' helps to bring out the complexity of these situations, which but for those arguments we might have overlooked.

From Berkeley onward, the introduction of sense data, or of any-thing that fulfilled roughly the same function, has fostered reductive analysis. The advantage of a phenomenalist as opposed, say, to a causal theory of perception is that if it works we do not have any problem about how we know that there are physical objects – or rather, we have only the general inductive problem of explaining how we can ever be justified in going beyond our data. We do not have any further problem because we are making what I call a 'horizontal inference' – extrapolating to entities of the same kind as those with which we started. On the other hand, if we regard ourselves as making a vertical inference, extrapolating to entities of a different kind, then we do have the further problem of supplying some proof that there are such external entities as our causal theory postulates, objects which according to the theory we do not and could not ever perceive.

But can it be doubtful whether there are physical objects? Must not an analysis of perceptual statements which allows this doubt be wrong? Not necessarily. The point which the champions of common sense overlooked is that there may be different sets of posits, as Quine called them, which might serve to account for our experiences; and that it depends upon contingent features of our experience that any such system works. It is a philosophical problem to make it intelligible how a system works, and the main objection to the causal theory of perception, at least in its classical form, is that it fails to do this. The difficulty is to see how we could possibly pick out any external objects as being the causes of our sense data unless these objects could be independently identified. So long as the identification of these objects is made to depend exclusively on physical theories, it remains a mystery how the theories themselves can ever get going. This argument is not, however, an objection to the inclusion of a causal clause in an analysis which allows for the objects to be independently identified.

From this point of view phenomenalism is superior. But the trouble with classical phenomenalism is that it was too ambitious. It assumed that analysis had to consist in furnishing translations, or at least descriptions of how translations might run; and this seems not to be feasible. One has to fall back, I believe, on showing how the common-sense conception of the physical world can be viewed as a theory with respect to a neutral basis of sensory elements. This is achieved by a method of fictive construction. One shows how the elements could get 'transformed' into enduring objects, and how the spatial and temporal relations found between them could be developed into a system. If this method is successful, it does, in a way, yield both an analysis and a justification. It shows *how* the theory works and *that* it works.

In this case a process of description seems to be enough. The positing of physical objects is not very hazardous, though it could conceivably go wrong. For example, in microscopic physics the ordinary criteria of identity through time break down, and one could imagine this happening on a larger scale. It might be the case that objects moved discontinuously or that many fewer things stayed put over any length of time, so that we were deprived of our traditional frames of reference. I think that I can imagine an everyday world in which the concepts of field theory would be more serviceable than the particle concepts with which we actually operate. But even then we could be philosophically content with description, a description of those features of our experience that favoured the concepts of field theory. We should just be describing a rather different world.

There are, however, more troublesome cases where description does not seem to be enough. One of the worst of them is the other-minds problem. Here we have no particular difficulty in describing the criteria that we actually use. 'How do you know that he is depressed?' 'He told me so.' 'Look at him.' 'He does not play with the children as he used to.' 'He tried to kill himself.' There is no question but that these are acceptable answers, at least in the sense that we unhesitatingly accept them when we are not philosophizing. 'We can be wrong, of course.' He was not depressed at all. 'He had fallen into a Byronic phase.' This comes out when the psychiatrist gets on to him. But then it does come out. More often than not our attributions of mental states to others are settled beyond serious doubt.

Why then should there be any philosophical doubt? The reason is not so much that things sometimes go wrong as that our procedures seem logically unsatisfactory. It is not that the accepted criteria do not work, but that we cannot account for their working in the way they do. The stages of the argument are well known. Propositions about people's behaviour do not entail propositions about their mental states. If mental and bodily states are connected inductively, it is an odd sort of inductive connection, in which one term of the relation is not observable. Of course it is observable in one's own case, and it is this that gives the theory that the connection is inductive what plausibility it has. But it is an uneasy position to hold. The empirical evidence does not seem strong enough for the weight which is put upon it.

This being so, why should the sceptic not prevail? Why do I not admit that I do not have any very good reason to attribute thoughts and feelings to anyone other than myself? I cannot in fact rid myself of the belief that other people do have a mental life, but I might be brought to admit that it was irrational. This seems to have been Hume's position in general, though he was surprisingly unconcerned with this particular problem. But it is not at all easy to hold a belief as firmly as I hold this one, and also think it irrational. So it is very tempting to fall back on saying that the evidence is *sui generis* but is nonetheless adequate for that. The trouble is that the sceptic's argument remains unmet.

In one way, indeed, the sceptic has prevailed. His victory is shown in the prevalence of physicalism. I cannot believe that the theory that sentences ascribing mental attributes to oneself or to others are equivalent to sentences ascribing physical attributes would ever have resulted from a dispassionate study of the way in which these sentences are used. If Carnap and, more hesitantly, Ryle made this suggestion, it was rather because they had become convinced that only by reducing the mental to the physical could they account for our ability to know about the mental states of others. The wildly implausible reduction of one's own mental states to physical ones was then forced on them by their acceptance of the valid argument that the analysis of statements about a person's experiences could not be radically different according as the statement was uttered by another person or by the person himself. I think that the same is true of the thesis that the mental and physical states are factually identical, though here a metaphysical preference for materialism is also at work.

In any event, the assumption of factual identity does not get rid of the problem. For here it is conceded that what is in fact a state of the patient's brain is perceived by him as a feeling of pain, so that the belief that he does so perceive it has still to be justified. And it surely cannot be deduced from our observations of his brain, even if we were equipped to make them. Consequently, even if we could be said to be witnessing his feeling when we examined his brain, it remains unclear how we could know that this was so. This difficulty would indeed be removed if we took the bold step, which some physicalists do recommend, of simply defining a mental state as whatever causes such and such behaviour and then applying Ockham's razor. But this does not seem an improper begging of the question.

The invocation of Ockham's razor, though surely unjustified in this instance, if only because of one's consciousness of one's own experiences, does, however, create a difficulty for the otherwise attractive suggestion that we are justified in attributing mental states to others because this makes better sense of the evidence than any other hypothesis. Perhaps the answer is that we do not in fact have the physiological theories which would enable us to explain such things as intelligent behaviour without attributing conscious purposes to the agent, and that even if we did have them we could not make very much use of them. For instance, it would hardly be practicable to keep people's brains under constant observation. Even so, the theoretical difficulty remains that even if we did possess these theories and could use them, it does not seem likely that we should cease to attribute mental states to others, any more than we should cease to attribute them to ourselves.

We have come a long way from the conception of philosophy as a system of definitions and closer to the Wittgensteinian idea of it as an attempt to rid ourselves of intellectual cramps. There is something in this idea, at least with regard to the problems which I have been discussing. It trades on the fact that when we tackle these problems we do not at this time of day expect to come up with anything startling, as it might be, some fresh clue to the existence or nonexistence of physical objects, or other minds, which everyone had overlooked. Again, this is not a commitment to common sense, though it has sometimes been so taken. Even though we do not expect any new evidence to be forthcoming, it is still possible to offer a radically new interpretation of the evidence, that we already have. And indeed this is just what Ryle and Wittgenstein did, rightly or wrongly, when they campaigned against inner processes.

If the idea that philosophy serves to remove intellectual cramps covers more of the ground than the idea that it provides a system of definitions, it still does not account for the whole range of philosophical activities. For instance, it has little if any bearing on the currently fashionable topics of reference and identity. I include under this heading such questions as 'What is the distinction between subjects and predicates?' 'Do proper names have a sense?' 'Are identity statements necessarily true if they are true at all?' 'Can indirect discourse be regimented in such a way that it comes to satisfy the criteria of extensionality?' In these cases we tend to proceed more scientifically. We advance hypotheses and test them by linguistic examples.

It may be thought improper to ask what is the interest of these questions, since it is surely legitimate to hold that they are interesting in themselves. To a certain extent, I share this attitude. For instance, I find identity statements puzzling and should like to see the puzzle resolved. But I am not quite content to leave it there. I do not agree with Austin's epigram that importance is not important, but truth is. Not every truth is important, or at least not to me. In the case of philosophical grammar, I find that my interest flags unless it leads to speculation.

But what further point can there be to discussions about reference or about indirect discourse? My answer is that they can be seen as having a bearing on ontology. I have a Humean picture of the world as consisting in discrete observable episodes, with no room in it for modalities or intentional objects. These objects belong, if anywhere, to a secondary system, but the notes of the secondary system have to be cashed in primary coin. We are free to make various arrangements of our primary elements, but there are only these elements to be arranged. I am therefore interested in any interpretation of intentional discourse which will make it compatible with this position. I attach less importance to the Quinean programme of eliminating singular terms, but I think that it has a value in doing justice to the fact, or what I take to be the fact, that we are presented not primarily with particulars, but with qualities or patterns out of which particulars can be constructed. In many ways, Quine follows Russell and there is an echo here of Russell's idea of making language reflect the structure of the world.

But what right have I to my Humean picture? For the answer I have to go back to the theory of knowledge. This is what I believe that I am given to build on. Or rather, it is a systematization of what I am given to build on, but one that is closer to the data than anything else I can think of, which would be sufficiently elaborate to deserve the appellation of a world picture. I do not want to say that this is what there really is, because I do not want to exclude other options. For instance, I do not want to rule out the possibility of opting for scientific realism. But if one did take this option, I think that the theory which one would then regard as supplying a description of the world would have to be justified as the Humean level, even though my primary facts will be explicable in terms of it.

One might indeed think that this was not a question of options but a question of fact. Scientific realism is true or it is false. But once you depart from the Russell-Frege treatment of existence, whereby to exist is just to satisfy some propositional function, you have to provide some other criterion. Russell himself made this departure when he talked about the ultimate furniture of the world. In terms of his own analysis of existence, his assertion that classes did not exist should have meant that no functions of any higher order than the first were satisfied; but of course this was not what he intended it to mean. He meant that classes were not part of the ultimate furniture of the world. He treated this as a question of fact, but gave no criteria for deciding it, and indeed it is hard to see what criterion he could have given other than that of the possibility of reduction to a selected basis. It is for this reason that I represent such a question as one of a choice of pictures. This is in line with Carnap's view of ontological questions as relating to a choice of languages, and perhaps also with Quine's doctrine of ontological relativity. The danger in any such view is that of opening the floodgates. We do not really want to legitimize the Homeric gods. It would seem that Quine has to legitimize them, if he is able to discover that anyone believes in them, so long as he can say nothing more than that they are excluded by his background theory. The question is whether his ontological relativity allows him to take the further step of saying that his background theory is superior to one in which the Homeric gods are accommodated. So far as I can see, one can take this further step only if one uses a theory to prove its own superiority, and I should in fact prefer to do this rather than succumb to total anthropological tolerance. It would indeed be more agreeable to have a noncircular proof. But in this case, as in that of the problem of induction, I fear that circularity may be inescapable.

FOUR

The Nature of Philosophical Inquiry[1]

I

PHILOSOPHY AS ELUCIDATING CONCEPTS

Disagreement among specialists about the very nature of their subject appears to be peculiar to philosophy. This is not, of course, to say that serious disputes do not occur in other subjects, or that these disputes may not be of a radical character. The disagreements between formalists and intuitionists in mathematics, or between Darwinists and Lamarckians in biology, or between Marxist and other historians provide obvious examples. But in all these cases the debate is staged against a background of accepted doctrine or, at the very least, a stock of accredited facts. This is not so in philosophy. In this respect, though in this respect only, it has something in common with theology. Even so, there is a greater measure of agreement among theologians as to what they are trying to achieve, however great the uncertainty as to whether they are succeeding.

The failure of philosophers to come to an agreement about the purposes of their activity, and the methods by which it should be pursued, has become more marked in recent years and has led, understandably, to a certain crisis of confidence. Philosophers of all schools increasingly feel the obligation to put the value of philosophy in question. Since this crisis has been building up for some time, it may be useful to trace its historical development.

[1] 'Philosophy as Elucidating Concepts', 'Philosophy as Constructively Critical of Conceptual Systems' and 'Berkeleianism and Physicalism as Constructively Critical' were delivered as three lectures at the University of Notre Dame, Indiana, in 1967, and published in Joseph Bobik (ed.), *The Nature of Philosophical Inquiry* (Notre Dame, Notre Dame University Press, 1970).

In the main, it is the outcome of the dissociation of philosophy from science. It did not affect the ancient Greeks, since they did not make any such distinction; for them, philosophy covered every kind of human knowledge. Neither was it a problem for medieval philosophers, who were content to take their premises from theology. Looking back, one can see the beginnings of a threat to the position of philosophy in the extraordinary development of the physical sciences which followed the Renaissance, but this was not apparent at the time. Philosophers like Descartes, Leibniz and Spinoza did not look upon their problems as being generically different from those of Galileo and Newton. Even philosophers like Locke, Berkeley, and Hume – who stood further away from the physical sciences – did not distinguish their subject from what we should nowadays call psychology. In particular, Locke was clearly aiming to produce a theory of mind which would be a counterpart to Newton's theory of matter. Kant was himself a distinguished cosmologist, and his *Critique of Pure Reason* is very largely an attempt to supply a foundation for the Newtonian system. Hegel, it must be admitted, was a good deal less scientific, but even he tried to incorporate the science of his day in his all-embracing metaphysical system.

It is in the nineteenth century that philosophy and science begin to take different paths. Indeed, the very word 'scientist' is a nineteenth-century coinage, introduced by the English philosopher of science, Whewell, in 1840. The need for its introduction marked the growing autonomy of the special sciences; until then they had been content with the title of natural philosophers. The new appellation declared their independence. This was conceded by the philosophers, though not (as we shall see) without some attempts to reassert their sovereignty; they were then left with the problem of finding some territory which they could still count as their private property. That there is such a territory (at least in the sense that there are activities which are distinctively philosophical) is perhaps the only point on which all contemporary philosophers are likely to be in full agreement. It is when we come to the characterization of this territory that the divergencies will appear. All that can be done, in these circumstances, is to describe it in my own way, at the same time setting out as clearly as possible the reasons why I believe this description to be correct.

I start with the assumption that there is some class of true propositions which it is the special business of philosophy to discover, and that their discovery is of some importance; in short, that philosophy is, or is capable of being, a worthwhile cognitive discipline. This assumption is itself not accepted by all contemporary philosophers, but my hope is to succeed in vindicating it. If I did not believe that it could be vindicated, I doubt if I should still be engaging in philosophy. Of course this is not an argument; it is only a confession of faith.

Our aim being to pin down the special province of philosophy (assuming provisionally that it has one), a good method will be to proceed by elimination. I shall try to dispose of various current views and then consider what possibilities remain. The answer at which I shall eventually arrive will be found to raise problems to which I do not know the solution. For our present purposes, I shall be satisfied if I can arouse your interest in the problems.

The first view to examine is that philosophy differs from the sciences only or mainly through its greater generality. The physicist, it is said, occupies himself only with one limited aspect of reality; the chemist with another, and the biologist with another. What uniquely distinguishes the philosopher is that he is concerned with reality as a whole.

There is some truth in this. What is true is that the subject matter of philosophy is not circumscribed in the way that the subject matter of any one of the special sciences may be held to be. On the other hand, it is false to say that the philosopher does the same work as the scientist, only on a larger scale. For what would this amount to? How would he set about depicting the whole of reality except through the depiction of its parts? I suppose that it would be possible to compose an encyclopaedia which would set out all the theories and hypotheses which were currently accepted in the various branches of science. It would be a difficult task for any one man to accomplish, and by the time that he had completed it, some parts of the work would almost certainly be obsolete. Even so, if it were well done it would have some utility. However, it is more than mere concern for the dignity of my profession that prompts me to reject the suggestion that the province of philosophy is limited to the compilation of scientific works of reference.

It may be thought that this is unfair to the view under consideration. What it requires of the philosopher is not that he should merely assemble the scientific theories of his time but that he should integrate them into a world picture; but again it is not clear what such a world picture could be. Perhaps one could envisage something of the following kind. It might turn out that physics could be unified; that is, a means might be found to fulfil Einstein's aim of constructing a unified theory of the utmost generality, incorporating both quantum theory and the theory of relativity. It might then be shown that the other sciences were all reducible to physics. To some extent this has already been achieved: there is good reason to think that chemical laws can be derived from those of physics and biological laws from chemical laws. If it could be shown that the laws of psychology and sociology were derivable from biological laws, the programme would be complete. If it were completed, one might then regard the ultimate physical theory (in terms of which everything else was explained) as affording a general picture of the world. Since the theory would be bound to be entirely abstract, it could only yield a very schematic picture; but it seems to me all that could be significantly looked for in this way.

But now it is surely clear that the question whether any programme of this kind is feasible is one of a highly technical character. Only a practising physiologist could be in a position to decide whether it is possible to construct a physiological theory which would account for what are ordinarily classified as mental phenomena. Equally, the question whether biochemistry provides a satisfactory bridge between the organic and the inorganic sciences is one that can be answered only by someone who is working in this field. Such questions certainly cannot be answered by a philosopher in his armchair, contemplating concepts. If any philosopher pretends to be able to answer them on purely *a priori* grounds, you should not listen to him.

You should listen to him even less if he claims to be introducing you to a different reality from that which is explored by science. This is an idea that has been most prevalent in the East, but it was also adopted by some Western philosophers in the nineteenth century, and still finds some adherents in the West. Among Western philosophers it has mainly taken the form of an attempt to show by purely *a priori* reasoning that the real world is quite unlike the world that we ordinarily believe in; that, for example, space and time and matter are illusory. In oriental philosophy, there is less that one can recognize as argument; you are exhorted rather to penetrate beyond appearances to a deeper level of being where everything is one.

I am afraid that this is just nonsense. There is no way of finding out what the world is like except by putting up hypotheses and testing them by observation. When people talk of a deeper reality, you will find that they are using the word 'reality' in such a way that no sense can be attached to it; there are no criteria, in this usage, for determining how it is to be applied. It is the same with the contention that everything is one (where this is construed not as implying that the stuff of which the world is made is homogeneous), or that everything is subject to the same laws, but that all distinctions are ultimately unreal. In any ordinary sense, it is just not true that I am identical with this glass, or this watch, or this chair, or that they are identical with one another.

Perhaps by the use of drugs or by some other method, one could get into a state in which one had the feeling that everything, including oneself was merging into everything else, but this feeling would have no cognitive import; it would have nothing to do with any matter of fact. It may, indeed, happen that things which seem to be distinct are not really so, as when some persistent object reappears under a disguise, but in all such cases there are recognized criteria for deciding whether or not identity has been preserved. To say that everything is one, in default of any criteria of identity, is to say nothing significant. I have chosen extreme examples, but the same objection would apply to any talk of an ultramundane reality.

A more intelligible view of the function of philosophy is that in which the philosopher is cast as a sage. What is expected of him is that he should (as Plato put it) tell people how they ought to live. This view, still very prevalent, was popularized by the Stoics who are also responsible for the popular usage of the word 'philosophical', in which to take something philosophically is not to mind about it. The idea is that the sage has his attention so firmly fixed upon higher things that he is not troubled by any of the ordinary cares of life. There is no particular reason to expect those who study philosophy to be philosophical in this sense of the word.

The role of the sage is one that philosophers can and sometimes do play; but it is not their professional perquisite. It is not anyone's professional perquisite, for the sufficient reason that morals is not a subject. This does not imply that it does not matter how people behave or that if one is in doubt about one's proper course of conduct there may not be persons from whom it is sensible to seek advice. Certain persons may be said to have good moral judgment, in the sense that the conduct of their lives or the verdicts which they pass upon the conduct of others command one's moral respect. What is meant by saying that morality is not a subject, is that there is no such thing as being learned in morals. It is not possible to have specialized knowledge in the field of morals, in the way that a chemist or an ornithologist has specialized knowledge. There is no repository of moral doctrine to which a philosopher, or anyone else for that matter, could have privileged access. To have had a philosophical training may be of advantage in helping one to see whether one's moral attitudes are self-consistent, and also perhaps in enabling one to discount prejudice. The study of moral philosophy may lead to a better understanding of the role of moral concepts and of the relation of judgments of value to statements of empirical fact. In so far as a philosopher may be expected to think clearly about such matters, his moral pronouncements may be held to carry a little extra weight.

Even so, if he does set up as a moral counsellor, his claim to our attention will depend rather on his character and his experience of the world than on his strictly professional attainments.

I come now to the conception of the philosopher's function which has played the most prominent part in the history of Western philosophy since the time of Descartes. This is the conception of the philosopher as a judge. The idea is that the philosopher does not investigate the world at first hand, but rather assesses the evidence which others set before him. His task is to pronounce on the claims to knowledge which are put forward by the scientist, or indeed by the ordinary man in the street. He raises the Socratic question whether we really know all that we think we know. He considers how far and in what manner our most fundamental beliefs are capable of being justified. 'Is there anything of which one can be absolutely certain?' was the question which Descartes posed in following his famous method of doubt and it is a question which has haunted Western philosophy to the present day. So empiricists from Locke to Bertrand Russell have started out with the 'hard' data of sense experience and tried to show how much could legitimately be built on this foundation. Kant attempted to fix the boundaries of the possible extent of human knowledge. Since the early work of Wittgenstein, the concern in recent philosophy has been with the boundaries of significant discourse rather than with the boundaries of knowledge, but though they are approached from a different angle the problems are substantially the same.

It is clear that in an inquiry of this sort everything depends upon one's criteria of significance or one's criteria of knowledge. Thus, with regard to the question of what can be known, someone like Descartes (who relies on intellectual intuition) is likely to come up with a different answer from that which would be given by an empiricist like Locke. Therefore, it is necessary for anyone who practises philosophy in this way to try to evaluate the criteria themselves. He is faced at the outset with the questions: What is a legitimate starting point? and What are the legitimate ways of advancing beyond it?

This is something with which I shall deal later on, but first I want to examine an argument which puts the whole of this enterprise in doubt. I attribute the argument to the Cambridge philosopher G. E. Moore, though he did not himself explicitly advance it. It does, however, seem to underline his distinctive approach to the problems of philosophy; an approach which has very largely coloured the development of contemporary British philosophy and has also had a considerable influence in the United States.

As many of you will know, Moore's chief contribution to philosophy was his defence of common sense. He was concerned to vindicate the common-sense view of the world against the attacks which had been made on it by metaphysicians, and his technique was to take the metaphysicians as meaning exactly what they said. The metaphysicians in whom he was mainly interested (for historical reasons) were the English neo-Hegelians who denied the reality of space and time and matter; and his procedure was to reduce their position to absurdity simply by showing what it literally implied. He argued that if time is unreal, it follows that nothing ever happens before or after anything else; nothing grows or changes; no event ever causes another event to happen; and no one ever acquires a belief, including the belief that time is unreal, since the acquisition of a belief is itself something that occurs in time. In the same way, he pointed out that if the proposition that matter is unreal were true, it would follow that nobody maintained it. For if matter is unreal, there are no physical bodies; and if there are no physical bodies, there are no human bodies; and if there are no human bodies, there are no metaphysicians to hold that matter is unreal. This does not strictly refute the proposition, since it could be true even though its truth was inconsistent with anyone's believing it, but it does remove it from serious consideration.

Against these metaphysical extravagancies, Moore simply set his knowledge of the truth of what he called the common-sense view of the world. He did not attempt to offer any vindication of this claim to knowledge; he merely insisted on the fact that he did know what he said he knew. Thus, in a famous lecture which he gave for the British Academy, he quoted Kant as saying that it was a scandal to philosophy that nobody had succeeded in proving the existence of the external world, where this is taken to imply the existence of objects in space, outside of our own minds. Moore undertook to put an end to this scandal by offering a proof. It took a very simple form. He held up his two hands and said that both he and his audience knew that these were two human hands. But, he went on, if we know that these are human hands, it follows that two human hands exist, and from this it follows that at least two physical objects exist; and since it is a defining characteristic of a physical object that it exists in space outside of any mind, you have your proof of an external world. For such a proof to be valid it is sufficient that the premisses be true, that they should not presuppose the conclusion, and that the conclusion should follow logically from the premisses. In this instance, as Moore pointed out, all three conditions are satisfied: consequently, the proof is valid. I shall show later on why one nevertheless feels it to be unsatisfactory.

It is to be remarked that when Moore claimed to know that the common-sense view of the world was wholly true he was not committing himself to upholding every proposition accepted by the man in the street. Among contemporary philosophers, common sense has a standing which few of their predecessors have been willing to accord it, but not even its most ardent champion among them would deny that it could sometimes go astray. It was once a mark of common sense to believe that the earth was flat, or that epilepsy was a symptom of possession by demons; it would be rash to assume that none of our common-sense beliefs will seem equally misguided to future generations. What Moore had in mind when he spoke of the common-sense view of the world was a set of very general beliefs which might be said to underlie all our more specific theories about the way the world works. Such is the belief that there are physical objects which are accessible to different observers and to different senses, so that, for example, the glass which I see on this table is identical with the glass which I touch, and identical with the glass which you see. It is also a part of this belief that objects like this glass have a temporal history and occupy positions in a public space. Another belief which Moore took as part of the common-sense view of the world is that some – but not all – physical objects have acts of consciousness attached to them, which is a way of expressing the fact that there are mental occurrences, without committing oneself to the postulation of mental substances. For Moore, there can be no doubt that these general propositions are true, since he takes them to follow logically from propositions which he knows to be true; for example, the proposition that I now perceive a glass is understood to entail both that there is at least one physical object – with all that this implies – and that there is an act of consciousness.

I shall now try to show how this championship of common sense can be used to throw doubt upon the conception of philosophy as having a judicial function. As stated earlier, Moore himself did not supply any justification of his claims to knowledge; he merely drew the conclusion that since he knew the common-sense view of the world to be true, the metaphysical theories which conflicted with it must be false. It seems to me, however, that he was in fact relying on a form of justification which neither he nor his followers have made fully explicit. If one does insist on asking how we know that this is a glass, the answer is not that we know it by divine revelation or by any form of purely intellectual intuition; we know it on the basis of our current sense experience. We can see the glass; and if this is not thought to be enough one can make sure by handling it. This justifies our assertion that the glass exists, for the very good reason that sentences like 'this is a glass' are used in such a way that our having just this sort of experience is the best possible evidence for the truth of what they express. Admittedly, the evidence is not conclusive; one can be deceived; as Moore himself was on a celebrated occasion when he pointed to a dummy skylight and claimed to know that it was a window to the sky. But in all such cases, there are ways to detect one's mistake. Even though the logical possibility of error may always remain, we can make observations which leave us in no serious doubt of the truth. In short, there are recognized criteria for deciding questions of this kind; and whether these criteria are satisfied in any given instance is not a philosophical but a purely empirical question. If someone calls out that the house is on fire, we know how to find out whether he is telling the truth; if our observations bear him out, we are likely to take some sort of action. There is no occasion here for an exercise of philosophical doubt.

But it is not only to statements at the common-sense level that this argument applies. It is equally true of the scientific or mathematical statements that there are accredited procedures for deciding whether they are valid. If someone is presented with the evidence which is taken as establishing a scientific theory, and still refuses to accept the theory, then unless he has some special reason for mistrusting the evidence, or supposing that it has been wrongly interpreted, his refusal to accept the theory simply shows that he does not understand it. If someone goes through a mathematical proof (for instance, the proof that there is no greatest prime number), and refuses to accept the conclusion, then unless he can advance some mathematical argument which casts doubt on the proof, he simply shows that he does not understand mathematics. It is a condition of the significance of any type of assertion that there should be criteria for deciding whether it is true or false; and whether the criteria are satisfied is always a question of material or formal fact. Consequently, there is no room for philosophy to intervene; there is no judicial function for it to exert. But in that case what use remains for it?

The next section will offer some criticisms of this argument. What I want to do now is to trace the consequence of accepting it. We saw earlier that the philosopher is not in a position to compete with the scientist in giving a description or explanation of the world. If now the function of a judge is also to be denied him, all that appears to be left is some work of clarification. At any rate this is the conclusion to which the followers of Moore and other modern philosophers have come. It is most commonly expressed by saying that the only legitimate contribution that the philosopher can hope to make to the advancement of knowledge is through engaging in philosophical analysis.

Though this is a view which has come to be very widely held (at least in English-speaking countries), there is no general agreement among those who subscribe to it as to what philosophical analysis consists in. In fact, I think it is possible to distinguish at least eight different activities which figure under this general heading. I shall conclude here by saying something about each of them in turn.

The most formal of these activities, and the one most closely allied to science is that in which the analysis consists in the structural description, perhaps even the axiomatization of a scientific theory. This is not very widely practised because the combination of scientific knowledge and logical skill which is required for it is rare. A good example is to be found in Professor Woodger's axiomatization of a part of biology.

A second and perhaps more fruitful proceeding is to give precision to terms which play an important part in scientific or in everyday discourse. Examples of this are Tarski's semantic definition of truth, Reichenbach's work on the concept of probability, and Carnap's and Hempel's attempts to develop a formal theory of confirmation. The idea is to take a concept which may be used loosely or ambiguously in ordinary speech, if necessary to break it down into a number of different concepts, and then by the use of formal methods to define a term, or a set of terms, which give a sharper rendering to the sense of the concept which you are replacing.

Thirdly, analysis may take the form of showing that certain types of linguistic expressions can be radically transformed or dispensed with altogether. I am thinking here of such things as Russell's theory of descriptions, or Quine's elimination of singular terms, or Goodman's and my own elimination of tenses. The motive for such undertakings may be that of removing some perplexity caused by the use of the expressions on which you are operating. Thus Russell was puzzled by the fact that apparently referential expressions like 'the present King of France' could have a meaning, even though they failed to denote anything. And he got rid of the difficulty by proving that the sentences in which such expressions typically occurred could be reformulated in such a way that the misleading show of reference disappeared. Another motive may be the desire to vindicate some general principle, as that everything that is shown in language by the use of demonstrative expressions could be explicitly said. This is one reason for trying to get rid of verbal forms (like tenses) which are tied to contexts. The fulfilment of the programme would require that proper nouns, pronouns and demonstratives like 'this' and 'that' be replaced by general descriptions of the person or object referred to, and that all spatiotemporal location be accomplished by specifying the relations of the things described to certain unique landmarks. It is interesting to note that the temporal landmark may be merely postulated. For instance, in the Roman dating system, the point of origin was the founding of the city by Romulus and Remus, most probably a mythical event. Neither does it affect the operation of our own dating system that the evidence points to the birth of Christ as having occurred in the year 4 BC. The statement that the battle of Waterloo was fought in AD 1815 is not held to be falsified by the fact that it was fought not 1815, but 1819 years after the occurrence of the unique event on which the whole system is supposed to be pegged. There is more to be said about the conditions which are required for a dating system to be viable, but it seems clear to me that if we have a viable dating system, we can dispense not only with tenses but with the concepts of past, present, and future. These are devices for indicating the temporal positions of the utterance in which they figure relatively to the event to which it refers; and this information can be made explicit by simply saying whether the event described occurs before or after or simultaneously with the description of it. How important it is to carry out this form of analysis is a debatable question; there are those who would dismiss it as little more than a technical exercise, but I think that in certain cases it can throw a useful light on the way in which our concepts work.

A variant of this procedure, important enough to deserve a place itself, is what may be called reductive analysis. This is the attempt to eliminate an alleged type of entity in favour of entities of another type which are thought to have a stronger grasp upon reality. For example, it is plausible to hold that nations do not exist independently of the individuals who compose them. The reduction would then consist in showing how everything that we want to say about a nation can be rephrased in the form of statements about its members. A more interesting but also more dubious example is the attempt to reduce mind to matter, or matter to mind. There are philosophers like my colleague Professor Ryle who say that there are no such things as mental processes over and above the fact that people behave or are disposed to behave in such and such ways. On the other hand there are the phenomenalists who claim that physical objects are reducible to sense data. The trouble with reductive analysis is that if the criterion of reducibility is the power to translate statements about the entities which you are treating as logical constructs into statements which refer only to the entities which you are treating as genuine, it never seems to work – except in trivial instances. It is easy to translate statements about the average plumber into statements about plumbers, but it is not easy to find a formula even for translating statements about nations into statements about their members. I shall have a good deal more to say about this topic in my succeeding essays.

A fifth type of analysis consists in the discrimination of different types of statement, not with respect to the objects to which they refer, but with respect to the function which they fulfil. The question of the nature of moral judgments (whether, for example, they can properly be said to be either true or false) would come under this heading. A notable recent contribution to this form of analysis is Professor Austin's discovery of what he called performative statements. These are statements which do not report activities but help to constitute them. For instance, the judge who sentences you to prison is not predicting that you will go to prison, but helping to bring it about. To say 'I promise' under the appropriate conditions, is not to report that one is making a promise but actually to make it.

Professor Austin was also largely responsible for the variety of analysis which consists in a meticulous examination of the ways in which English words, or the words of some other natural language, are actually used. This kind of linguistic philosophy – as it came to be called – is going out of fashion, even in Oxford where it took hold most strongly. But it can be valuable in certain fields, such as the philosophy of law.

A point which the vogue of linguistic philosophy helped to emphasize was that not all explanations of the use of concepts result in definitions. For instance, one might set out to elucidate the concept of memory, not by defining it, but by making such points as that remembering does not necessarily involve the presence of a memory image; that even when such images do occur the part which they play is logically inessential. A great deal of what is known as the philosophy of mind consists in advancing considerations of this sort. Such informal explanations make up my seventh category.

Finally, there is the approach of Wittgenstein and his followers, who see philosophy as an attempt to free us from the perplexities into which we fall when we misinterpret the workings of our language. By a suitable choice of examples, an attempt is made to expose such naive assumptions as that the things to which a common noun applies necessarily possess a common quality or that words like 'intending' or 'undertaking' stand for mental acts. In Wittgenstein's hands this method can be most illuminating; the same cannot always be said of his imitators.

This classification of the various types of analysis is not intended to be sharp. Neither am I putting forward my eight versions as competitors; different methods may suit different persons or different problems. There has indeed been a certain tension between those who tend to think that only a formal approach can yield anything of cognitive interest and those who believe that the really interesting questions are not of a nature to yield to formal treatment. But I can see no reason *a priori* why both parties should not achieve significant results. What we do need (especially in the cases where the approach is informal) is a clearer understanding of the purpose for which the analysis is undertaken, and of the ways in which we are to determine whether it has been successful.

Even if we suppose this to have been achieved, the question still remains whether the practice of analysis, in one or other of these different forms, exhausts the legitimate scope of philosophy. To answer this question we shall have to return to Moore's argument. Is there any possibility of escaping from its restrictive implications? And if there is such a possibility, for what kind of critical or even speculative activity does it leave room? These problems will be considered next.

II

PHILOSOPHY AS CONSTRUCTIVELY CRITICAL OF CONCEPTUAL SYSTEMS

Let us begin this lecture by taking another look at the argument underlying Moore's defence of common sense. It rests on the premiss that every type of statement has its own criteria built into it; if we understand the sentence by which the statement is expressed, we know under what conditions it is to be accepted. It is then pointed out that whether these conditions are satisfied in any given instance is a plain matter of empirical or formal fact. There is, therefore, no place for any philosophical decision.

A version of this argument which has played a leading part in recent philosophical discussions is the so-called argument from paradigm cases, mainly used to rebut scepticism. Suppose, for example, that a sceptic tries to put in question the existence of physical objects, such as a table. It is argued that if the sceptic were right there would at least be some doubt whether the criteria which govern the use of the English word 'table' were ever satisfied. But since it is a matter of common experience that the criteria are satisfied (since we constantly do apply words like 'table' successfully), it follows that the sceptic must be wrong. Or again, take the vexed question of free will. Surely, it is said, there is a manifest difference between doing something of one's own free will and being constrained to do it. We can easily distinguish between a shotgun wedding and one in which the bridegroom willingly goes to the altar. Distinctions of this kind are provided for in our language, and we know perfectly well how to make them. But from this alone it follows that the sceptic who denies or even queries the existence of free will is simply going against the obvious facts.

This argument is suspect, and in showing you why it is suspect, I hope to be able to throw some more light on our general theme of the nature of philosophical inquiry. The point which Moore and his followers have overlooked is that every word or – if you prefer to talk of concepts – every concept, carries its load of theory. This is obvious in the case of scientific concepts, but the amount of theory which is embodied even in the use of such everyday words as 'table' or 'glass' is much greater than is generally allowed for. Thus the objects to which such words are understood to apply are required to be accessible to different senses and to different persons; they have to occupy positions in public space and to endure through time. They have to be capable of existing unperceived, and it is part of the common-sense view of the world to assume that they exist unperceived in very much the same form as they normally appear to us when we do perceive them. This last point is of special interest as it threatens to bring common sense into conflict with science, which tends to draw a distinction between things as they appear to us and things as they really are. For instance, on the scientific level, physical objects are divested of their colour. The question whether there is a genuine conflict here (and if so, how it is to be resolved) is a very good example of a serious philosophical problem.

This should clarify what is meant by saying that even the most ordinary words of our language carry some theoretic load. The point to make now is that the mere fact of our recognizing that a word has application does not commit us to the acceptance of its theoretical background. I will give two illustrations, both of them used before; but as they effectively establish the point, I hope you will not mind.

Suppose there is a tribe whose custom it is to interpret everything in terms of the moods of their deity. When it rains they say that Mumbo-Jumbo is grieving; when the sun shines, they say that Mumbo-Jumbo is happy, and so forth. This is not just a linguistic oddity; their language represents what Wittgenstein called a form of life: it embodies their conception of reality. To make this fully clear, we can develop the story by supposing that their talk of Mumbo-Jumbo is bound up with religious practices, that they attempt to influence his moods in order to bring about whatever they desire. Now consider the position of an anthropologist who is studying this tribe. There is a sense in which he will wish to dismiss everything that they say. Since he does not believe in the existence of Mumbo-Jumbo, he rejects their whole conceptual apparatus. At the same time, the argument from paradigm cases operates against him. There are recognized criteria for deciding whether the statements which are made in this language are true or false; for example, the criterion for the truth of the statement that Mumbo-Jumbo is grieving is that it is raining. It is a matter of empirical fact in any give instance whether or not these criteria are satisfied.

What are we to say in a case of this kind? There are three courses that might be taken. The first would be to apply the verification principle and simply cash these people's statements in terms of the observations by which they were taken to be verified. The conclusion would be that all that these people really meant by saying that Mumbo-Jumbo was grieving was that it was raining. They themselves would deny this, but this would just prove their ignorance of semantics. A second more flexible course would be not to force this reduction on them but to argue, along Moore's lines, that since there are empirical criteria for deciding what mood Mumbo-Jumbo is in, then in the case where these criteria are satisfied, the statements which describe his moods are true. The third course, which seems to me the right one, is to distinguish the core of fact to which the statement corresponds from its questionable theoretical setting. This leaves us free to admit that there is some truth in what these people are saying – there is, after all, a sense in which they do record empirical facts – but also permits us to reject their statements as embodying a false, or even nonsensical conception of the way in which the world works.

This is a fanciful example, but the same point can be illustrated historically. At a time when the belief in evil spirits was a part of common sense, there were recognized criteria for deciding when people were demoniacally possessed. Since these criteria were empirically satisfied in many instances, we should have to conclude (if we rigorously applied the argument from paradigm cases), that the tales of demoniac possession were often true. But this is a conclusion which no rational person nowadays would be willing to accept. We can avoid it quite easily by distinguishing (1) the undoubted fact that certain people displayed the symptoms in question from (2) the erroneous interpretation which was put upon it.

It is in this way, I think, that we should approach the problem of free will. Of course, if we only look at the phenomena, there is a difference between an ordinary wedding and a shotgun wedding. However, it is possible to admit this difference without accepting the interpretations which the concept of free will carries. To put it summarily, free will is a condition of responsibility. It is, in general, only for things which we have done of our own free will (in the sense that we are believed to have been free not to do them), that we are held to deserve praise or blame, punishment or reward. But a philosopher who acknowledges there is a manifest difference between doing something which you have decided you want to do and doing something because you have a gun pointed at your head, may still wish to say that this difference is not sufficient to justify your being held responsible in the one case and not the other. He will argue that so far as responsibility goes, the two are on a level, since causality operates in both. It is only that in the case where you are said to have acted of your own free will, the determining factors are less obvious. This argument may be open to criticism, but it is certainly not refuted by a mere appeal to paradigm cases. Though the question will not be pursued here, there are good grounds for saying that the idea of desert is incoherent, so that if we were rational we should give up our current notions of merit or guilt. We could still continue to praise and blame, reward and punish, on utilitarian grounds; but even so, this would make a considerable difference to our moral outlook and even to the operation of our penal system.

It is already becoming clear that once we distinguish between the extension of a concept and its theoretical background (so that we can admit that a concept has application without being obliged to accept the theory from which it emerges), Moore's argument loses its force. It no longer guarantees the validity of the common-sense view of the world. For instance, a disciple of Berkeley's would not have to disagree with anybody else about the application of ordinary words like 'glass' and 'table'. If he followed Berkeley's injunction to think with the learned and speak with the vulgar, his use of common-sense expressions would not noticeably differ from that of the man in the street; but what his thinking with the learned would come to would be his rejecting the assumptions which common-sense statements are ordinarily understood to carry, beginning with the assumption that things exist unperceived. In current philosophical jargon, he would be adopting a different conceptual system.

I am not going to try to define the rather vague notion of a conceptual system, though I hope that the remainder of this essay and the following one may help to make it rather more precise. Obviously the most important questions with which we shall have to deal are what is required of a conceptual system, how one discriminates between them, and what grounds there can be for criticizing one or another. But before discussing any of this, I want to pose a more general question to which I do not know the answer. It might be held that there were certain general features which any conceptual system must possess for it to be possible for us to make any use of it at all. This is the position which Kant took; and one of his principal aims in the *Critique of Pure Reason* was to disclose what these general features were. As you know, he represented them as conditions of the possibility of human experience. A similar assumption is made by contemporary philosophers who have been influenced by Kant.

The difficulty here is that I do not see what foundation there can be for this sort of *a priori* anthropology. I do not see how one could arrive, otherwise than experimentally, at any universal generalization about the way in which the human understanding works. At the same time I am so far in sympathy with Kant that it is difficult to see how any possible world could be other than spatiotemporal. I am inclined to hold, therefore, that any conceptual system which can serve as a framework for an intelligible account of the world must contain the means of ordering things in space and time. But it is not at all clear what sort of necessity this is, or how it could be shown to obtain. As I do not think that I have anything of value to say about this question, I shall not pursue it further.

A less puzzling version of the Kantian approach is to be found in the claim that our conceptual system must have certain features if we are to be able to make certain distinctions that we should naturally wish to make. Thus Strawson has recently argued that if we are to distinguish between an objective world – not necessarily a world of things in themselves in the Kantian sense, but at least an objective world of phenomena – and our subjective experiences of it, then certain objects must be reidentifiable. This is substantially the argument of Kant's first analogy. Or again, there is Wittgenstein's contention that if we are representing a world in which there is communication, then certain objects must be represented as being public, in the sense that they satisfy criteria of identity which allow for the same object to be perceived by different observers. If this contention were valid, it would rule out the most radical form of phenomenalism, in which the world is broken down into a set of mutually exclusive private domains. But it might still allow for a weaker version in which an attempt was made to construct a public world out of neutral data. My difficulty, once again, is in seeing how such conclusions could be established by purely *a priori* arguments. It seems to be rather a matter of our having to try out possible counterexamples and finding, perhaps, that they break down. So if one were unable to devise any form of phenomenalism that met one's requirements, one might give up the whole idea, even in default of an argument that showed it to be contradictory. This takes us back to the problem of what these requirements are.

One way to approach it is to ask what motive there can be for trying to elaborate a conceptual system which is significantly different from the one that we ordinarily employ. It might, indeed, be undertaken for its own sake, simply as a technical exercise. The aim might be to throw light upon the workings of our current system, by showing in what ways and to what extent it is replaceable by a system of a different structure. I think that this motive has been operative, especially in recent times. But what seems to me to have been the most common motive for developing a different system is the belief that our existing system is in some way unsatisfactory.

All this may become a little more clear if we consider examples. I am going now to examine four philosophical positions, each of which I interpret as an attempt to substitute a different conceptual system for the one that we have. In general, this is not what their proponents have thought that they were doing. In most cases, they have thought that they were seeing more clearly into the nature of reality.

The first example is the philosophy of Absolute Idealism; the second an animistic or theological system. You may remember that Professor Quine, at the end of his celebrated paper, 'Two Dogmas of Empiricism', maintained that from a cognitive point of view, physical objects were in no better position than the Homeric gods: they are both cultural posits which are brought in to account for our experiences. We will develop this idea by considering a system in which things are supposed to happen by divine agency. This purpose could also be served by the third example, the system of Bishop Berkeley. However, we intend to ignore the theological aspect of Berkeley's philosophy and concentrate solely on his denial of matter or, in other words, his attempt to replace physical objects by collections of sensible qualities which exist only when perceived. Finally, we will go to the other extreme, considering that version of materialism which has come to be known as physicalism, in that it aims at the elimination of states of consciousness, or at any rate their reduction to physical processes. All these systems differ significantly from our present-day system of common sense, and apart from the second example, they are all philosophical in the sense that they result from the kind of speculation in which philosophers typically engage.

The main point to be made about the philosophy of Absolute Idealism, is that its interest is purely negative. On the positive side, the Absolute Idealists are even worse off than our Mumbo-Jumbo people, who at least have a going concern. Though it cannot be supposed that their methods of divination would enable them to understand or control their environment to any very profitable extent, we have represented them as making statements over which there is some empirical control. But what way could there possibly be of controlling such idealist claims as that all that there really can be is the Absolute, self-expressing and self-expressed, or that what masquerades as a system of material bodies in space and time is in reality a collection of immaterial selves timelessly loving one another? We do not know how to handle such statements; we cannot relate them to anything that we actually experience. The philosophers who put them forward were indeed willing to allow that our everyday statements contained some degrees of truth, but they did not have any viable method by which these degrees of truth could be assessed. It seemed almost to come down to vulgar worship of size. Any collection was thought to be more real than its elements, and everything culminated in the grand collection which alone was wholly real. But just because it was so grand one could not say anything significant about it. If you take a book like Bradley's *Appearance and Reality*, you will find that the section on 'reality' is very sad stuff.

By contrast, the section on 'appearance' is of considerable interest. The weakness of the Absolute Idealists is that when they reject the common-sense view of the world, they have nothing intelligible to put in its place. Nonetheless, their reasons for rejecting the common-sense view are worth looking into. It is not a question of their trying out an alternative to see if it will work; this sophisticated approach is found in some contemporary philosophers like Nelson Goodman, but it is a product of our own times. The philosophers we are speaking of, who flourished at the close of the nineteenth century, sought an alternative to the common-sense view because they believed that this view was untenable. Their reasons for saying that space and time and matter were unreal were that they could not find an answer to the intellectual difficulties which they detected in the notion of continuity, or of infinite divisibility, or of things possessing material properties independently of our perceiving them. They certainly went too far in claiming that the assumptions shared by the common-sense and scientific views of the world were self-contradictory, but they did call attention to genuine logical difficulties, not all of which have yet been satisfactorily disposed of (as the continuing interest in Zeno's paradoxes shows).

For example, the Cambridge philosopher McTaggart was one of those who denied the reality of time, which made him an easy victim of Moore's literalism. What could be more ridiculous than to suggest that nothing ever happens before anything else; that it is not, for example, true of us that we commonly have our breakfast after we wake up, or that we are all a day older than we were yesterday? But if instead of concentrating on McTaggart's conclusion we look at the arguments which led him to it, we find that they are not ridiculous. He begins by pointing out that the characteristics of being past, present, and future (which every event is supposed to possess) are mutually incompatible. To avoid a contradiction, we therefore have to say that events possess them at different moments. Our position then becomes that every event is past at a present or future moment, present at a present moment, and future at a present or past moment. But then the same difficulty arises with respect to the moments. We either relapse into contradiction or embark upon an infinite regress: This is a perfectly valid argument. What it proves, of course, is not that time is unreal, but rather that the relation of temporal priority has to be taken as fundamental; and past, present and future defined in terms of it by reference to the temporal position of the speaker, this position itself being characterized by its temporal relation to other arbitrarily chosen events. But since the effect of this is to spatialize time in Bergson's sense, since it leads to a 'static' picture of the universe as a four-dimensional continuum, there is a sense in which McTaggart is vindicated. His conclusion is absurd if you take it literally, but his argument does throw light on the workings of temporal concepts.

Now to the second example. Here again the main difficulty is in seeing how the alternative system could be operated. What criteria would there be for deciding whether Zeus was angry, whether Hera was jealous, and so forth? As in the Mumbo-Jumbo fantasy, you could more or less arbitrarily correlate the moods of the gods with natural phenomena, but in default of anything which enables you to correlate their moods independently of these actual manifestations, the system would have no explanatory value. To be able to make any predictions, we should have to correlate our experiences in some more practical fashion, and the introduction of the Homeric gods, though not entirely nugatory (since there is a sense in which someone who believed in them would see the world differently), would not extend the range of these correlations in any useful way.

The same is true of all religious views of the world. The explanations which they furnish of the course of events are always *ex post facto*. We are given no criteria for determining what the gods intend other than the observation of what actually happens, and this means that the explanations in question are empty. A theory which accounts for every possible occurrence has no explanatory value; it cannot lead us to expect any one thing to happen rather than any other. This objection would not hold if there were alleged to be reliable methods of receiving communications from the gods. The criticism would then be that these processes of divination did not achieve their purpose; that in comparison, for example, with scientific theories, their yield in terms of true predictions was very small.

It might be argued, however, that this was not a fair test. What it shows is that theological systems come off badly when their results are measured by scientific standards. But why should they not supply their own standards? Why should not their adherents rely on divination not only as a source of predictions but also as a means of determining whether or not the predictions are satisfied? In that event, they might come out very well.

This may seem an absurd suggestion, but it brings out a point of fundamental importance. It is a point to which empiricists pay too little attention and one that I should probably have gone on missing if I had not been engaged in a study of pragmatism. Those of you who have read the works of Peirce will remember that his pragmatism is based on the principle that the sole object of inquiry is the fixation of belief. His reason for saying this in preference to saying that the object of inquiry is the discovery of truth, is that the attainment of stable beliefs is what the pursuit of truth comes down to in practice. Though truth may not be formally definable in terms of belief, the question of what is true or false – as a question that one puts to oneself – is practically equivalent to asking what propositions one is or is not willing to accept.

I have a favourite illustration to illustrate this point. Consider the following game. You are asked to take two sheets of paper and write down on one of them a list of true propositions and on the other a list of propositions which you firmly believe. The rule of the game is that the lists are to be mutually exclusive; no proposition that is eligible for one list is to appear on the other. Now this is an instruction that you cannot rationally carry out – what you are asked to do is not self-contradictory. It is conceivable, and indeed not improbable, that among the propositions which you firmly believe there are some that are false, and there are certainly a great many true propositions which you do not believe – if only because you have never considered them. So you could fulfil the instructions by accident. What you could not do is to fulfil them by following any rational procedure. If you are asked to give any examples of true propositions, your only honest course is to mention propositions which you firmly believe.

The moral of this is that whatever is put forward as a method for arriving at truth will in fact operate as a method for fixing belief. You may remember that Peirce distinguishes four such methods: the method of tenacity, which consists in holding on to whatever beliefs you happen to have, no matter what evidence may be brought against them; the method of authority, which consists in believing what you are told by those who are placed in authority over you; the *a priori* method, as practised by some philosophers who deduce their beliefs from first principles which they find 'agreeable to reason'; and finally, the method of science. On various grounds, Peirce himself comes out in favour of the method of science, while still insisting – perhaps a little disingenuously – that it is in the end a matter of choice.

But suppose now that one has decided to operate not with the fourth method – the method of science – but with some variant of the second method, the method of authority. Consider a primitive society in which all beliefs are formed in accordance with the pronouncements of the spirits, which there is some accredited method for ascertaining. So long as they employ the same method for testing their beliefs as they do for arriving at them, they will be able to claim that their theories are in accordance with the facts. The spirits tell them what expectations to form and the spirits assure them that these expectations are satisfied.

Obviously these people move in a circle; but, it may be argued, so do we. To a certain extent, at least, we employ scientific method in testing the theories at which we arrive by the use of scientific method. What valid ground can we then have for thinking that our ways are superior? An answer suggested by Peirce is that although our recognition of anything as a fact is always the result of some process of interpretation, neverthe-less – at the level of sense perception – the latitude which this allows us is severely limited. The very nature of our sense experience, as it were, forces certain beliefs upon us. The superiority of our method would then consist in its yielding theories which were more closely in accord with these 'natural' beliefs. The devotees of the method of authority would try to maintain the same accord by suitably interpreting their observations, but they would not be able to make it work; the data themselves would not permit it. Since I dislike the extreme relativism to which the argument would otherwise commit us, I hope that this answer is correct.

The relevance of this rather crude example to our central theme is that it leads us to face the fundamental problem of the criteria of truth. In another way, however, it has been irrelevant, since we are not supposing that the members of the primitive tribe arrive at their system by a process of philosophical argument. Neither is it suggested that their conceptual scheme (any more than that of the Absolute Idealists) is to be regarded as a serious rival to our own. In this respect, the first two examples differ from the third. For the great interest of Berkeley's system is that it not only puts the common-sense view of the physical world into question on philosophical grounds, but also develops what may be a viable alterna-tive to it.

This is not exactly how Berkeley saw it. The idea (found in a book like Nelson Goodman's *Structure of Appearance*) that it is of interest to construct a phenomenal system just to see what can be made of it, is a modern development. Berkeley and those who have followed him (like John Stuart Mill and Bertrand Russell) have taken the position that only a phenomenal system could be legitimate, because it alone sticks to what is observable. As we shall try to show, there is a sense in which Berkeley's denial of the existence of matter is perfectly serious. He rejects the concept of matter, which he attributes to Locke and Newton, on the ground that it does not apply to anything that could possibly be observed. This demand that every concept be put to the touchstone of observation occurs throughout the history of philosophy. It stands at the opposite pole to the Platonic view, in which pre-eminence is given to the unchanging world of abstract ideas. The difficult question for those who make it is how much of the world of science – or indeed of common sense – they can reconstruct on the basis of what they take to be directly observable.

In recent years, this whole approach has come under severe criticism. Doubt has been thrown upon Berkeley's initial assumption that the data with which we are presented in sense perception are sensible qualities, existing only when they are perceived. The attempt to construct a viable system on the basis of these data is dismissed as an obvious failure; the reasons for which this attempt has been made have themselves been put in question. These criticisms will be examined next.

III

BERKELEIANISM AND PHYSICALISM AS CONSTRUCTIVELY CRITICAL

Berkeley's denial of the existence of matter is the kind of statement that only a philosopher would make: it impresses but also irritates the plain man. He thinks that he is being told that his world is entirely different from what he takes it to be, and he finds this hard to believe – even though he cannot spot the fallacy. So Boswell, discussing Berkeley's 'ingenious sophistry' with Dr Johnson, remarked that 'though we are satisfied his doctrine is not true, it is impossible to refute it.' And Johnson answered, 'striking his foot with mighty force against a large stone, till he rebounded from it, "I refute it *thus*." '

If Berkeley's assertion that there are no material things were to be taken literally, then Dr Johnson's refutation would be valid. For Johnson's procedure exactly foreshadows that which we have seen

Moore adopting in his proof of an external world. They both prove that there are material things by indicating examples of them. It is clear, however, that whatever Berkeley was maintaining it was not something that could be refuted by holding up hands, or kicking stones. To this extent, then, his assertion is not to be taken literally. But how then are we to interpret it?

It is tempting to say that what Berkeley was really doing was not to deny the truth of statements which are ordinarily thought to imply the existence of material things, but to give an unfamiliar analysis of them. His own words support this interpretation, insofar as he insisted that he was not depriving the plain man of anything that he believed in. His analysis is not one that it would occur to the plain man to give, but then so long as the plain man can be sure of the truth of the statements that he makes about the things in his environment, he is not concerned with their analysis. That is the province of philosophers.

I am not prepared to say that this is a wholly incorrect description of what Berkeley was doing, but I can no longer regard it as explaining all that needs to be explained, partly because of the obscurity of the notion of analysis. To say that Berkeley was trying to tell us what we really mean when we talk about stones and hands and chairs and tables, etc., is to invite at least two obvious objections. In the first place, if this is Berkeley's concern, he sets about it in a very odd way; he does not engage in any linguistic or sociological investigations. And secondly, if he were giving an account of the meaning which statements of this kind are commonly understood to have, he would appear to be straightforwardly mistaken. It seems quite clear that our ordinary usage of words like 'stone' and 'glass' and 'chair' is such that we conceive of the things to which they apply as being capable of existing without being perceived. But if Berkeley's denial of the existence of matter implies anything, it is that nothing (other than a spiritual substance) exists unperceived. The words which we use to apply to physical objects are used by him to apply to things which have only a strange manner of persistence, as ideas in the mind of God. But it is surely obvious that what we ordinarily mean when we speak of the things in our environment is not anything which entails the existence of God. It would seem, therefore, that whatever Berkeley is doing, he is not giving a faithful account of ordinary usage. It is still open to us to say that he is refining ordinary usage; or, better still, that he is engaging in a form of reductive analysis. But this needs further explanation.

As we saw last time, in cases where a philosopher makes what is obviously an outrageously false statement (as that nothing moves, or that time is unreal, or that there are no material objects), the interest lies not in the statement considered on its own, but in the arguments which lead up to it – in the proof which the philosopher offers. Let us now apply this to Berkeley. The central proposition in his system (from which the denial of the existence of matter follows) is that for anything other than a spiritual substance, to exist is to be perceived. How then is this proposition proved?

The proof which Berkeley offers is very simple. It can most easily be set out in the form of a syllogism. Let us use the general term 'things' to refer to what Berkeley took such ordinary words as 'table', 'chair', 'glass', 'watch', 'stone', to denote. The major premiss of the syllogism is that things consist of sensible qualities; the minor premiss is that for a sensible quality to exist is for it to be perceived; and the conclusion is that for anything to exist is for it to be perceived.

There is clearly nothing wrong with the logic of this argument. If the premisses are true, the conclusion must also be true. But are the premisses true? The first point to notice is that they are intended to be necessary propositions. For Berkeley, it does not just happen to be the case that things consist of sensible qualities: for then it would be at least conceivable that we should come across a counterexample. He takes the much stronger view that it is only in so far as the things to which we refer do satisfy this condition that it is possible for our reference to them to be successful. In the same way, he does not regard it as a mere matter of empirical fact that sensible qualities exist only when perceived. He treats it rather as a defining characteristic: anything of which this were not true would not be a sensible quality.

Now what Berkeley means by a sensible quality is very much what modern philosophers have meant by a sense datum. A sensible quality is to be taken, at least in this context, as an instance of colour, or sound, or taste, or smell, existing as a particular entity only as an item in the private experience of the person who senses it, and enduring no longer than the occasion on which it is sensed. All this is a matter of stipulation. But it is one thing to make a stipulative definition and another to show that anything answers to it. It has not been so obvious to all other philosophers, as it was to Berkeley, that these sensible qualities exist. But if there is doubt about the minor premiss of Berkeley's syllogism, the major premiss is more doubtful still. For even if there are sensible qualities (in the sense here intended), it is a tall order to assume that any collection of them can be an adequate substitute for a physical object – in the sense in which this term is commonly understood. Berkeley assumes it because he is convinced that if we ask what the plain man is referring to when he speaks of the things in his environment, the only possible alternatives are to say that he is referring to collections of sensible qualities or to say that he fails to refer to anything at all. But this again is by no means obvious.

We now see that to get a proper understanding of Berkeley's position, we have to look at the epistemological assumptions underlying it. I propose, therefore, to restate his major premiss in a way that will bring this out more clearly. Let us restore to words like 'stone' and 'watch' and 'table' the meaning that they would commonly be understood to have. Then Berkeley's premiss may be taken to be that the only evidence we can have for the existence of anything to which such words apply is our perception of sensible qualities.

This is plainly a weaker proposition than the proposition that things consist of sensible qualities. Is it acceptable? If we are to accept it, we have to make a distinction which has recently come under attack. The distinction is between the hard core of observable facts and the interpretation which we put upon them. I am not conceiving of what I called 'hard data' as being altogether uninterpreted; nothing can be called a 'datum' unless it is in some way classified. Even a reference to sensible qualities, in Berkeley's usage of the term, allows for some latitude, since there could be other ways of classifying such things as colours and shapes than the ones we actually employ. But even if this is granted, it may still be possible to distinguish between the direct evidence of our senses (in the form of data which involve the minimum of interpretation) and the more far-reaching constructions which we put upon it. A distinction of this kind is, indeed, implicit in the works of classical empiricists from Locke and Berkeley, through Hume and John Stuart Mill, to Russell, Broad, and Price and other sense-datum theorists of our own day. By attacking it, or attacking the use which has been made of it, contemporary philosophers like Austin, Ryle, and Wittgenstein have struck at the roots of this whole philosophical tradition.

Against the trend of current opinion it can be argued that the distinction can be maintained. In order to try to show this, we will reconsider something previously stated. You may remember that I called your attention to the amount of theory that was carried even by so simple a statement as 'this is a watch.' In claiming to perceive anything of this kind, we were assuming that the thing was tangible as well as visible; that it was accessible to any number of different observers, but also capable of existing unperceived; that it preserved its identity through time, and occupied positions in a public space. I took it to be part of the common-sense view of the world that things of this kind persisted unperceived in much the same form as that in which we normally perceived them. There are also special assumptions which are involved in identifying anything as a watch, or a chair, or whatever it may be, but consideration of the more general assumptions which I have listed should be enough for my present purpose.

Now it seems clear (and here I can only state it dogmatically) that there is a very good sense in which to make a statement which carries all these assumptions is to go beyond the immediate sensory evidence. This is not to suggest that the sense experience which I am now having does not justify me in claiming that I perceive a watch on this table. What I am suggesting is that there is much more to such a claim than is strictly contained in the experience on which it is based. If I may use the word 'see' in a way in which it might be used by a psychologist who was interested in the quality of my vision rather than in the identification of the objects which come within my view, I am claiming more than I see. This does not mean that it is incorrect for me to say that I see the watch; it means only that in such cases the description of what is seen covers more than what is visually presented. That the watch is tangible, that it is visible to others besides myself, that it persists at times when no one is observing it: all this is a construction which I put upon my present visual data. I confess that I do not see how this can be seriously disputed.

But then the question arises whether it is not possible to devise what might be called a language of minimal commitment. Could we not formulate statements which were designed to do no more than describe what was sensibly given, in the way that I have just been trying to explain? For instance, we could proceed upon some such lines as Nelson Goodman's in his *Structure of Appearance*. Our statements would just record the presence of sense qualia, without carrying any implication as to the states of these qualia; whether, for example, they are public or private entities, and without containing any reference to what occurs or would occur on any other occasion. One could regard these statements as featuring in a kind of primitive language game (if I may be allowed to pervert a favourite expression of Wittgenstein's) in which the rule is just that when you are confronted with certain sensory patterns, you salute them with the corresponding words. The only element of interpretation is in the selection of the sensory patterns. Though this argument will not be pursued here, it can be shown that such a game is playable.

Since we are speaking in this context of Berkeley's system, it should be made clear that in referring to sense qualia we are not making the assumption that Berkeley makes when he refers to sensible qualities. The main difference is that Berkeley takes it for granted that there are entities to which his sensible qualities are given. He assumes the existence of minds as spiritual substances, and speaks of his primitive data as their ideas. But this not only commits him to the objectionable course of starting with what are defined as private objects; it also saddles him at the outset with a heavy and very questionable load of theory. One has no right to take it as a datum that there are minds, in Berkeley's sense, let alone that their experiences are concordant. Neither does he need to make these assumptions in order to obtain an adequate starting point. One advantage which we gain from starting with a very primitive language is that since persons do not figure in it, the question of privacy or publicity of our hard data does not arise.

Our first step might be described as a refinement of Berkeley's. If you allow it to be taken, how will it help us to understand Berkeley's denial of the existence of matter? The answer is that we can then think of it as imposing a restriction on the possible interpretations of the primitive data. What Berkeley is claiming is that the common-sense interpretation is illegitimate. This does not prevent him from attaching a meaning to statements like 'this is a watch', which allows them to be true. He simply takes them as being established by the occurrence of the appropriate sensible qualities. What he rejects is the common-sense view of the way in which such statements go beyond the data by which they are verified, and the reason why he rejects it is that he thinks it impossible to conceive of material things as existing apart from the data of sense.

The principle which underlies Berkeley's argument is that whereas horizontal extrapolation is permissable, vertical extrapolation is not. What I mean by horizontal extrapolation is a form of inference in which, starting with entities of a given type, you predict or postulate the existence of further entities of the same type, whether actual or hypothetical. Vertical extrapolation, on the other hand, is a form of inference in which you move from one level to another, concluding with entities which are held to be manifested by (and therefore of a different type from) those with which you start. This is well illustrated by the fourth example, the thesis of physicalism. One motive for taking a physicalist view of other persons is that it enables us to substitute horizontal for vertical inferences. A horizontal inference, in this context, would be an inference from present to future behaviour; a vertical inference would be an inference from observed behaviour to a state of mind, conceived as lying behind it.

The reason for preferring horizontal inferences to vertical inferences is that you then avoid having to postulate entities which are relatively inaccessible. So the mental states of other persons, if not subjected to a physicalist reduction, are inaccessible relatively to their own behaviour. So again, physical objects, if not treated phenomenalistically, are inaccessible relatively to sense data. Whenever you can substitute a horizontal for a vertical inference you avoid an epistemological problem. This leaves us, however, with the question when this procedure is justified. We have in fact returned by another route to the problem of the criteria of reductive analysis.

An argument which is often brought against these attempts at reduction is that they presuppose what they are designed to eliminate. For instance, if one takes my restatement of Berkeley's starting point, one may perhaps allow onself to imagine that there are people who play my primitive language game. One might even go so far as to imagine that there are people whose use of language goes no further than this. But in indulging our imagination in this way (even in formulating the rules of the game), we are making use of concepts for which the game itself makes no provision – in this instance, the concepts which are involved in thinking of groups of persons inhabiting a common physical world. This is not objectionable so long as the use of these concepts can eventually be justified on the basis of the elements which they help you to introduce. It would not do if the elements were actually defined by means of these concepts; but I can see no reason why, in giving an explanation of your procedure, you should not make use of all your linguistic resources – the only limitation being that you must not bring in entities which you are not in a position to construct.

But this brings us back to the question: What is to count as a construction? If we continue to follow Berkeley to the extent of dispensing with any vertical extrapolation, we shall be able to admit only what is explicitly definable in terms of our primitive data, or anyhow reducible to them by the process of translation. But this will not give us all that we need. I assume that we want to arrive at some sort of public world containing persistent entities, not necessarily such objects as glasses and watches, but – at any rate – regions of space. Also, we want to be able to distinguish between the objective course of events and their various reflections in the experiences of different persons. The work which has been done on phenomenalism shows that it is not possible to tell so elaborate a story exclusively in terms of sense qualia. If we adopt the useful distinction which F. P. Ramsey made in his last papers between a secondary theoretical system and a primary system which is treated as factual, relatively to the theory, then we have to say that the secondary system, in this instance, is not translatable into the primary one.

Does it follow then that we cannot represent physical objects as being constructible out of our primary data? Not necessarily. It depends on what we are going to count as a construction. The best procedure will be to see what the relation between the two systems is and then to consider what status we want to assign to the constituents of the secondary one.

The answer to the first question is not at all simple, and can here be dealt with only summarily. It is possible to exhibit the physical world of common sense as a natural projection of our primary data. The empirical fact on which this mainly depends is that qualia form relatively stable clusters. If one considers any fairly elaborate sensory pattern, there will be, as a general rule, only a small number of contexts in which any given observer comes upon it. The consequence is that these patterns are found to be reinstatable, by traversing similar sensory routes. This means that by projecting the spatial and temporal relations which are sensibly presented, one is able to conceive of certain configurations of qualia as being permanently accessible. In this way one arrives at the notion of a phenomenal continuant. Among phenomenal continuants there is one that has the distinctive property of being almost totally pervasive. It is the observer's body, not characterized as such (since we have not yet credited our observer with the notion of himself), but characterizable as the central body. The concept of the central body, since it allows for the observer's movement, assists in the process of fusing visual and tactual space.

By correlating different states of the phenomenal continuants, an observer can now form a rudimentary picture of the way the world works. There are, however, a certain number of presentations which do not fit into the general picture. This leads him to distinguish between those data which fit into his main account, and those which do not. With the arrival on the scene of other observers, characterized in the first instance as continuants which resemble the central body in that they are also producers of signs, he is able to obtain corroboration of his main account of the world and also to acquire the idea of himself not only as a figure in this main account, but also as a maker of signs corresponding to nothing that the others recognize and so as a recorder of worlds existing only for him. This lays the foundation of the public-private distinction from which self-consciousness arises and the attribution of consciousness to others. And so, having proceeded from an entirely neutral basis one is finally able to develop the distinction between mind and matter.

This piece of science fiction – it is only a rough sketch – is intended as a model of the way in which our common-sense view of the world is 'cashed' at the sensory level. If it is acceptable in this light, one might follow Quine in speaking of the physical objects of common sense as cultural posits. The positing of them would be regarded as a device for linking one's data together and for predicting the course of one's experience. In the same way, the positing of scientific entities, like atoms and electrons, could be regarded as a device for linking together the physical observations that are made at the level of common sense. The positing of unconscious mental states could be regarded as a device for linking together certain sorts of overt behaviour. On the other hand, since one arrives at all these entities by processes of vertical extrapolation, one might feel obliged – or at any rate prefer – to treat them realistically. One might think not only of chairs and tables, but also of atoms and electrons, and even of unconscious mental states, as literally existing.

How does one decide this issue? What is actually at stake in the controversy between someone who takes a realistic view of scientific entities and one who conceives of them as operational devices? The dispute is taken seriously by philosophers of science, but it is not at all clear to me what it involves. There may, indeed, be an analytical question about the adequacy of suggested operational definition, but once this is cleared out of the way, it is not easy to see what theoretical issue remains. It comes down to a question of how one chooses to look at the world and what picture one prefers to form of it. There would then be no question of truth or falsehood here, but only of convenience. This is not to say, however, that the issue is trivial; it may have great psychological importance. For instance, it can plausibly be argued that the adoption of a realistic view is necessary for the progress of a science at certain stages of its development.

Let us look at a case in which the realistic view appears to impose itself, although (from a logical point of view) it does not appear to differ in any essential way from those which we have so far been considering. This is the case of propositions about the past. Two illustrations can be used. The first is taken from a book called *Father and Son* by the late nineteenth-century English critic, Edmund Gosse. The elder Mr Gosse was a member of the sect of Plymouth Brethren, who tended to be fundamentalists. At any rate they accepted the conclusion, which Archbishop Usher had derived from his study of the chronology of the Old Testament, that the world was created in the year 4004 BC. For such people the development of the science of geology was a great stumbling block, for it appeared to indicate the world had existed for very much longer than was provided for in the Bible, if the archbishop's calculations were correct. However, the elder Mr Gosse found a very ingenious way of getting round the difficulty. He maintained that God had indeed created the world in 4004 BC, but filled it with delusive signs of greater antiquity in order to test men's faith. The stronger the geological evidence appeared to be, the farther it showed that the Deity was prepared to go in carrying out this test.

The point of this illustration is that if we allow Mr Gosse his notion of a Creator, if we allow even that the world had a beginning in time, there is no way of refuting his position. Any evidence which the geologists interpret in their way, he can interpret in his; it is simply a multiplication of the deceptive signs. Of course if we put it to the vote, hardly anyone would be found to side with Mr Gosse, but that would not have worried him, except as a proof of human weakness. The only argument that we can think of is that if you are going to accept the findings of science in other fields, it is hardly consistent to assume that its laws break down at just this point. It would seem extraordinary that a generalization concerning the rate at which radio-atoms disintegrate should fail only when we draw references from it which apply to time earlier than 4004 BC. But all that this shows is that Mr Gosse's system is uneconomical; it does not show that it comes into conflict with any observed facts. In the end we deal with Mr Gosse in the same sort of way as we would deal with the Mumbo-Jumbo people. His conception of the way the world works is one that we simply refuse to accept.

The second illustration is taken from my own work, *Language, Truth and Logic*, where I maintained that statements about the past were equivalent to statements which described the present or future observations which would be counted as establishing them. So, to assert (for example) that Julius Caesar crossed the Rubicon was to make an assertion about what you would see if you looked into history books. My reasons for taking this implausible view were the same as those which led Peirce to the same conclusion, though I did not discover this until quite recently. The past events themselves being inaccessible, the only grounds that one could have for asserting their existence must lie in the nature of the present evidence; to deny that some received opinion about the past was true would be a completely idle performance unless one were either setting out the existing evidence in a new light or predicting that further evidence would favour a different view. This is in line with Peirce's saying that practically speaking the meaning of every factual proposition lies in the future.

I have long given up this view. For one thing, it is inconsistent with the view that tenses are eliminable; for another, I cannot accept the consequence that the meaning of every sentence which expresses a statement about the past is constantly subject to change, as further evidence comes to light. But mainly it now seems obvious that a statement like 'Caesar crossed the Rubicon' can neither entail nor be entailed by any description of what is to be found in history books. It is logically possible that the event should have occurred without its being subsequently recorded, and it is logically possible that the historians should all be giving a false account. I am bound to acknowledge, however, that the significance of these possibilities is purely formal. If there is no record of a past event, one is not in a position to say anything about it; if all the records go to show that a given event occurred, one can have no reason to assert that it did not. In postulating the existence of the past, independently of any record, one is therefore making a formal concession to realism.

This is in accordance with common sense. It is to be noted, however, that the common-sense view of the world is not consistent in its treatment of time. The past, but not the future, is treated realistically. Yet logically there is no difference between them. In either case, the objective fact is that an event of such and such a kind is located at such and such a date. From this point of view, the question whether this date precedes or succeeds the date of our reference to the event, is irrelevant.

The fourth example is the thesis of physicalism. This is again a question about the existence of a certain class of entities, in this case mental states and processes. The thesis of physicalism is that there is no need to postulate such entities, in addition to physical processes. Another way of putting it would be to say that statements about mental entities are reducible to statements about physical ones. If one starts with qualia, this is a question that arises only at the secondary level; and here I am inclined to think that this applies to ontological questions as a whole. I am inclined to think that the question what there is, at any rate as it figures in discussions of this kind, is a question of what we want to put into our picture of the world, and therefore that it does not relate to our primitive data, but only to the construction which we put upon them. Once again, this brings me close to Peirce, who assigns existence to the category of Secondness (the category of relation), and not to that of Firstness (the category of quality). It is to be assumed that our secondary system provides for the existence of physical objects. Whether it can admit the reality both of the physical world as it is represented in science, and of the physical objects of common sense, is an interesting and difficult question, not entered into here. In whatever way it is answered, the thesis of physicalism will not be affected.

What are the motives for adopting this thesis? The main motive is epistemological. We constantly make judgments about other people's states of mind, and in many cases are confident of their truth. We do not believe that these judgments are infallible, but we do believe that they are well-grounded. Very often we should say that we knew what another person was thinking or feeling; whether, for example, he was angry or in pain. But now if we have to conceive of the mental states of others as being hidden from us, in the sense that all we can ever hope to observe is their physical effects, it is not clear how we can be justified in claiming any such knowledge. It is not clear what warrant we can have for making a vertical inference from people's overt behaviour to the mental processes which are believed to underlie it. On the other hand, if mental processes can be identified with physical ones, this difficulty is removed. It will then be only a matter of our having to justify horizontal inferences, from one piece of behaviour to another or from the agent's behaviour to his physical condition.

Another motive is a semi-scientific one. If you believe that everything that happens in the world can be explained in terms of the laws of physics, you will be driven to conclude that the postulation of mental occurrences serves no scientific purpose. As Professor Feigl puts it, they are in the position of 'nomological danglers', and in the interest of economy one should try to shave them off. Against this, it may be said that the fact that a class of entities was scientifically superfluous would not be a sufficient reason for ruling them out of existence, if there were other grounds for taking them to exist. In any case, it has yet to be shown that the laws of physics are capable of accounting for everything that happens.

The scientific motive, for what it is worth, applies to the existence of any mental state; the epistemological motive applies, in the first instance, only to the attribution of mental states to persons other than oneself. There are, however, very good grounds for holding that the meaning of a statement in which a mental state or process is attributed to a given person must be essentially the same, whether the attribution is made by the person himself or by others; and in that case if you accept a physicalistic account of other people's mental states you will have to extend it to your own.

This consideration also goes the other way. The strongest objection to physicalism is that one seems clearly able to distinguish between one's own mental state and any physical event: and if one acknowledges this distinction in one's own case, it will follow by the foregoing argument that one must also acknowledge it in the case of other people.

This objection tells most strongly against the thesis which Carnap has put forward, that statements which apparently refer to mental states or processes are logically equivalent to statements about physical events. The difficulty here is that there is no sure method of determining logical equivalences when they are not governed by the rules of a formal system. One may adduce what seem to be obvious counterexamples, but the proponent of the thesis may refuse to acknowledge them. At the same time, it can safely be said that this interpretation of the meaning of statements about mental occurrences would not be likely to result from any dispassionate examination of the way in which these statements are actually used. The reason why some philosophers have accepted it is that their epistemological or metaphysical presuppositions appeared to leave them no alternative.

This objection does not apply, or anyhow not with the same force, to the thesis (which for some reason appears to be especially attractive to Australian philosophers) that mental states are not logically but factually identical with states of the central nervous system. This thesis depends on the assumption that all our experiences are causally determined by the condition of our brains. Its proponents recognize that this is an empirical and not a logical assumption, and are therefore careful not to claim that the identity for which they are arguing is a logical identity. They do believe, however, that there are strong empirical grounds for taking their assumption to be true. If it is true, they think that one would be entitled to regard mental states as being identical with states of the central nervous system in the factual sense in which, for example, the Morning Star is identical with the Evening Star, or lightning is identical with a discharge of electricity. But since they put forward no criterion of identity, apart from the assumed causal dependence of mental upon physical states, it is doubtful if their thesis amounts to anything more than a recommendation to adopt a certain way of speaking. Even if their causal hypothesis is granted, it is still open to anyone to regard mental states as existing concurrently with physical states, without being identical with them. In the absence of any further criteria, this is not a question that can be decided empirically. The choice is between two different ways of conceiving what there really is.

One advantage of physicalism is that it simplifies the problem of personal identity. Though I think that this price is too high to pay, I must also confess that I have never yet found an analysis of personal identity with which I could be satisfied. In these circumstances, one may be tempted to take the lazy course of postulating a soul, or spiritual substance. But since this supplies us with no criterion for determining when two different mental states are states of the same soul, it hardly deserves to be considered as a genuine theory; it is rather an admission that the notion of personal identity is not able to be analyzed. We may in the end be driven to this, but it is not a position that we should allow ourselves to adopt until we have thoroughly explored all the forms of analysis that seem to have any chance of succeeding, and we have found decisive objections to them.

The point of these examples has been to show how philosophers can legitimately engage not only in the work of elucidating concepts but also in that of constructive criticism. I doubt if my treatment of them has provided you with a sufficiently clear answer to the question what philosophy is; but I hope that I have succeeded in doing some philosophy along the way.

FIVE

The Glass is on the Table – A Discussion[1]

ELDERS: Ladies and gentlemen, I would like to welcome you to a debate which will, I suppose, be of interest in many respects. I would like to lose as little time as possible in beginning this philosophical contest, in which you will see an avid football fan, Sir Alfred, and a lover of boxing and alpinism, Arne Naess, debating with each other on central issues of their own philosophies. First of all, we have to discover what kinds of philosophical views both philosophers have. Sir Alfred and Mr Naess, would you each explain to the audience what you consider to be your tasks as philosophers? Sir Alfred?

AYER: Well, I suppose to try to answer a certain quite specific range of questions which are classified as philosophical questions – and are very much the same questions as, I think, have been asked since the Greeks, mainly about what can be known, how it can be known, what kind of things there are, how they relate to one another.

In general, I would think of philosophy as an activity of questioning accepted beliefs, trying to find criteria and to evaluate these criteria; trying to unearth the assumptions behind thinking, scientific thinking and ordinary thinking, and then trying to see if they are valid. In practice this generally comes down to answering fairly concrete specific questions.

And I hope, in a sense, to finding the truth.

ELDERS: And you, Mr Naess?

NAESS: Well, I see it a little differently, I think, because I would

[1] 'The Glass is on the Table' was originally a discussion between A. J. Ayer and Arne Naess with Fons Elders as interviewer, broadcast in English on Dutch television in 1971 and subsequently published, along with discussions from the same series by other philosophers in Fons Elders (ed.), *Reflexive Water: The Basic Concerns of Mankind* (London, Souvenir Press; Ontario, J. M. Dent & Co., 1974).

rather say that to philosophy belong the most profound, the deepest, the most fundamental problems. They will change very little, and they have not changed much over the last two thousand years. So we have different conceptions of philosophy, but we agree that the epistemological question, 'what can we know?' and the ontological one, 'what main kinds of things are there?' belong to philosophy. As I see it, they are among the most profound questions we can ask.

AYER: Yes, but how do you measure the profundity of a problem? I mean, a problem may often look quite trivial and then turn out to be profound. In a sense, you try to answer what you are puzzled by. Now this may be something very profound; it may even look quite superficial, then turn out to be profound.

NAESS: How do we measure? Well, that's one of the most profound questions of all. How do we know? I suppose it will vary with cultural and social circumstances. It involves fundamental valuations, not only investigations of fact or logic.

ELDERS: Sir Alfred, would you give an outline of a sceptic?

AYER: Well, I was going to talk about this. It seems to me that, perhaps not so much in ancient philosophy, but certainly in modern philosophy since Descartes, a lot of problems have arisen out of a certain very characteristic sceptical argument. I should say that a sceptic is always someone who questions one's right to make certain assumptions – often assumptions about the existence of certain kinds of things – on the ground of their going beyond the evidence.

I mean, a very obvious and classical example would be scepticism about other minds. People will say, well, all you observe is other people's behaviour; all you observe is their actions, the expressions on their faces. How do you know that anything goes on behind? How do you know that everybody isn't a robot, or whatever? And so you get scepticism also tied up with a certain neurosis. It has also a certain emotional tone.

Or again, take the classical example of the scepticism of David Hume, the scepticism about induction. Hitherto, when you lit a cigarette, it would smoke; when you have walked on the floor it has supported you. How do you know that this will happen in the future? How can you extrapolate from past evidence to future occurrences? And then it is shown that the argument is, in a sense, circular, always presupposing something that you can't justify. And a lot of philosophy comes out as the posing of arguments of this kind and the attempts to find replies to them. And you could even characterize different sorts of philosophy by their different ways of meeting the sceptic. Now, I think one mark of a philosopher, why I think that Arne Naess is a profound philosopher, is to take scepticism seriously. Would you?

ELDERS: But in *The Problem of Knowledge* you are quite critical about scepticism.

AYER: I think I rather cheated in *The Problem of Knowledge*. It seems to me that I gave scepticism a good run, and then in the end somehow some little strong John Bull common sense came out in me and I took away from the sceptic the victory he had won, like a corrupt referee in a boxing match.

NAESS: I had the same impression when I read your book. Ultimately you would say: 'Hm, no! Common sense, after all, tells me there is something rotten here, so there is something rotten.' But . . . well, I don't know your mind.

ELDERS: Speaking about this common sense, Sir Alfred, has it something in common with what the Germans call *Gesundenes Volksempfinden*?

AYER: I do not know whether it has or not, because I don't know really which Germans you are talking of, or what they would mean by this.

ELDERS: But what do *you* mean by common sense?

AYER: By common sense I mean what Hume calls natural belief. For instance, take the case of the past. Now, in fact, you can't justify any belief about the past, because any attempt to justify it will be circular. The most you can do is check one memory by another one, one memory report by another one; or check the records, and this again presupposes the reliability of memory, because how do you test the records? So you really have no non-circular justification.

So it is perfectly true to say, as Russell said, that for all we can *prove*, for all we can demonstrate, the world might have begun five minutes ago, with people already fully grown who delusively remember a totally unreal past.

Now I suppose, Naess, you want to leave it there and say: I really don't know. But I'd say, well, the argument for it may be circular, nevertheless I'm going to assume it. This will be what I would call common sense. At a certain point I say, no, no, no, this is carrying scepticism too far: to hell with it.

And possibly that is a remarkable weakness in a philosopher: I should be more heroic. I mean are you more heroic, more heroic in this way? Would *you* say we have no reason to believe that the world has existed for more than five minutes?

NAESS: I think it is reasonable to say that it has existed for a very long time, and that it is reasonable that we should assume this. But that still leaves open the question of truth. Reasonableness does not rule out mistakes. Our concept of known truth is such that you must have a guarantee. But are we ever justified in saying that our research is over, we need not bother to test our beliefs any more, fifty thousand years ago there were people living on this earth? We do not have any guarantees – or do we? I have not found any. The more I think about this, the less I come to feel that I know. That's a feeling you don't have every time you take a tram or walk on the floor. But in the moments when, as Heidegger would say, you live more authentically, that's to say you . . .

AYER: Let's keep him out of this.

NAESS: I knew it, I knew it, and therefore I had my small pleasure!

AYER: We ought to maintain certain standards.

NAESS: Well, a man whose name begins with H and ends with R thinks, and other philosophers also, that we are more or less concentrated and integrated. In moments of high concentration and integration, not at the times when I am merely functioning, I have this feeling – and it is not just a feeling – that we don't have any decisive arguments for any conclusions whatsoever. That is, when the conclusion starts with 'It is true that. . . .'

AYER: And yet there is something peculiar here, in the way I view it, because we have got all the evidence. It is not like a palaeontologist, who might be doubtful about dating some fossils, because perhaps more evidence will come in; perhaps some day more archaeological work will show him in what way his dating is wrong.

But with sceptical questions, in a sense there literally isn't any more evidence to come in. No experiment could be made that would show us, one way or the other, that we *were* justified in assuming the existence of other minds. No psychoanalyst is going to still our doubts on questions of this kind. They are in a sense logical doubts; in a sense all the evidence is there.

NAESS: There are so many conceptions of logic and of intelligibility, and of what an argument is, and of what is evidence. I feel that in questions of conceptual analysis you can never say: now we have all the evidence here, now the cake is complete. Who knows the baker? Even in logical questions our situation resembles that of the palaeontologist: we do not have all the evidence about the evidence. I am also against the idea that the collecting of evidence should always be a kind of collecting of the results of external experiments. Experiments should also be made with our logic and ourselves. What does the I, the ego mean? We use the distinction between the I and the rest – what does it mean? Philosophers have many, but doubtful, solutions, and I will probably go on trying to collect evidence until I die.

The mysteries that we 'know' include those of 'I', 'know' and the link between the knower and the known.

AYER: Yes, I'm not dissenting from what you say, I'm merely trying to get at what's behind what you're saying. Do you think we might discover any quite different criteria even of validity; I mean that we might suddenly say, no, we don't want to use this logic? That you envisage even finding a different form of logic?

NAESS: Yes, I expect the future here will resemble the past: continued modification of the conceptions of inference, criteria and evidence. I don't think that in the year 2000 we will have a completely different conception of what constitutes evidence. But sometimes you add or subtract some kinds of evidence; and in a most unexpected way. As, for example, the concepts of proof in mathematics.

AYER: Indeed, indeed.

ELDERS: Mr Naess, I think we're still speaking a little evasively, because we can also formulate the problem of the past and the present in our own terms. Perhaps Sir Alfred will tell us how certain, how convinced he is that we are here now; and perhaps you could also speak on this question.

AYER: Yes, I would say, if I were in a law court, I was convinced beyond reasonable doubt. I wouldn't say it's certain; it is certainly logically conceivable that I should wake up and find myself back in my bed in London: that I've dreamt the whole thing. Although, of course, *that* experience might be the dream one. In that case, however, the question would be how things went on from then. But I would be convinced beyond reasonable doubt. I would bet on it. I would bet at least as much as you're paying me, for instance. And I think Naess would too; he's more sceptical than I am, but he will risk a bet.

NAESS: A little less willingly than you, I feel.

AYER: But of course it's not simply a question of the fact of our being here: it's also how you are going to interpret that fact. We say we are here; but what are *we*? I mean, are these just bodies or do they have minds too; what's meant by their having minds? Are we going to regard them just as little bits of atoms, or are we going to regard them in a common-sense way as being consciousness looking outward? All these questions come up.

Just saying 'We're all here', represents, I think, something that you are pretty confident of. How, then, are you going to analyze that? What ontology do you envisage? This is again disputable.

NAESS: You are now speaking as a sceptic here, Sir Alfred. We don't disagree on a single point here. But an important thing in scepticism is this: that anything can happen somehow, and that perhaps all things are somehow interconnected. Perhaps no question can be solved in isolation.

The question 'Is this a glass?' is somehow irrelevant in relation to the basic problem that all things are interconnected. The particular question 'Is this a glass?' evades the fact that there are several different ways of looking at the glass, that there are different relationships between human beings and a thing, and that all these interconnect.

ELDERS: But you still presuppose the entity of the glass.

NAESS: If you say 'presuppose' an 'entity', that raises a tremendously difficult question. Do I ever presuppose?

AYER: Well, of course, an enormous number of presuppositions are built even into the language we are using. If we talk about our being here at all it presupposes, first of all, an assumption of human beings, in some sense or other; a whole spatiotemporal system; the glass you're looking at; even the very terms we're talking in. But I wanted in fact to ask you: how serious is your scepticism? You say anything can happen. Now I perfectly agree that it is logically possible; there is no contradiction, no formal contradiction, in the idea of all these people turning into swans, and even Jupiter coming – I think Jupiter is going too far, but some human analogue of Jupiter coming in – and behaving as he did to swans. This is logically possible, but you don't envisage it as a serious possibility.

ELDERS: As an empirical possibility.

AYER: I mean, it seems to me that although one admits the logical possibility, one doesn't think it will happen. One's scepticism in actual life, in one's actual beliefs, in the way one plans one's life, is pretty narrow because of the extreme force of what Hume called 'natural belief'.

We are conditioned to make certain assumptions, to take for granted that things *do* go in regular patterns. A really serious scepticism might be represented by someone who really would refrain from taking action because, after all, the man that I shake hands with, *might* suddenly explode; therefore, he says, I won't go near him. This is, if you like, an armchair scepticism, but I would not for this reason say that it was not serious, for I think that purely intellectual problems are serious. But it is, in this sense, theoretical.

ELDERS: You agree with this sharp distinction between logical and empirical possibility?

NAESS: Well, this is not as important as certain other things which were said at the time, if you will excuse me.

I would say that sometimes I'm just functioning. When I buy a ticket to Groningen I neither assert anything nor deny anything; therefore I do not presuppose anything. I just walk, talk and go. I don't quite feel a philosopher at such moments. I do not assert the truth or falsity of any proposition: I just function. I act with a certain *trust*. A trusting attitude in walking and buying things for paper money. I think it's a trust towards things, not propositions. And that's different from making an assertion; this *is* true and the other *is* false. That's one point.

The second point is this, that I could easily imagine that a certain lady here in the room might become a swan at any moment. I also tend to think something completely different – so many different, incompatible things, that they must collide with each other.

Therefore I am not afraid that we shall explode, for if anything and everything can happen, you're no longer afraid. You may explode but it may not hurt you. If you only think something dangerous will happen, you're afraid; but if anything can happen, you simply calm down. And that's how I feel.

ELDERS: So as a sceptic you are less afraid than Sir Alfred?

AYER: I think that if I thought anything could happen I should be afraid, yes. Anything whatsoever.

NAESS: Well, that may be because you have had some bad experiences, but I have mainly had good experiences.

AYER: No – I think it's just because I have a more feverish imagination.

NAESS: Basically I have had good experiences with other people.

AYER: But in *this*, you see, you're now doing exactly what you ought not to be doing: you're generalizing from past experiences. You say you've had good experiences, therefore you expect only good things to happen. But this is not just allowing anything to happen, it's allowing only what has happened to you to happen.

NAESS: That's a misconception of scepticism.

AYER: It's in your natural belief.

NAESS: This is a first semester scepticism. Not generalizing and using a lot of 'perhaps'es'. In the second semester you utter generalizations, because you do not strongly resist your own tendency to utter what strikes you. So I say something about all people and I don't believe it to be a truth in the sense that I'm convinced it is true in the moment I say it. But if you say, 'Oh, Mr Naess, you are generalizing and speaking about all good experiences with all people', then I would say, 'Yes, yes; I generalize quite naturally, but I couldn't give a good argument for the truth of what I am saying.'

So, generalizing is okay for a sceptic; if he is relaxed as a sceptic he will make a lot of generalizations, but *without taking them too seriously*.

AYER: Yes, I mean, every moment it's true; of course, you're taking generalizations seriously now in reaching forward confidently and drinking your orange juice. You are taking generalizations seriously because a huge amount of theory goes into this. Theories about the behaviour of the glass, about the liquid that's in the glass, about your own body, about the behaviour of your neighbours, deciding that they will not suddenly go mad and start to be violent, all sorts of theories. Every minute you're making an enormous number of assumptions of this kind.

NAESS: But do I assume the truth of any proposition? Scepticism has to do with claims about the truth. During the war and during the Hitler regime, and when I meet people who are really convinced that what Marx says is true, then I feel the importance of a sceptical attitude; these people take the attitude that what they're saying just couldn't be false, an attitude of unshakability and incorrigibility. This I fight. I can be shaken and I wish others to be able to be shaken! The stand against incorrigibility somehow becomes generalized until it colours one's total view. But I think one of the roots of unshakability and incorrigibility must lie in political and social conflicts.

ELDERS: Well, will you try to apply what you are saying now to the concept of democracy?

AYER: That's a big jump!

NAESS: Well, I have, for instance, discussed and published more than three hundred different definitions of democracy, in order to undermine politicians who say that democracy requires so-and-so; Soviet theorists who say that *they* breed 'real' democracy; and British democratic politicians who say that 'real' democracy is very different. But I only undermine, not accuse of error. The British traditions go back to certain authors in the Greek world and the Soviet conceptions go back to Plato and Aristotle. So they all have a 'big shot' behind them. What I do is merely to make it complicated for propagandists to monopolize the term.

AYER: Ah, something I was interested in: you used the phrase 'real' democracy and I think this brings out an interesting, indeed philosophical point, namely what Stevenson called 'persuasive definitions'. When you say real democracy, the word 'real' here is, as it were, an okay word, it is trying to capture assent for your conception of democracy. Not essence, I'm not saying that there is an essence of democracy; the word 'democracy' means what we choose it to mean.

And you're therefore trying to capture assent for a certain definition of the word, and of course not simply assent for a certain use of language, but trying to gain adherence to a type of behaviour that is associated with the language. Someone might say, well, real democracy consists not in the right to vote, but in economic equality, shall we say. What he's then doing is trying to capture the favourable word 'democracy' for a policy that he advocates. And I think that with questions like how you define democracy, what they're really asking is not in the least how you define the word, they're not asking questions of lexicography, they're asking you for some kind of political programme; the word 'democracy' now being one that has got favourable sentiments attached to it. And presumably you arranged your three hundred definitions in some order of desirability. I mean there were some you wanted to be accepted more than others, that even reflected your own political opinions, presumably.

NAESS: Sure, to do that is very tempting. So far, I have only undermined the use of the slogan 'democratic'. But, I'm sorry to say, in some ways I feel miserable to be defending scepticism now, because there is a very tragic conflict between the attitude I hold in my integrated and concentrated moments, which is more or less sceptical, and the requirements of consistent action. For instance, when we believe that we really must do something about some terribly pressing problem, we must somehow narrow down our perspective. The vast plurality of possible worlds – and how do we know in which world we live – are suddenly not only irrelevant, but contemplation of them undermines the willingness and capacity to act. Most people are only willing to act forcefully and consistently when they have a belief in *the* truth and close their minds to all else.

AYER: But I should have thought this was a field in which a certain kind of scepticism anyhow was very desirable and fruitful. It's very healthy indeed not to listen to the rhetoric about democracy, but to look at the facts. Look and see what actually happens: see how people live their lives, see what is actually done in the law courts, look behind the words to realities. This is in a sense a form of scepticism, although you're not sceptical about the words that we use to mark the realities with. And I would think there that your approach is thoroughly sceptical and at the same time constructive in this field.

NAESS: Yes, it's desirable that people should be like you in this way, but mostly they seem not to be like that. The students say that we must get rid of particular textbooks of Naess because they undermine convictions and will undermine collective action now and over the next five years. And this is real; it is a tragedy, because they need rhetoric and dogmatism, I think. Scepticism breeds passivity. I do not feel that way, but the students do.

ELDERS: But, Sir Alfred, if you are stressing this point of the relationships between certain philosophical schools on one hand and certain values on the other hand, do you see any relation between your empiricism and your role as director of the Humanist movement in Great Britain?

AYER: Yes, I see some relation. I don't see a relation in the sense that I would be able to deduce my political or my social views from any set of metaphysical or epistemological principles. I don't think that, in this sense, I have a coherent system or that there can be one. But of course I think that there is some relation, inasmuch that if one has an empirical, even sceptical temper of mind, then one will be hostile to rhetoric, or at least one will look for the facts behind the rhetoric.

I've been a humanist, for example, partly because I could see no reason to believe in the existence of God. And therefore I would be opposed to people who not only maintained this, but also based political or social programmes on it.

I would be a humanist inasmuch as I think I would be professionally opposed to humbug of any kind: the kind of humbug that you too often find in people in power, in judges and people of that sort. And, in a sense, I would expect an empirical philosopher to be radical, although if one looks at history, this isn't always so: Hume, who was the greatest of all empiricists, was in fact, if anything, a Tory. This was partly because of his scepticism. He was sceptical about schemes of human improvement.

ELDERS: Like Schopenhauer.

AYER: Yes. But in general it has certainly been true in the last century or so that there has been a close association, *so* close an association between empiricism and radicalism that it couldn't entirely be an accident. But I think it's a matter of a certain habit of mind, a certain critical temper in the examination of political and social as well as philosophical questions, that is responsible for this, rather than some deduction from first principles.

ELDERS: Yes, but these are not really arguments, but merely a piece of history.

AYER: I'm giving you an explanation. You asked me what I thought the connection was, and I . . .

ELDERS: The historical explanation. But we're talking now on the level of arguments about the relation between empiricism and humanism.

AYER: But it's slightly more than this, because I think a certain habit of mind, a certain critical temper that you would develop if you did philosophy in the sort of way that Naess and I do it, would on the whole tend . . . after all, you bring the same intelligence to bear on any of a wide range of problems, even though they aren't necessarily the same problems, and this would, I think, tend to have the effect of making you a liberal radical in social and political questions. This would be more than just a historical accident, as it might be if I happened to be both protestant and have brown eyes; it's not as accidental as that. There is, I think, some causal connection of a very close kind.

But I don't think that I can, from any kind of empiricist premisses, deduce a political programme. I mean, you can't get rabbits out of hats that don't contain them. Do you agree?

NAESS: Well, no! First of all, you expect that as philosophers we should somehow be able to deduce them, whereas I would say our responsibility is to connect our views – our ethical and epistemological as well as our political views – in a fairly decent way so that we get a coherent whole. The connections may be looser than ordinary scientific connections, looser than deductions. I think we disagree here on how we conceive of our roles as philosophers. I consider myself a philosopher when I'm trying to convince people of non-violence, consistent non-violence whatever happens. That is a fairly fantastic doctrine, considered descriptively or empirically. I must therefore make clear, to myself and others, what kind of normative principles I also make use of, and derive from them the special norms and hypotheses characteristic of Gandhian strategy of conflict behaviour. I think I believe in the ultimate unity of all living beings. This is a very vague and ambiguous phrase, but I have to rely on it. It is a task for analytical philosophy to suggest more precise formulations. Because I have such principles, I also have a programme of action, the main outline of which is part of my philosophy. So I might suddenly try to win you over to consistent non-violence and to persuade you to join some kind of movement – and this in spite of my not believing that I possess any guarantee that I have found any truths.

AYER: I can see you might indeed try to persuade me of this, but I don't think you'd persuade me of these methods. The ultimate unity of living things: I mean . . .

ELDERS: Is this metaphysics, in your opinion?

AYER: Well it could be an ordinary scientific statement. In fact it would include not only living things but also inanimate things, if they are all made of atoms; in this sense they are homogeneous. Then I suppose there is more homogeneity between organic things, although the difference between organic and inorganic is so slight.

It doesn't seem to me that on any scientific basis of this sort, one is going to build an ethical view. After all, civil wars take place, and the people who fight each other in them don't deny that they're each human beings and even belong to the same nation: but it doesn't stop the fighting.

So, in fact, this alone is not going to be sufficient. You have to put up some moral principle, which is not going to be deducible from any factual or metaphysical one; that it is wrong to take life of any kind. But do you then extend this to all life, mosquitoes and the like, or just human life? I'm not saying this ironically: I think that it's a perfectly defensible position to be vegetarian and so on – I'm not, but I think . . .

ELDERS: But will you try, Mr Naess, to give the metaphysical foundation for your belief in non-violence, about which we can speak later? We are still at the level of principles and arguments for or against metaphysics.

AYER: And it's partly political too, isn't it? It's not just metaphysical. However well Gandhi did against the British, he would have done less well against the Nazis.

NAESS: Yes, metaphysical and political and anthropological, all at once, all in one: therefore systems are unavoidable. Gandhi as a leader in Germany? Perhaps one million Jews killed before 1938, none after. He advised resistance, not submission. The metaphysical principle here of course belongs more to the Indian than to the European tradition.

AYER: Yes, I would say so.

NAESS: But the ecological movement may change the European tradition. The formulation 'all living beings are ultimately one', is neither a norm nor a description. The distinction between descriptions and norms and even imperatives can be put in afterwards, semantically speaking. It is the kind of utterance you make in support of something I would call an intuition, by which I do not mean that it is necessarily true. In moments of concentration you are aware of vast perspectives: yes, that is the thing, ultimately life is one!

And then you start to ask yourself how you can argue for this and what does it mean; and at this moment you need a norm, a system of ethics and an ontology and plenty of hypotheses in many fields covered by the sciences. And you say: a mosquito and myself are obviously not biologically the same, so I must mean something different from it. For instance, something like: if I hurt you, I hurt myself. My self is not my ego, but something capable of immense development. Think of a picture from the war: a young man is just going to throw a grenade and there is another young man, the so-called enemy, very similar to him, also intending to do the same at exactly the same moment. It's a case of 'him or me', but they are also obviously aware of the fact that they are the same kind of being and that to throw grenades at each other is really nonsense. They are one.

AYER: Well, I share your moral sentiments, but I think what you've been saying is very largely just false. It's like the schoolmaster who is going to beat the boy and says 'This is going to hurt me more than it'll hurt you.' That's an absolute lie; it isn't going to hurt the schoolmaster at all – on the contrary, in only too many cases it's going to give him pleasure.

NAESS: The boy also if he's a masochist.

AYER: The boy also if he's a masochist, yes. But, in fact, what you are saying simply isn't true. I mean, not only I and a mosquito, but even you and I are not one. Of course, if I sympathize with you and you are hurt I shall be sorry, but I shan't be hurt in the same way. It's indeed true, empirically true, that to a rather limited extent human beings sympathize with one another; with people they know and like, and people they feel in some way close to. But to say that they're one is in any literal sense just false. I'm not identical with you, and it would be a terrible thing if I were, in a way. I mean, this discussion would be very difficult.

ELDERS: Or it would be much more easy.

AYER: Ah, well, yes, it would be. It would be even more solipsistic than it sometimes tends to become.

ELDERS: Growing more and more together.

AYER: It seems to me that clearly, if one takes these things literally, they're false; and therefore you take them metaphorically. Now, it's just when you take them metaphorically that they become moral principles of a perfectly respectable kind: that you ought to treat other people as though they . . . I mean, if you like, as in the Christian way of thinking . . . I mean, deal with other people as you wish them to deal with you. They wouldn't necessarily have the same tastes, but in a sense one should treat other people as if they were as important to you as yourself. This is a perfectly good moral principle. But why pretend that we are identical when we are not?

ELDERS: Now you need some whisky, Mr Naess?

NAESS: No, no. You are too rash.

AYER: He doesn't want to identify with me too much, does he?

NAESS: Too rash, you are too rash. First of all, there is no definite literal sense of an utterance like this in relation to its metaphorical sense. You have to analyze it from a great many points of view. Its so-called literal meaning is hardly exemplified in any available text; what is the literal sense of the identity of all living beings?

AYER: Well, I mean it in the sense in which the Evening Star is identical with the Morning Star; in the sense in which the Young Pretender is identical with Charles Edward Stuart; in the sense in which the author of *Pickwick* is identical with the author of *Oliver Twist*: this is what I would call the literal sense of identity. Now it's up to you, since you're not using it in that sense, to define a sense in which you are using it.

NAESS: That's right.

AYER: And now I subside.

NAESS: Good. That's better. Have patience!

When we say that we are the same, three concepts may profitably be interconnected. The ego, the self with a small s, and then this great Self, with a capital S, the atman, which you hear so much about in Indian philosophy, but also, of course, in certain Western traditions. If you as a boy had had a very much wider development, your self, what you take to be part of you, would not only include your body, it would include everything that's yours, so to speak; so what is yours would have been much wider.

This justifies the tentative introduction of an entity, the Self, with a capital S, the power of which gradually increases. You might still say your limits are those of your body, but there you would have to include units of your central nervous systems such as, for instance, those corresponding to the Milky Way and the Andromeda nebula in so far as you have sensuous or other bodily interactions with them.

And in this kind of philosophy they ultimately believe that human beings can develop in such a way, that in a sense their selfs include the other selfs in a certain way.

AYER: But in *what* sense? In *what* sense does my self include Fons'? Or could it ever, however much I thought of him?

NAESS: Now you are too impolite. Fons is not utterly different.

ELDERS: I should like that.

AYER: I'm sorry, but I don't know, I . . . Fons would like it.

NAESS: Philosophy is just this; that you develop something that I've started and gradually you introduce preciseness from different directions. Then you breathe three times, reinforce your intuition, and go a little further towards precision. But there is no hurry, this process will take a long time. And of course sometimes intuitions vanish for some of us; for instance, those of 'absolute movement' or of an absolute 'voice of conscience'.

I suppose you would say that the limits of the self gradually increase from infancy to puberty; and the sense in which it increases is, I would say, what you are concerned about. What you identify yourself with . . . the norms you internalize.

AYER: Ah! Now that's, yes . . .

NAESS: And concern in the sense in which you say *my*! You use the possessive term, my – *my* mother, for instance.

ELDERS: I think in a biological sense we form a chain of divisions; so for example, in this sense, you can use the meaning of the greater Self, against the small self or ego.

NAESS: Yes, biologically we are just centres of interactions in one great field.

AYER: But why put things in a portentous way when they can be put in a simple way? Why not say that as you grow older you come to comprehend more things; your knowledge perhaps increases, and then after a certain point, I'm afraid, diminishes again. But up to a point it increases. Perhaps your range of sympathy is greater; perhaps you identify with more things and sometimes again with less.

Again, one can't always generalize; some people differ in this respect, some people narrow themselves in the sense of concentrating more on themselves. When one has a fairly precise method, a precise way of describing all these facts, why does one have to make such portentous statements about one's self expanding and including everything. It sounds romantic, but it's quite superfluous when what you mean can be put quite definitely: that these things happen, and these things are empirically testable. I would say that what you're describing is true of some people, not of others.

NAESS: Well, what is pretentious depends on at which university you are studying.

AYER: Portentous. I did not say pretentious, that would have been rude, I said portentous.

NAESS: I meant portentous also: and that depends on the university. If you had been at Oxford or Cambridge at the time of Wittgenstein, it would have been a different thing than what it was at the time of Bradley and of the Hegelians. Trivialism is portentous if carried to extremes. But let us go back to the belief in the pervasiveness of the 'I'. Well, people then used certain terms about which we now would say 'Oh, my God, don't be so portentous.' So this is completely relative, I think. There are a million things to be said: must they all begin with 'I'? Spinoza introduces the 'I' in part two, not in part one, of his system. Do we have a definite ego all the time? Isn't that a weird construction? A Cartesian prejudice? 'I developed from this to that' or 'Now I am developing more in this direction' or 'I was very different when I was thirteen from when I was twelve', and so on – I, I, I!

Must we think that there is such an entity? I wouldn't simply think there is a definite entity there. Without this scepticism I would not feel 'all living things are ultimately one' to be a good slogan.

AYER: I don't think I disagree with you there. I certainly don't want to postulate any sort of Cartesian substance, anything of which the ego could be a name. I'm very puzzled about this, I don't at all know the answer to it, but I'm inclined to think that you can't find a personal identity except in terms of the identity of the body.

But of course, if that's right, if you can only define personal identity in terms of bodily identity, then your thesis that one's identity could include other people would become false, except if some kind of bodily identification were to take place. I'm not very positive about this, but let us take, say, the relation between you and me. We're about the same age, your self and my self are sitting here now, and two small boys went to school so many years ago. Now clearly there is a physical relation, in the sense that there is a spatiotemporal continuity between these bodies and those ones, and there are also certain causal connections. I mean that what we are thinking now is causally dependent upon what happened to those bodies then. Whether there is more than this I would be inclined to dispute – except for memory, but that again could be held to be a function of physical stimuli.

So I'm inclined, I think, to equate personal identity with bodily identity, but I'm not sure about this.

But even if this equation were shown to be wrong, as it easily might be, I wouldn't want a Cartesian substance. I would want something like a Humean theory of a series of experiences linked by memory and the overlapping of consciousness and so on, so that in this sense I don't want to attach too much importance to the I.

But I think I wanted to say that in whatever way you define the series of experiences which are properly called mine, they are always exclusive of those properly called yours. I don't think that series of experiences from different persons can logically intersect. Although paranormal psychology might produce phenomena that one might want to describe in this sort of way, I don't want to be at all dogmatic about this.

NAESS: I'm genuinely glad to hear this. I agree concerning the term 'experience'. Its logic is subjective: insisting on using that term, you are caught in the same trap as Hume.

Perhaps before the year 3000 there will be 'hardware' people, let us say people who have abandoned their brains, taking in computers instead. Collectivists may prefer this: it might herald the end of egos. But it couldn't be quite the end, and is perhaps not central to what we are speaking about. More central is the fact that, as a philosopher, I think I have a kind of total view, which would include logic, epistemology and ontology, but also evaluations, and that I do not escape from the relevance of them at any moment. When I'm saying who I am, so to speak, I cannot avoid indicating what kind of evaluations I make, what kind of priorities or values I have, etc. And there it seems to me that we get into a metaphysical area, a 'portentous' area, because only there do we realize just how many different conceptions of fact and experience are possible.

I have a feeling that the empiricism that I suspect you are inclined to accept is too narrow, in the sense that you do not admit a commitment to statements which are untestable empirically. I am inclined to say 'your thinking is too narrow'. Would this hurt you slightly? If I hurt you I hurt myself, which means that if, for instance, I now said something to you and the next moment I thought that it had been unfair of me to say that when I realized that it had hurt you somehow – not that you couldn't easily win an argument – but if it had hurt you, I would have a moment of identification. Phenomenologically there would be 'one' hurt, which was not yet 'my' experience. I expect you now to jump into psychology and say that when you identify yourself with somebody else this is a matter of psychology, not philosophy, and that we have the empirical evidence from more or less good experiments which can show us to what extent we identify with each other. It has no ontological consequences. If A identifies with B, he remains A.

But for me it is more a question of what in German they would call *Einstellung*; it's something that is not reducible to empirical psychology, because whatever the psychologists find, I would stick to it probably. They are committed to a definite conceptual framework from the very beginning.

AYER: Yes, I wasn't going to make that move, because I don't think these labels matter all that much: these are classifications for librarians. I think we should be free to say what we like in every field if we like. I was rather going to take up what you said earlier about this question of who I am. I think when I was arguing before, I was using it more in what could be called a 'passport' sense; for example, who is Arne Naess? I would say that he is someone who answers to such and such a description, whereas you were clearly using it in a wider sense than this. You were meaning by 'who am I?' something which has to do with your own conception of yourself. When you said that hurting me would hurt you, this means that it would in some way be injurious not to your identity as the passport Arne Naess, but injurious to your conception of yourself, injurious to the sort of man you like to think of yourself as being. And possibly also if you hurt me it would have repercussions on your own character, and therefore in this sense you've injured yourself. You wouldn't literally feel the pain that I felt, but you would be damaging yourself; which means that you are, in a certain sense, identifying with me, because you regard it as part of your conception of yourself that you don't gratuitously or voluntarily or deliberately hurt other human beings.

Now there seems to be no quarrel here whatsoever. But I think that if there is a difference between us, it is that I make a sharper distinction than you do between what's descriptive and what's normative. I would say that this was simply an announcement of what rightly, to put it in this way, could be called a policy.

I mean, it is perhaps not quite right, it's somehow not so deliberate as that, and it's more important to you than that. But this is a form of life that you're adopting, and something that goes very deep, and you put this forward, if you like, for me either to imitate you or disagree with you.

But, I think that a mistake could only arise, and I should only have a quarrel with you, if you tried to prove it by deducing it from what masqueraded as a statement of fact. If you accept what I have just said as what you mean by 'you and I are one' or 'you identify with me', then we are talking in sympathy. It's only if you say that you have this policy *because*, and then make this appear as a factual statement, that we then quarrel on intellectual grounds.

ELDERS: So, in fact, the central question is the relationship between metaphysics and morality.

NAESS: A norm or a moral injunction should not masquerade as a description; but neither should a statement involving description, for instance factual description, masquerade as a norm. 'All living beings are ultimately one' admits partial interpretations or analyses in various directions, descriptive and normative. None seem to be exhaustive, which is typical of good old metaphysical formulae.

Incidentally, the distinction between fact and norm, or injunction, is ultimate: it is not that I think the norms are less normative, but that the descriptions are less descriptive. Description presupposes, for instance, a methodology of description. A methodology includes at least one postulate, at least one rule. A change of postulates and rules changes the description. This makes the notion of description as opposed to norm a little shaky: therefore I no longer use the term fact. It suggests independence of postulates and rules.

ELDERS: There we go, Sir Alfred.

NAESS: I am sorry. I would feel badly if you were to take me as just a Heideggerian or some kind of . . .

AYER: No, no, on the contrary, I mean, I wouldn't . . .

NAESS: I'm not so sure I'm not. I'm quite near Heidegger in a certain sense.

AYER: Nonsense!

NAESS: Yes, we are *Geworfen*. I feel very much that I have been thrown into the world, and that I am still being thrown.

AYER: Now *why* do yourself this injustice? Why spoil it? Now leave him out, keep him out. How do you know we are thrown into existence. You may have had a very difficult birth for all you remember.

NAESS: How do I know? How do I know the relevance here of knowledge?

AYER: Thrown into existence, nonsense.

NAESS: Perhaps you use the term 'know' too often.

AYER: This should be eliminated.

NAESS: Let's get away from being thrown into existence . . . Yes, I shall try to trust you when you say that I am not thrown!

AYER: Good, but I take your earlier point, which I think is an extremely important one, about the vulnerability of the notion of fact.

I think we need the notion of fact, because we do need a distinction between fact and theory at some level: we need some kind of distinction between the deliverances of observation and the explanation for them. But of course it is not a sharp distinction. And if you like to say that what we call facts are already theory-laden, I would say it is a fact that there were more than two glasses on this table, and I should agree that an enormous amount of theory has already gone into this.

And I would share your scepticism about anything that might be called 'pure unadulterated fact'. I think probably that doesn't exist, that there is already some conceptualization here, and if you like, conceptualization is already to some extent normative; pragmatic considerations have already come in, in the way we classify things, since the classifications are based on what we find it useful to do. So I quite agree that the distinction isn't an absolute one. The only question is whether it's relatively strong enough to bear the sort of weight I want to put on it. And I'm again hesitant about this.

NAESS: I'm glad you are hesitant. But of course, when you say we need a concept of fact, of hard fact, I say some need it sometimes. But who, and when? It's not the great Self, it is the small self that needs limitation: it is when I'm functioning in tough practical situations, but not when I'm deciding what it is worthwhile doing in life, when the very widest perspectives are involved and when one is concentrating and meditating.

AYER: One needs to make certain distinctions in order to move forward a little bit. You must take certain things for granted in order to make a further step, and then possibly you go back and question other things; otherwise you never start.

NAESS: Yes, I agree. But it doesn't help you when you're saying that we need a concept of fact, e.g. that this is a glass.

I do not think we need a concept of fact, and we do not even need a concept of knowledge, in what I would call fundamental philosophical discussion. After a lengthy discussion, when we really get down to subtleties and refinements and also fundamentals, the term fact no longer occurs in your speech; neither does the term 'I know' occur in mine as far as I can see. But there is this kind of vanishing – somebody said that the state would vanish, though they say it less and less now, I think – and I would talk about the vanishing distinction between description and norm, fact and non-fact: the vanishing distinction, not vanishing facts, but the vanishing distinction . . .

AYER: Well, the vanishing distinction between truth and falsehood?

ELDERS: No, between fact and interpretation.

AYER: Well, then I would say I would need the concept of fact to maintain the distinction between truth and falsehood, to maintain some notion of truth as stating *what is so* and falsehood as stating *what is not so*, and using 'fact' as a purely general term to cover *what is so*.

NAESS: But you don't need the term fact in order to maintain the very general distinction between true and false . . .

AYER: I don't need the actual term, but I need some term doing that work.

NAESS: I don't think so.

AYER: You don't admit it – you do?

NAESS: Well, not in order to uphold the distinction between true and false. There is a need for the term 'fact' in everyday trivialities, like when I pick up this glass and . . .

ELDERS: Well, but in a logical sense you don't need any fact . . .

AYER: No. You could certainly do without the actual term fact, because one can talk of propositions as being made true by states of affairs, by events, by things having certain properties, or whatever. But I still think you need something to stand for what stands on the right-hand side of the equation. You have an equation: such and such a statement is true, if and only if . . . and then you assert whatever it is. For instance, 'you and I are sitting here' is true *if and only if* you and I are sitting here. Then you want some generic term, it seems to me, to describe these states of affairs that in the last resort verify or falsify all the statements that we make.

I do want some residue of realism, I want something out there that in the last resort makes our statements acceptable or not acceptable: in the end one can't say that anything goes. It's all very well my wanting to believe that I have a thousand pounds, or a million pounds in the bank. I go to the bank and I try to draw it out and it's a fact that the cashier doesn't pay it to me.

And in the last resort one wants some, I don't mind what term you use, but some term, it seems to me, to characterize, in any philosophy, really this . . . the brutishness of things, the hard thing you stub your toe against. Yes this, like Dr Johnson. [*Strikes his fist on the table.*]

NAESS: Excellent. But it is highly characteristic, I think, of your monumental tradition of empiricism in England, in Britain, I should rather say.

AYER: England I prefer. I'm not a Scot.

NAESS: I would say British: the Scots were wonderful empiricists. But when you need a term for something, if you say this: it snows, it does not snow; this is true if something, something . . .

AYER: That's right, the actual stuff.

NAESS: . . . then you get the idea: ha, facts. No, that is British, that is not universal. The Bengali seem never to get the idea, think of Tagore and others . . .

AYER: If it were British, alas, we should be in a much more powerful position than we are. I'm afraid it's becoming American.

NAESS: Well, I learnt from housewives and schoolgirls another way of putting it. They say that something is true *if* it *is* so. Marvellous. It is a little wider than 'it *is* so', and much wider than 'it *is* a fact.' It's true *if* it *is* so, it's false *if* it *isn't* so. Marvellous. But very little is said, of course, concerning testability.

AYER: But 'it's being so' is what I call a fact.

NAESS: '*If* it *is* so'; we have a conditional there, and there we agree.

AYER: Yes.

NAESS: It is only true '*if* it *is* so'.

AYER: Certainly.

NAESS: But what *is*? What *is* there? And here we must be terribly comprehensive, if we are to include all living ontological traditions. And to narrow it down to facts, is to narrow it down to the British Isles first of all.

AYER: Oh no, you mean that only in the British Isles anything is so? I'd be very sorry to hear this.

NAESS: No, on the contrary, 'anything is so that is so' is more, is broader than 'what is a fact?' And the British tradition, which politically speaking is sometimes, I'm glad to say, very good in comparison with the opposite German attitude . . .

ELDERS: With the Labour government or with the Conservatives?

NAESS: Both, they are identical as far as . . .

ELDERS: Do you agree, Sir Alfred?

AYER: They're much more similar than I care for.

NAESS: Yes, and very British.

AYER: No, when the last government was in power, I thought these are no better than the Conservatives. But now that the Conservative government is in power, they are worse.

NAESS: When you say 'they are worse', would you add: well I just talk like this, it is not part of my philosophy. Personally I would say: this is part or should be part of both our philosophies. 'They are worse', you should be able to say that . . .

AYER: I do say that, constantly.

NAESS: But you might do more than say it, you might take it as part of your personal philosophy, or your *total view*. And there we are; the total view, which is considered unclear, unempirical, metaphysical in a bad sense. Because if you have a total view, somehow it hangs together and you always see the facts only as structures within a great body of hypotheses.

AYER: You can't seriously maintain, can you, that every opinion that I hold, or every emotional preference that I have, must be tied up with my philosophy. For example, I'm a lifelong supporter of Tottenham Hotspur, a football team: it is absurd to say this is part of my philosophy and that, had I happened to support Arsenal instead of Spurs, I could not be the positivist pragmatist that I am, but some sort of absolute idealist.

This is being ludicrous. I have lots and lots of opinions about all sorts of things: political opinions, aesthetic opinions. If you like, they're all unified in the sense that it's the same person who holds them; and possibly some very clever psychologist could trace some connection, could realize that there was something in the Spurs type of play that would appeal to philosophers of my sort possibly more than something, shall we say, in the play of Manchester United. But why do we have to go so far? Why not leave me in my compartment?

NAESS: No, not today. No, if you say 'they are worse' and you think of a Labour government, or any other government, you do not mean worse as football players, you mean worse . . .

AYER: I make a moral judgment, yes, certainly.

NAESS: Partly moral, partly political and economic.

AYER: Mainly moral.

NAESS: And to me that means that you are already involved in philosophy. There are degrees of philosophical relevance. Not all moral judgments are part of your system, but all moral judgments of yours should hang together within the framework of your philosophy; let us distinguish frame and details. So every moral judgment you make is relevant to your philosophy without being part of it. The mythical fall of the apple which struck Newton is not described in a physical system, but it is a physically relevant fall.

AYER: In this sense I don't think I have a philosophy.

NAESS: I suspect you don't have.

AYER: I don't think so, no. I don't think that anyone *should* have in this sense.

NAESS: Should! Another ethical judgment.

AYER: It seems to me that I have an intelligence such as it is that I . . .

NAESS: Here is a moral issue for you. I shouldn't have such a philosophy – your general statement included me.

AYER: I think it tends to confuse your thought. I think you'd be a better philosopher if you did not have a such a philosophy.

But I don't know, it is such a silly question: are you speaking as a philosopher? What does it matter? Am I speaking as an Old Etonian, am I speaking as a former member of a regiment and so on. I mean, it's irrelevant. The question is: what are you saying and what are the grounds for it and how would you defend it? But this 'are you speaking as a such and such?' seems to me to be somehow a red herring. I'm not speaking as a fisherman, I am not a fisherman in fact . . . not even of souls. [*Laughter*] The point is to say: well all right, you hold these principles about the Conservatives; why do you think they're so bad? And then I would say something about the dislike of the kind of businessman's outlook they seem to represent, this 'let me make as much money as I can' that is the true characteristic of many of them. This, in a sense, is the theme that runs through their policy and attitudes.

And then you say: 'Are you speaking as a philosopher?' I don't know how to answer this if you mean 'Do you deduce this from your views about the problem of perception?' No, I don't. If you mean 'Is this in any psychologically recognizable sense the same person as wrote those books?' Yes, it is. What more do you want?

NAESS: I wonder, if you said . . .

AYER: Or was it already enough?

NAESS: . . . you shouldn't have a total philosophy; you would be a better philosopher . . .

AYER: I don't say 'you should', I say you haven't got a total philosophy.

NAESS: But you said 'you should' . . .

AYER: I also shouldn't have . . .

NAESS: I do not forget it. You said, 'I shouldn't have it.'

AYER: Yes, I will maintain that. I'll maintain 'you should not.' Liking you as much as I do, I change this to 'you do not.'

NAESS: Too late!

AYER: But I'm prepared to maintain also 'you should not.'

NAESS: We probably agree that a dogmatic view of all things lacks value, even if it were possible to work it out. But implicitly we pretend to coherence, implicitly we pretend to have methods of how to establish views, empirically or otherwise. In short we implicitly pretend to have views relevant to whatever we say. And those views are personal, not something found in libraries.

I'm inviting you to let us get hold of more of you; and not psychologically or socially, as Mr So-and-So or Sir So-and-So, but to get to know how you perceive the world, its relation to yourself, the basic features of the condition of man as *you* experience them.

And I call this a philosophy and approximations to a total view.

AYER: Oh, no, no, no.

NAESS: Now you try to take that back?

AYER: No, no, no.

NAESS: You have said 'I don't have.'

AYER: No I don't take it back. Let me put it this way. I don't think that the term 'total philosophy' . . .

NAESS: Total view.

AYER: . . . has any very useful application. What would having a total philosophy imply? Assuming that you do and I don't, in what way, in what concrete way, do we differ? I mean, I also have opinions about politics, ethics, aesthetics and express them and act on them. But these are not part of a total philosophy in your sense. How would I have to change, either in these opinions or in the meta-language, in order to have a total philosophy in your sense?

ELDERS: May I try to formulate a question by which you could perhaps illustrate your point of view? Does your offensive non-violence, Mr Naess, imply that you would prefer to be killed by someone else rather than kill someone else? Is it part of your philosophy?

NAESS: It would be more than a preference, actually. It might be that I would *prefer* to kill the other person, but I value the preference negatively. Norms have to do with evaluations, with pretensions to objectivity, rather than preferences. Let me formulate it thus: I hope I would prefer to be killed by someone else rather than to kill, and I *ought* to prefer it.

ELDERS: And this is a part of your philosophy?

NAESS: Yes. And it has empirical, logical, methodological, ontological etc. ramifications, like other philosophical issues. It belongs to a greater unity of opinions which *in part* are derived from certain principles of descriptive and normative kinds.

ELDERS: And how is it for you, Sir Alfred?

AYER: I should, I think, disagree. Although it's a very difficult question I can imagine situations certainly in which I should prefer to kill someone rather than be killed by them, in which I should in fact try to kill someone rather than allow him to kill me.

After all we were both, I assume, in the war and there these situations arose. But I don't see in fact how this fits in. Because supposing I gave a different answer from the answer that he gave or indeed suppose I gave the same one, how would this in either case be part or not be part of a total philosophy?

It might of course in some situations be an extremely important concrete moral question; but what I am denying when I reject that sort of philosophy is that the way either of us answers a question of this kind has any relation, any logical relation, to our views, for example, on probability or on the theory of knowledge, or on the mind-body question, even on such questions as the freedom of the will. Whatever our theoretical views about the freedom of the will, I can't see that they would settle a question of this kind one way or the other. I mean, we might both be determinists in theory and yet take different views about this; or we might one of us believe in free will, the other in determinism and take the same view. When I was sceptical and said you shouldn't have this total philosophy, what I meant was that I can't see what the links are supposed to be to make the totality.

But of course I have opinions on all these matters and very strong ones, although in this particular case I think I would probably dissent from you. I think I'm not a total pacifist. I haven't been in the past, and I think I can imagine circumstances in which I shouldn't be in the future. I think if something like the Nazis were to reappear, I would want to defend myself against them as I did then.

NAESS: There is a relation between not wanting to kill somebody else, even in a fight, and epistemology; because any question which you answer implies a methodology. And this also holds good for the question 'Would you prefer to be killed rather than to kill?' In order to answer this I must have a kind of methodology to find out whether I would. All fields of inquiry are interrelated, therefore we implicitly must pretend to cover them all when giving any answer whatsoever. We presuppose a total survey from mathematics to politics.

AYER: May I put this concretely? Suppose that either you or I held a physicalist's view of human beings, something like Gilbert Ryle's in *The Concept of Mind*. Suppose you were a behaviourist and thought of the mind as the ghost in the machine and so on, do you think that this would then entail an answer one way or the other to your question? Do you think that Ryle, for example, is in some way logically committed to giving a different answer to this question from the one that you would give?

NAESS: No, I don't think it would entail this. But I think that certain views cohere more or less and that it's the business of a philosopher today to try out to what extent they cohere; to what extent they're not only logically consistent, for that would leave us too free, but also coherent in their non-logical aspects.

AYER: Do you think that this view of the mind would even favour one answer to this moral question more than another? I mean, could you deduce simply from Ryle's book, other than psychologically, even in a semi-logical way, what moral position, what view he would take on this moral question?

NAESS: I think that if you made different combinations of interpretations, it favours, so to speak statistically, the acceptance of violence. But we would be capable of reconstructing it in such a way that it would not favour violence. And this is an important thing. A book like Ryle's leaves things implicit: presuppositions, postulates, methodological rules. No single, *definite* set can be said to be presumed, therefore there will be a plurality of interpretations and a plurality of reconstructions.

And I agree with you, it is too easy to talk about a total view and to say 'I have one.' I detest questions like 'What is your total view?'

AYER: Yes.

NAESS: Yes.

AYER: Well, there you see how much I sympathize with you.

NAESS: We cannot have a total view in the sense that we are somehow inescapably linked to certain definite opinions; nor can we behave like a general surveying an army of possible views and pick out some, saying these are my views – the relationship between ourselves and our views are too intimate.

AYER: I should have thought, in fact, that your general philosophical position, with which I sympathize, went entirely the opposite way, and that the tendency would be to see each question independently on its own merits; not to feel that you were committed by your answer to this one, by any answer to that one.

NAESS: Not any longer.

AYER: Not any longer?

NAESS: No, because I feel that as a philosopher I am an acting person, not an abstract researcher. Even this discussion is not really some kind of a contemplative affair; it is also a kind of continuous action all the time.

AYER: Indeed, indeed. In certain things you then require more coherence in action than you do in theory. You do not mind your theories being incoherent, but you want your actions to be coherent.

NAESS: In research I tend to adopt an almost playful attitude in the sense of looking at and pleasurably contemplating more combinations of views than anybody else. More kinds of common sense even! But as an acting person I take a stand, I implicitly assume very many things, and with my Spinozist leanings towards integrity – being an integrated person as the most important thing – I'm now trying to close down on all these vagaries. I am inviting you to do the same.

AYER: But, why should I . . .

NAESS: As a person you may have such a high level of integration that if you took some years off and tried to meditate a little more, you would be able to articulate some of your basic evaluations. These are more than inclinations; Jaspers calls them *Einstellungen*. They determine or at least express an important part of what would be your total view.

AYER: It's not a prospect that I find at all desirable. Failure to be articulate has never been my problem, I think.

NAESS: I think so.

AYER: Well, there are hidden problems perhaps, I don't know.

NAESS: Too fast, you're too fast.

AYER: Yes, but I say a lot of things twice, that's all right, I catch it on the second time round.

I don't know; why should integrity demand consistency? One thinks that it does, but why shouldn't one judge things differently when the circumstances are always different? Why shouldn't one have the same flexibility in one's moral and political judgments as one wants for one's theoretical ones? I suppose one thinks that people are insincere if they don't maintain similar opinions in similar cases; but then the question of even what cases are similar is theoretically difficult.

I don't know: I dislike what you have just said – I think it's really the first thing that you have said at all, that I *have* disliked. This seems to me to be really a conception of, well, I don't mind if it's called philosophy or not, and I don't mind if someone's trying in all honesty to solve problems that he thinks important, theoretically important or even practically important, but somehow this represents a kind of deep narcissism, a digging down into oneself, contemplating: I'm not concerned with this. All right, it is possible that if I spent a year meditating I should perhaps dig up some very pleasant things; I don't know, I don't care. I've got better things to do in a way. I've got this problem, that problem, the other problem, I've got a certain intelligence, I'm going to use it for as long as it lasts. And perhaps, when I'm gaga I'll start contemplating in your sense.

NAESS: Too late!

AYER: And of what interest will that be to anybody?

ELDERS: I'll ask the same question, but not on a personal level. Would you say Mr Naess, that in your total philosophy intellectuals have a special responsibility at this moment?

NAESS: Yes, because they are highly articulate. They are trained at universities in situations where they have at least three-quarters of an hour to think what could be argued against this, what could be argued against that; they get to be narrow and clever, too clever. I think that intellectuals might consider their intellects in a more Spinozistic way, as *intellectus* in the Spinoza way, and cultivate *amor intellectualis*.

ELDERS: Can you translate it?

NAESS: *Amor intellectualis* would be a kind of loving attitude towards what you have insight into, while considering it in an extremely wide perspective. And intellectuals might do this without making the terrible mistake of becoming sentimental or fanatical. They would be able to say things to people in a more direct way and to articulate evaluations, their attitudes – *Einstellungen* or total attitudes – in a very forceful way while at the same time using some of the, in a narrow sense, intellectual training they have acquired in the universities.

They should be able to make us feel that to elaborate total views that are not expressive of something like 'I am more clever than you are' is neither portentous nor necessarily favours some kind of fanaticism. When I say that you are, perhaps, deficient in articulation, it is because I feel you jump too fast to particular opinions on so-called facts, instead of taking a broad view and letting yourself say things which sound portentous and which might make you sound like a rhetorician or a politician, or even a prophet.

In this way I think that the intellectual of today, and especially the philosophically educated one, has a larger and wider function than that of being analytically minded. I'm sorry I use that catchphrase.

AYER: Well, I don't disagree with you on the question he asked. I do think that intellectuals obviously have a responsibility to do their job as they see it, and as well as they can do it; and also, I think, a social responsibility. I'm not a believer in the ivory tower at all; I think that anyone who has the capacity to think and to reason and perhaps believes, rightly or wrongly, that he can see things clearly, *should* try to contribute to social and even to political questions, so I don't in the least dissent from you there. I don't think that we quarrel at all about what we should be doing. What I think we may quarrel about is perhaps *how* we should do our job, and you might think that I do it in the wrong way.

NAESS: Well, couldn't you send me a copy of a speech made by you about a political situation?

AYER: Indeed, I could send many. I mean, I'm constantly doing this; I've even stood for office, but I lost. I've stood on soapboxes on street corners . . .

NAESS: And there you use descriptions and norms.

AYER: Ah, mainly normative, my language is then pretty emotive.

NAESS: May I ask for instance, could you act as if you were now on a political platform? Say something real, 'Bang!' like this.

AYER: Well, I think that you can't. Political speeches are not made in the abstract. But if I knew local politics, I daresay I could make quite an effective political speech. I would point out how one side was acting in its own interest, more than the other, and how such and such a measure was perhaps an attempt to preserve privileges, or was associated with corruption, and all this would be highly charged emotionally.

Of course, we have to have facts behind it; it's no good saying so-and-so is corrupt, unless you produce some evidence. But these two elements are mixed, obviously; and political speech has got to be factual, but with emotive overtones.

ELDERS: What's your attitude towards the Common Market?

AYER: This I regard as a factual and technical question. I'm emotionally in favour of it, in the sense that I'm in favour certainly of larger units, against nationalism.

But economically I simply don't know; whether from the point of view of the ordinary Englishman in the street the economic price will become too high or not. And the economists are totally in disagreement. So, as a rational man, I suspend judgment. But I myself, if you like, feel European. I am by origin not purely English, I have some French blood, even on my mother's side Dutch, and therefore I'm emotionally in favour of a larger unit.

But I think this is partly a question of fact where I acknowledge ignorance. Whereas Naess, with his total philosophy, brings in different little facts. If he doesn't believe in facts, then why should he joke about them on this issue?

NAESS: This is rhetoric, isn't it?

AYER: Of course it was, yes.

NAESS: You shouldn't immediately give up so quickly in this way. Behind the rhetoric there are sets of value judgments.

I'm in a fight against Norway joining the Common Market. And one of the main things I'm against is putting larger units in place of smaller ones. I think that the larger units achieve greater technological advances and larger units of production instead of getting together with other people in a nice personal way. We will get bigger markets, more standardized products, and we will take over some clever ideas from British universities instead of using our own less clever ideas about the university.

AYER: I would think that some ideas from Norwegian universities might even be more clever than the ones I get at Oxford.

NAESS: I doubt it, really. On the whole we are not clever, but we are provincial in the good sense of living our own way undisturbed by pressures from the great centres.

For me the question of whether to join the Common Market is not merely a factual and technical question. I am trying to connect my fight against the Common Market with basic evaluations. What are our value priorities? I see other people without analytical training taking up a philosophical point of view. I try to help them articulate their implicit systems in order to connect their ways of feeling with ways of asserting and evaluating things. Doing this I still feel myself to be philosophical and intellectual, whereas you would say it's more emotional, it's my emotional inclinations.

AYER: No, I don't think so: on the contrary. I just said I thought it was partly a rational question, but I suspended judgment because I don't believe I have enough evidence. I mean I don't let my emotions dominate me here, because emotionally I'm attracted to the idea, but I suspend judgment as I'm not convinced of it intellectually.

ELDERS: So you couldn't be a good politician?

AYER: I'd be a rotten politician, yes.

NAESS: Just a minute. You couldn't be convinced intellectually? There I think you again use too narrow a concept of intellect . . .

AYER: No, I mean that if I were to take a final decision, it would depend, in part, upon the answers to certain economic questions, to which I don't think I know the answers.

NAESS: Well, again you are displaying something narrow, I think – no, not narrow, but something peculiarly empirical – when you talk of a final judgment. But I can't make a final judgment about anything political, in a sense, because all the time that I am acting and being acted upon here all my judgments will be provisional.

But in spite of being decidedly against the Common Market, I could say that the range of facts known to me is probably narrower than yours, I know perhaps less about the Common Market. Decisions cannot wait until all the facts are gathered: they are never all available.

AYER: Well, I hope the judgment is only final in the sense in which the reaction might be irreversible.

ELDERS: Irreversible, yes. Well, perhaps I could now ask my final and I think most difficult question; a question about the audience: do you think we have managed to get through to the audience, both here and at home?

AYER: Yes, I think, in part. I mean, how can one possibly tell? I do think that we have got through to the audience here, in the sense that nobody walked out, and nobody threw things.

But inasmuch as we were both talking seriously and saying things we believed and things that interested us, and on the whole not trying to score off one another but trying to get at what truth there is in these matters, then I should hope that this at least would get through.

And perhaps, when one looks at two philosophers talking, this is what one wants to get through: the idea that these questions are important, some idea of what sort of questions they are, and some idea that one can really seek the truth about them without, perhaps, any notions of personal advancement.

ELDERS: And you, Mr Naess?

NAESS: I trust that we have got through to a limited extent, of course. I feel sure many people have turned off and are looking at something else.

ELDERS: Well, may I now suggest that we have a short discussion with the audience? Perhaps we could agree about time; I suggest a discussion of half an hour.

AYER: It has taken very long already.

ELDERS: You would like to relax a little?

AYER: I must say it was not an easy passage of time.

ELDERS: Yet you have not walked out, Sir Alfred, after an hour and ten minutes. Well, may I have the first question?

AYER: Get one done, yes.

QUESTION: In the beginning, Sir Alfred, you gave a definition of philosophy which was entirely a negative definition. Philosophy is a kind of criticism, a criticism of belief and a criticism of knowledge, but I feel a certain tension between that kind of definition of philosophy and the opinions on everyday matters that you have, and which you derive from what you call natural belief, or what is part of natural belief.

AYER: Or common sense.

QUESTION: Well, what is the relation between that positive conception of a rational belief or a rational certainty of the world that you have, and your negative definition of philosophy? And that question is related to another one – and here I feel that perhaps Mr Naess would have another opinion – namely that natural belief is a thing which for itself has a criterion; you have criteria in order to be certain about certain things. But there can be different kinds of certainty, and so different kinds of natural belief. Why do you have *this* kind of natural belief and not another?

I don't know if this is perfectly clear, but I could elucidate this by giving an example. For instance, I imagine that I believe in ghosts, or I believe in the existence of Australia, where I have never been. I could give criteria for believing in ghosts, as I could give criteria for believing that Australia exists.

They would be the same kind of criteria. I've never seen either of them, never perceived them, never heard them, but I've read about Australia, and I've read about ghosts.

And I think that if you conceive natural belief in that way, then it could be possible to have another kind of natural belief; for instance in werewolves. I could be instantly afraid of you, for instance, because I saw a certain glance in your eyes which would be for me an indication that you were a werewolf.

ELDERS: Is the question clear?

AYER: Yes, it's clear to me, I think. On the first part, I didn't intend my definition to be a purely negative one, and wouldn't in fact think it to be so. I mean that in one's questioning of accepted beliefs, or really of the criteria underlining accepted beliefs, one's attempt to clarify concepts, one can quite often come up with a positive answer. And I think there are examples in the history of philosophy; for example, Hume clarified the concept of cause, and I think that as a result of Hume's work one understands much better than people understood before what is involved in causation. I think he showed that the popular concept of causation was, to a very large extent, if you like, superstitious; but that there is then a residue remaining which can be clarified and be made quite precise. And I think, for example, that the concept of truth has been clarified, first by Aristotle and more recently by Tarski and so on; and, at present, I am myself working on the concept of probability, and other people have worked on it. And I think that through this, one often arrives at something positive.

I don't at all want to say that one has to come to rest in scepticism, but only that scepticism was a kind of challenge posed to the philosopher, one which sometimes he didn't need, sometimes he left alone, but sometimes at least it provoked him into providing an answer, which was at least provisionally acceptable. I think I agree with Naess here that it's always only provisional.

I think the second half of your question was in fact very important and profound, because I think there is a kind of relativism here that is in a sense inescapable. The reason why we all believe in Australia when many of us haven't been there, is that it fits in with our general conceptual scheme; there is nothing surprising to us that there should be a country on the other side of the world. We have a spatiotemporal framework into which you fit things: we already have a scientific, and after all, very fine, well-tested belief that the earth is round, so that there should be a country at the antipodes is something that comes quite naturally to us, so that here we accept testimony; we could go there and see for ourselves, but we don't bother to.

Now ghosts, even though they might be well attested – let's assume, for the sake of your question, that the evidence in favour of apparitions is even stronger than it is, or, much stronger than it is – there we become more cautious because it doesn't fit into our way of organizing the world.

Now you might say, why not? After all this has been true of some primitive peoples, so why don't I see you, not just as another man, but as, potentially, a werewolf, a being with all sorts of magical powers and so on?

Now, this could be a way of organizing my experience and it's a way in which people of other communities have, to some extent, organized their experience; and, in a sense, I can't refute it, except by begging the question against it; except by assuming all sorts of methodological criteria which are inconsistent with it.

So, in the last resort, I think, the answer here is pragmatic, in the way that it seems to me that, with a system of explanation of the sort I have, I explain phenomena more satisfactorily, I make more successful predictions, than I do with an animistic system.

But if someone likes to see the world animistically, I don't think that I can refute him, because as Naess pointed out in our discussion earlier on, the notion of fact is itself a dubious one, itself infected by theory. And I could say, well . . .

ELDERS: You've nearly converted him.

AYER: . . . in a sense I'm more successful with my type of theory than he would be with his.

ELDERS: Well, Sir Alfred, he has nearly converted you.

NAESS: No, no, what I would say is that I listened with pleasure, because there you used some kind of a concept of *total view*. And so I congratulate *you* for making Sir Alfred show in practice that he is very near to thinking in terms of a total view.

AYER: Oh, in this sense, if you like to think of one's language and what's implied by one's language and one's general method as a total view, then certainly. I think connections are much looser within the conceptual system than you're making them out to be. But to this extent, certainly.

ELDERS: Ladies and gentlemen, this has to be the end of this debate. Sir Alfred, Mr Naess, thank you very much for your total, clear discussion, on behalf of the audience, here and at home.

SIX

The Concept of Freedom [1]

Nowadays a nation is commonly said to be free if it is autonomous, but a free nation in this sense is not necessarily a nation of free men. The elimination of foreign rulers may indeed be regarded as a means towards the acquisition of individual freedom, but the securing of the end remains a practical problem. There is also the theoretical problem of discovering in what this individual freedom consists.

An apparently simple answer to this theoretical question is that a man is free to the extent that he is able to do what he chooses. This indeed is the view that was taken by the utilitarian philosophers, who may be regarded as the spokesmen of nineteenth-century English liberalism. The value that they attached to freedom can thus be represented as a corollary of their belief that the appropriate end of all moral and political action was the promotion of happiness. For they assumed that to allow people the greatest possible measure of individual freedom was equivalent to giving them the fullest opportunity for the satisfaction of their desires; and they supposed that this would lead to the general preponderance of pleasure over pain in which they took happiness to consist. In consequence, they were largely concerned with the ways in which people might make their desires known, and it is partly for this reason that so much importance was attached to freedom of speech and freedom of the press. Similarly, the preoccupation with electoral reform may be held to have issued from the belief that a man's political desires were revealed by his exercise of the vote. The same assumption had been made by Rousseau, when he said that the English people was free only at election times, for he was implying that it was only during the course of an election that any means existed by which the ordinary English citizen could effectively express his political will.

[1] 'The Concept of Freedom' appeared in Cyril Connolly (ed.), Horizon, Vol. IX, No. 52, 1944.

It is characteristic of this liberal attitude to government that it is taken for granted that men can but trusted to know what they themselves desire. But this is by no means a universally accepted axiom. In particular it has been rejected by the numerous political theorists, who, in one way or another, have attempted to draw a distinction between what men think they will and what they really will. Thus Rousseau, who was not a consistent writer, differentiated the general will of a society from the individual wills of its members, and made accordance with the general will the criterion of freedom. As a result, he was able to speak of the criminal who was dragged unwillingly off to execution as being forced to be free. This author-itarian view of freedom was perpetuated by Hegel, who finding Rousseau's general will to be a somewhat nebulous entity, inasmuch as it was a will which nobody could definitely be said to exercise, gave it an owner in the person of the state. The result is justly described in Russell's malicious dictum that, for Hegelians, true freedom consists in the right to obey the police. In the same way, the modern apologists for Fascism have been able to claim, not merely that their dictator's subjects enjoyed the benefits of a better government than the citizens of the pluto-democracies, but also that they were more truly free. This is not perhaps a distinctively Christian idea, but it finds its parallel in the religious conception of a deity 'whose service is perfect freedom'. And indeed the theory that the dictator incarnates the real will of the people can easily be made to carry the metaphysical rider that he also exemplifies the will of God.

At first sight, it may seem that these accounts of freedom, which make a man's liberty consist in his complete subservience to some form of authority, are diametrically opposed to the ordinary liberal notion that a man is free to the extent that he is able to be a law unto himself. Whatever advantages may be enjoyed by the inhabitants of a totalitarian state, it would not ordinarily be said that they were conspicuously free; and it would seem more honest for the advocates of this form of government to argue that the attainment of these advantages necessitated some sacrifice of freedom than to maintain the paradox that no such sacrifice occurred at all. It is tempting therefore to dismiss the whole of the authoritarian conception of freedom by saying simply that it is based upon a palpable misuse of language. But this would be to misplace the incidence of the paradox. It is not necessarily in their definition of freedom that the authoritarians depart from common sense; they might well be prepared to accept the ordinary view that freedom for the individual consists in some form of self-deter-mination. What leads to the paradox is the further assumption which they make that, in surrendering to the will of a superior authority, whether that of God, or the leader, or whatever agents may be concealed by the abstraction of the state, a man is really obeying himself. On this showing, Rousseau's criminal who is forced to be free, is really conveying himself to execution, though he may not be aware of it, and the subject whose actions are completely governed by the decrees of a dictator is not really subordinate to another's will, because, in some mysterious way, the dictator is really the subject in disguise. And while it is in the authoritarian systems that this assumption is carried to the farthest lengths and entails the strangest consequences, it has made its appearance also in democratic theory. Indeed, the very use of the word democracy in its application to a modern state conveys a suggestion of this sort; for it implies that, for a man to be governed by an assembly in the election of which he has the opportunity to participate, is really equivalent to his governing himself.

It is a dictum of G. E. Moore's that, when a philosopher tells you that something is really so and so, what he actually means is that it is not so really; and this is surely an instance in point. For suppose, to take the most favourable case, that I am living in what is now called a democratic country, and that the man for whom I record my vote at an election is returned to parliament as a member of the numerically superior party; suppose even that he then becomes an active promoter of legislation; it is still not true that the acts of the assembly to which he belongs are really my acts. I may approve of these acts, and, generally speaking, I must acquiesce in them, but they are not mine, because it does not depend upon the exercise of my will that they should be either done or forborne. This is not intended to imply that any system in which I did govern myself would be either practicable or desirable. The point is only that it is a piece of chicanery for politicians to tell me that I myself really do govern, when I really do not. The chicanery is still greater in the cases where I am subject to a dictatorship. Here again, it is possible that I approve of the acts of my rulers, and probable that I acquiesce in them, but neither my acquiescence nor my approval, however fervent, renders them my acts. The dictator may happen to reflect my will, but he cannot incarnate it. His actions are not really mine, because it is in no sense I who do them. For the most part they have not even that remote connection with the subject's will that gives to the institution of representative government its claim to be accounted democratic.

I conclude then that the assumption on which the authoritarian view of freedom is based is manifestly false. But independently of this assumption there appears to be nothing to recommend the departure from ordinary usage which is involved in identifying freedom with subjection to authority. Accordingly, we may return to the liberal view that the freedom of the individual is to be measured by his power to do what he himself actually wills. And we may begin by taking it as established that it is a necessary condition of a man's acting freely that he should be doing what he has chosen to do, and as the result of his choosing it; that is to say, it must be true in some sense that he could have acted otherwise if he had chosen. The next question is whether it is also a sufficient condition. If it were, there would be no need to continue the discussion, though the question as to whether it is ever possible to act otherwise that one does raises a separate philosophical problem. The fact is, however, that it is not sufficient.

The reason why it is not is that it takes no account of the factors that govern a man's choice. It is, of course, open to anyone to decide so to use the word freedom that its application depends only upon the occurrence of a process of choice, irrespective of the way in which the choice is determined. But, in the first place, this would not be in accordance with customary usage, which requires that, at least in some cases, a restriction of the field of choice should be regarded as a limitation of freedom. And secondly, it would fail to bring out the actual complexity of the political problem. For the practical aim of those who represent themselves as advocates of greater personal freedom is not merely to remove the hindrances which prevent men from doing what they choose, but also to transform the factors which limit and pervert the nature of their choice.

Among the most important of these factors are poverty and ignorance. It was one of the achievements of Marx that he exposed the current pretence that men were in a position to act freely, when in fact they were the prisoners of an economic system which put most of the commonly accepted goods of life entirely beyond their reach. It is indeed hard to believe that the utilitarians did not perceive that the freedom of contract, which they sought to establish between workers and employers, was bound to be an illusion so long as one party to the contract was economically at the mercy of the other. Probably they did perceive this, but did not regard it as an objection to their system, because they did not believe that the facts could be altered. They were misled by the theories of Malthus into thinking that the poverty of the mass of the population was the outcome of a natural law, so that to try to mitigate it by social and industrial legislation was futile, if not mischievous. Today, these theories are discredited, but there are still those who object to such modern developments as the interference of the government with private enterprise, or the concession of power to trade unions, on the ground that they put restraints upon individual liberty. And, in the narrow sense in which they conceive the question, these objectors are right. What they ignore, however, is that, without such restraints upon the liberty of some, the liberty of others, who constitute the greater number, would be very much more restricted. In themselves, the facts to which objection is taken are indeed limitations of freedom, but some such limitations are necessary to make a wider enjoyment of freedom possible.

The ground for taking ignorance to be restrictive of freedom is that it causes people to make choices which they would not have made if they had seen what the realization of their choices involved. The distinction, which we have already noticed, between what people think they want and what they really want, is valid if it is taken only as a way of expressing the fact that people do very often desire what actually fails to satisfy them when they obtain it. Their dissatisfaction may arise from the fact that they find the situation which constitutes the fulfilment of their aim to be essentially different from what they had expected; or they may discover too late that the events which they have sought to bring about have natural consequences which are so undesirable from their point of view as to outweigh the value of the events themselves. So long indeed as there is no obvious ground for fixing the responsibility for such errors elsewhere than on the person who commits them, it would not conventionally be held that his commission of them was incompatible with his acting freely; but it is a different matter when he has clearly been denied the opportunity of acquiring the knowledge which would have saved him from the errors in question. In other words, what is thought to diminish a man's freedom is not so much his actual unenlightenment, as the fact that it appears to issue from the malevolence or neglect of others, or from the operations of the political or economic system under which he lives. The consequence is that, in assessing a man's freedom, it is necessary to take some account of the education which he has received.

At this point, however, the difficulty arises that every system of education is to some degree tendentious. It is impossible to bring up a child without encouraging him, whether intentionally or not, to make some judgments of values; the precept and example of those with whom he is in contact is bound to have some influence, even if it is mainly negative, upon his subsequent interests and tastes. This is a fact that has been strangely neglected by most liberal theorists, who, in supposing that men were rational, have seemed also to assume that they grew up in a moral vacuum. It has not, however, been neglected by the modern exponents of autocratic government. The dictator who claims that he represents the will of his people may eventually be justified, if he takes sufficient care to condition them in such a way that they come to believe and desire only what he thinks it expedient that they should. That this is possible is not indeed a new discovery. The Jesuits, for example, have long been credited with the belief that, if they were allowed to have the control of a child during his early years, he would be theirs for life. But the modern improvements in the technique of propaganda have made the process of conditioning very much more effective and far-reaching. It is perhaps the ultimate refinement of tyranny that the slave is induced to glory in his chains. Neither need the tyranny be in any way maleficent. In a completely planned society, the members of which were trained from birth for their respective functions and who were so thoroughly conditioned that they never conceived any desires but those that were appropriate to their station, the subjects would be perfectly happy; and since they would be granted the ability to satisfy their desires, they would seem to themselves to be free. But we, surveying the whole system from the outside, would judge, without hesitation, that they were not really free.

To most of us, including those who say that they approve of governmental planning, the picture of such a society is not attractive, and the reason why it is not attractive is precisely that it seems to involve a negation of freedom. But now it may be asked whether it is in this respect essentially different from our own. The difference is that the planned action of a ruling caste is substituted for the largely unplanned action of parents, or nurses, or schoolmasters, or writers, or politicians, or lovers, or friends, but the conditioning is there in either case. Where then are we to draw the line? Our natural tendency is to say that a man chooses freely if the conditions of his choice are relatively obscure and haphazard, and to deny that he is free in proportion as the external influences to which he is subject are manifest and purposive. This is, however, a very vague distinction, besides being arbitrary; and it seems paradoxical that a man's freedom should be measured, not merely by the influences to which he has been subjected, but also by other people's knowledge of them. One might expect that other people's knowledge would enter into the question only in so far as it actually affected the agent, but this appears not to be the case. That a man's own knowledge should be held to be relevant independently of its affecting his actions, is less surprising. Indeed, Spinoza went so far as to identify freedom with awareness of necessity. But this, though a workable definition, runs exactly counter to our normal tendency to regard an action as lacking in freedom if its necessitation is obvious either to others or to the agent himself.

In view of these difficulties, I do not think it possible to give any precise definition of freedom that would correspond at all closely to ordinary usage. This does not mean, however, that there is nothing further to be done in the way of its analysis. For even if there is no rule available for determining that a person is, or is not, unqualifiedly free, it may still be possible to indicate the criteria by which we judge that one person is freer than another. And this, if it can be achieved, is probably as good a solution as the character of the problem admits.

To bring to light what I believe to be the nature of these criteria, I propose to borrow from a theory of probability the concept of a *spielraum*. In connection with the judgments which we make about freedom, this metaphor of a playing-space can be applied in three ways. For our assessment of a man's freedom may be held to depend first upon the degree to which his *spielraum* is encumbered, secondly upon its extent, and thirdly upon the manner in which its boundaries are fixed. These three criteria are logically independent of one another, and do not always reveal a similar result when they are severally applied to a given case. There appears, however, to be no established rule for giving any one of them the preference over the others in the case where they conflict.

The first of these criteria is the one that is employed when we test a person's freedom by his ability to satisfy his desires. So long as we confine ourselves to this criterion, it does not matter what these desires are, or how they came to be acquired. All that is relevant is the degree to which they succeed in being satisfied. To return to the metaphor, it does not matter how small the *spielraum* is, or what its size depends on; the only test is the ability of its owner to move about it without being checked. It is in this sense that the stoic who is immured in prison can still claim to be free, for he deliberately adapts his movements to the configuration of the *spielraum*; that is, he schools himself to conceive only those desires that his situation permits him to satisfy. It is in this sense also that the ascetic achieves freedom through limiting the range of his desires. It is not the fact that his *spielraum* is small that makes him free, but the fact that, in making it small, he empties it of obstacles; because his desires are few and simple, the ratio of their satisfaction is high. In this particular case, the first of our criteria is reinforced by the third, for the limitation in the *spielraum* is conceived to be the consequence of his own deliberate choice. But, as far as the operation of the first criterion alone is concerned, the result would be the same if the limitation was held to have been forced upon him. The only point to be considered is the actual ratio of satisfaction that he is able to obtain.

The fact that the first criterion tends to favour asceticism brings it, however, into conflict with the second; for the effect of using the second criterion is to establish a positive correlation between the extent of the *spielraum* and the freedom which its owner enjoys. It is by this criterion that most social and economic, as opposed to penal, legislation is judged to be productive of freedom; for, by raising people's standards of living and improving their education, it serves to widen their field of choice. It is true that the effect of amplifying the *spielraum* is usually to add to the possibilities of its being encumbered, but this is a consideration which is generally disregarded in politics, except by a few romantics, who vainly advocate a return to a more Spartan economy and a simpler way of life. Whether their policy is justifiable or not is here beside the question. The point is that, if freedom is taken as a value, the second of our criteria operates against them. It is in the light of this criterion also that objection is chiefly taken to restrictions upon freedom of speech and the freedom of the press. For the effect of such restrictions is to limit the *spielraum*, not merely of those who are directly restrained by them, but of the whole public that their utterances would have reached. Furthermore, it may be noted that the factors which limit the *spielraum* are not necessarily external to its owner. Thus, the justification for holding, as Plato did, that a man is not free when he is governed by the passional side of his nature, is that this slavery to his passions excessively restricts his field of choice. In this case, indeed, our first criterion tends to come into play also; for we are more ready to say that such a man is not free if we know that in his cooler hours he entertains desires which his dominant obsessions actually prevent him from satisfying.

There remains the third criterion, which differs from the others in being concerned, not with the character of the *spielraum*, but with its provenance. The ideal of freedom which it presupposes is that a man's choice must depend as little as possible upon external factors, including the will of others, and as much as possible upon himself. It is by this criterion that most of our moral judgments are guided; for, in praising or blaming people for their actions, we tend to make the assumption that they were genuinely responsible for them in a sense which goes beyond the mere fact that they willed to do them. It may, however, be argued that this assumption is irrational, for we are also inclined to think that, if we had sufficient information about the agent's ante-cedents, we could always find a reason for his acting as he does, and this chain of reasons must eventually carry us to facts which are not in any way attributable to the agent himself. Even in the case where the ground for blaming a man is that his will is weak or perverted, it seems justifiable to ask why this is so; and, though the man himself may be held to be immediately responsible, he will not appear to be so ultimately if the explanation is sufficiently far pursued. It is for this reason indeed that those who are at all deeply influenced by the work of modern psychologists are disposed to abandon the notion of personal responsibility, at least in its prevalent form, and to put their moral judgments upon a utilitarian basis, if they consciously give them any basis at all. Nevertheless, our third criterion continues to function, at any rate negatively. It still seems paradoxical to say that a man is free if his course of action clearly depends upon decisions which he did not take, or material factors over which he had no control. To return to the example of the scientifically planned society, the reason for judging as, surely, nearly everyone would, that its members would not be free, is that the whole pattern of their lives would have been antecedently determined, even though they might not be aware of it themselves. If we considered only the first two criteria, we should allow that members of such a society could enjoy a high degree of freedom; for, if the planning were successful, their *spielraum* might be both extensive and unencumbered. It is the influence of the third criterion that turns the scale. No doubt the use of this third criterion is illogical, since it is hard to see how any choice can fail to be somehow conditioned; and it may be that an increased awareness of this will eventually resolve the conflict that now exists between our desire for the advantages of a planned society and our attachment to the idea of freedom. The fact is, however, that the emotions which are based upon the acceptance of the third criterion remain extremely strong; and any faithful analysis of the current conception of freedom is therefore bound to take it into account.

SEVEN

John Stuart Mill[1]

If 'The proper study of mankind is man', it is curious that men of science have done so little to promote it, compared with the progress that they have made in the study of other organisms and in that of the inanimate parts of nature. This discrepancy has grown less in recent years, thanks to the advances made in the domains of human physiology and genetics. In 1862, when John Stuart Mill devoted the sixth and final book of his *A System of Logic* to a disquisition 'On the Logic of the Moral Sciences', it was still very great. Empiricist philosophers of the seventeenth and eighteenth centuries, like John Locke and David Hume, had, indeed, aspired to inaugurate a science of man which would stand comparison with the chemistry and physics of Boyle and Newton, but for all their philosophical acumen, the contributions which they made to political theory and the acuteness of many of Hume's remarks about the passions, they did not leave a legacy on which the social sciences could capitalize. The impression which they had given was that the way to progress lay in the exploration of the principles which governed the association of our ideas, but the attempt made in the early nineteenth century by such men as David Hartley and James Mill, John Stuart Mill's father, to develop this 'associationist psychology' in a systematic fashion had achieved nothing of substantial importance. To all appearances one could learn more about human nature by reading history or even fiction than by trying to subject it to the discipline of science.

This was not a conclusion which John Stuart Mill was willing to accept, at least if it was taken to imply that the application of scientific method to human thought and action was subject to any limitation of principle. He believed that all natural phenomena were governed by

[1] 'John Stuart Mill' was the introduction to a new edition of Mill's Book VI, *On the Logic of the Moral Sciences*, in *A System of Logic*.

universal laws, so that the operations of men's minds were no exception. Not only that, but he believed that the psychological laws in question were discoverable, and even, it would seem, that they were not especially difficult to discover. In his view, the principal reason why the moral had lagged behind the natural sciences was not that men's thoughts and feelings and motives in any way escaped the rule of law, but that the 'ultimate' laws which they obeyed were excessively remote from their concrete instances. The source of this remoteness was not only the number and variety of the 'minor causes' which joined with the major causes in producing specific effects, but also the vast quantity of particular facts which went to determine how even the conjunction of major with minor causes operated in detail. Indeed, at one point, Mill goes so far as to say that nothing which has ever happened to a person is 'without its portion of influence'. The result, since we can never take account of all the relevant factors, is that the generalizations on which we rely 'for predicting phenomena in the concrete' will never be more than approximately true; and so long as they are approximately true, it would not seem to matter whether they are prised out of works of literature or obtained from controlled experiments, which have, as Mill himself acknowledges, a very limited reach in this domain. Nevertheless he thinks it both important and feasible to connect these approximate generalizations 'with the laws of nature from which they result'. Not only is this a necessary condition for our possessing a science of human nature, but it should have the practical advantage of enabling us to make our own approximate generalizations cover a larger range of circumstances, and so increase our success in predicting future experience.

It is interesting to note that Mill, who is often accused of underestimating the part that the deductive procedure of framing hypotheses and testing their consequences plays in the natural sciences, maintains that 'The Social Science . . . (which, by a convenient barbarism, has been termed Sociology) is a deductive science: not, indeed, after the model of geometry, but after that of the more complex physical sciences.' It might be thought that the model of geometry was obviously inapplicable, but here we must remember that Mill regarded all mathematical propositions as empirical generalizations: his reason for thinking that geometry was not a suitable model for social science was that it allowed no room for 'the case of conflicting forces'; the mistake made by those who took it as a model was that of supposing that social phenomena could be deduced from a single principle. Since Mill passes for being a Utilitarian in moral philosophy, it is again interesting to note that he finds the most remarkable example of this error in the attempt made by Jeremy Bentham and his followers to base a theory of government on the single premiss 'that men's actions are always determined by their interests'. Mill points out that it is just not true 'that the actions even of average rulers are wholly, or anything approaching to wholly, determined by their personal interest, or even by their own opinion of their personal interest', and that it is still further from being a universal truth that the rulers' 'sense of an identity of interest with the community' is uniquely the effect of their being held responsible to those whom they govern. This is not to decry the system of representative government, which Mill himself advocated, but merely to object to its merits being attributed to a single false premiss. Mill does not refer to Karl Marx, but there is no doubt that he would have raised a similar objection to the use of the notion of class conflict as the universal explanation of historical change.

The geometrical method being excluded, there remain what Mill calls the physical and the historical methods, each of which can, under the appropriate conditions, yield trustworthy results. The difference between them is that in the physical method we try to verify, by observation, hypotheses which we have derived from a mixture of what we take to be the laws of human nature with an evaluation of the circumstances which affect their operation in some particular branch of human activity. The historical method proceeds, as it were, inversely. It starts with rough generalizations suggested by the lessons of history. These generalizations would acquire the status of empirical laws if we were able to deduce them from psychological laws or from the laws of Ethology, which is Mill's name for the 'Science of the Formation of Character'. In practice, this will not be possible, because there are more factors at work than we are able to reckon with, but we may hope to show that the success of the generalizations, in the cases under review, is at least a likely outcome of the dominant laws. There is thus a double process of verification: the proof, so far as we can achieve it, that our historical generalizations conform to the laws of human nature, and once again the observational tests.

Because the explanations of social phenomena are so complex, we have usually to be content with the historical method, but there are cases in which the stronger physical method can be used. They are those in which a form of human activity functions almost as a separate department within the whole body of social science. An example is Political Economy, which can show what actions would result if men's principal object were the acquisition of wealth. This is by no means always the case, but it covers a wide enough field for the science to yield general consequences from which, if we proceed with the proper caution, we can derive a reasonable number of successful predictions.

It is to be remarked that Mill does not think that his famous inductive methods are applicable to the social sciences. He conjoins them in this book under the slightly odd heading of the 'Chemical Method'. There is the overall difficulty that the subject matter is such as to afford us little or no opportunity for making artificial experiments. We have to rely on the 'spontaneous instances' with which history naturally provides us, and they do not supply the conditions which are requisite for any of the divisions of the Chemical Method to be fruitful. The Method of Difference, considered by Mill to be 'the most perfect of the methods of experimental inquiry', obliges us to find an instance where a phenomenon is present, and one where it is absent, which are the same in every relevant respect except one, to which we then infer that the phenomenon is causally related; and plainly this is a condition that is not historically satisfied. Nor do we fare any better if we resort to what Mill calls the Indirect Method of Difference, where the requirement is that two classes of instances differ only in the one crucial respect. Here, too, we are defeated by the multiplicity of causes. The same axe falls upon the Method of Agreement, where it is required that two instances of a phenomenon have nothing relevant in common except the circumstance which is our candidate for its cause. To take Mill's own example, let us suppose that we discover a set of prosperous nations which, within the limits of our inquiry, agree only in practising commercial protection. We cannot infer that this common practice is the cause of their prosperity. The reason why we cannot is that we have not proved either that protectionism would in any case be sufficient on its own, or that various combinations of the divergent factors would not yield prosperity even in the absence of protectionism. Similar objections apply to the Method of Concomitant Variations, and the Method of Resideas presupposes, what is not here the case, that 'the causes from which part of the effect proceeded are already known'. To the extent that they can be known, it must be by deduction from the 'principles of human nature'. But then the Method of Resideas becomes superfluous. The use of one or other of the appropriate deductive methods will do its work.

But will it? Or rather, can there be any method that comes anywhere near achieving Mill's objective, the discovery and application of the laws which govern all the acts of men? By what right does he assume that there are such laws? Is it not possible that the mind of man is not, in this sense, a subject for science at all?

The most common reason for denying that man is a legitimate subject for science is his alleged possession of free will. Mill considers this objection and dismisses it. He does not deny that we possess free will, in the sense that we have reasons for our actions and act upon them. We are not prisoners of fate, in the sense that the course of our lives proceeds independently of the choices that we make. A man's choices are, indeed, conditioned by his character, but his character is not something that he has no power to alter. The circumstances which form it include his own desires, and one such desire, which can often be realized, is the desire to make himself, in some degree, a different sort of person. In Mill's view 'this feeling, of our being able to modify our own character *if we wish*', is what constitutes our feeling of moral freedom.

None of this, however, is inconsistent with determinism. It remains true, according to Mill, 'that if we knew the person thoroughly, and knew all the inducements which are acting upon him, we could foretell his conduct with as much certainty as we can predict any physical event'. It is simply that his being the sort of person that he is, his consequently having such and such motives, and the manner and degree in which he acts upon these motives, are all matters of fact which fit into a regular pattern, when the attendant circumstances are taken into account: the uniformity of these patterns is captured by the generalizations to which we give the name of natural laws. To say that all human actions are predictable is, thus, to say no more than that with respect to any statement which truly describes a human action there is a set of laws and a set of true statements about the attendant circumstances from the conjunction of which the statement in question follows.

Why then should the thesis of determinism have been so widely seen as robbing us of our pretensions to free will? Mill's answer is that people have been misled by the improper use of the word 'necessity' to express 'the simple fact of causation'. 'Necessity' suggests constraint. If people are told that they necessarily think and feel and act as they do, they conclude that they are being represented as the helpless prisoners of fate. When it is explained to them that 'necessity' in this context implies no more than 'mere uniformity of sequence', they should cease to feel that their dignity or even their autonomy is threatened.

There is something in this. If a man is said to be acting under constraint only in cases where his choice is not a causal factor, or those in which it is subject to obvious pressures, such as his having a pistol pointed at his head, then the fact that an action is causally explicable does not entail that it is performed under constraint: and if it is only the factor of constraint that removes or greatly diminishes the freedom of the will, we can consistently hold that most human actions are done freely while also holding that they are causally determined. Even so, I doubt if this would be enough to satisfy any fervent believer in the existence of free will. He would argue that the issue is not merely whether we find ourselves able to realize our choices, but also how we come to make the choices that we do, and if the answer involves a chain of causes which takes us back to our genetic endowment and its responses to external stimuli, over which we have no control, he would conclude that we are not really free. But the trouble with such people is that they are making a demand which cannot possibly be met. They would be no happier with the answer that our choices are ascribable, at least in some degree, to chance. They stand by a concept of self-determination to which no sense can be attached.

This is not to say that the case for determinism in the domain of the social sciences has been made out. The most that can be claimed is that we have no good reason for dismissing it without further inquiry. The likelihood that the laws which govern the behaviour of atomic particles are fundamentally statistical allows room for causal laws to prevail at the macro-level of human thought and conduct. But then we need some proof that they do prevail. We need to discover and apply them successfully. This is not something that we have the right to take for granted *a priori*. To say, as Mill does, that we should be able to predict a person's conduct if only we knew enough about his character and circumstances is nothing more than an encouragement to pursue research, unless the laws which support the predictions are at least roughly specified. The claim will be deprived of content if no amount of failure is allowed to affect it, if, however unsuccessful we are, we protect our thesis by appealing to our lack of knowledge. If we are to proceed scientifically, we must allow our continued failure to light upon causal laws as bestowing at least some probability on the conclusion that they are not discoverable.

In fact, 'The Laws of Mind' which Mill himself adduces are certainly not sufficient to generate either of his deductive methods. Apart from the major generalization, which may not even be true, that every state of consciousness can be reproduced in memory, he relies on three laws of association: first, that similar ideas tend to excite one another; secondly, that where two impressions have frequently occurred in close temporal conjunction, the recurrence or the idea of one of them tends to excite the idea of the other; and, thirdly, that the more intense either or both of the impressions are, the more frequently will this excitement operate. No doubt these generalizations could be given more factual content, but the mass of detail required would appear too great for them to be transformable into manageable laws.

A more promising approach would be to have recourse to physiology. We should need an established theory accounting for the succession of states of the central nervous system, and a set of well-supported hypotheses serving to correlate these states with states of consciousness. Mill allows this to be possible, but dismisses it as impractical, which, indeed, it still remains. For all the advances that have been made in physiology, we are still very far from being able to meet such ambitious demands. We must continue to be content with explaining human conduct in terms of desires and purposes, attributed on the basis of statements of tendency, and arriving at predictions of which the best that can be said is that, so long as they allow for a fair amount of variation in detail, and do not venture very far into the future, they are successful in the main.

There remains the question whether we are able to discover social laws which, like the proportion of male to female births or the expectation of life in a given community, can be taken as holding good, without our having to inquire into the particular facts concerning individual persons on which their truth finally depends. It is widely believed that there are such laws, but the candidates which have been put forward, such as the dependence of social institutions upon economic interests, have at best a limited application. There is also the major difficulty that the cultural and technological developments which play so great a part in all our lives are, directly or indirectly, the outcome of the work of a few exceptionally gifted men: and even though the birth of such men is subject to the laws of genetics, we cannot make use of these laws or any others at our disposal in order to predict the ways in which these gifts will actually be manifested. It is all very well to say that the social conditions were such that if Newton or Darwin or Mozart or Cézanne had not existed, someone else would have achieved similar results at much the same time. As Mill himself acknowledges, this claim is not supported by anything approaching sufficient evidence. If we confine ourselves, therefore, to what the state of our knowledge reasonably allows us to count as predictable, eschewing idle talk of what might be predicted if only we knew more, we have to conclude that a decisive part in human affairs is played by a factor of chance which we are not, and probably never shall be, in a position to eliminate.

EIGHT

Bertrand Russell as a Philosopher[1]

I

Russell's Approach to Philosophy

The popular conception of a philosopher as one who combines universal learning with the direction of human conduct was more nearly satisfied by Bertrand Russell than by any other philosopher of our time. Other philosophers, though not many in this country, have taken an active part in public life, but none of these matches Russell in the width of his interest in the natural and social sciences or in the range of the contributions which he made to philosophy itself. He himself, no doubt with good reason, attached the greatest value to the work which he did on mathematical logic, both in its philosophical and technical aspects, but the interest which he also paid to the theory of knowledge, to the philosophy of mind, to the philosophy of science and to metaphysics in the form of ontology was comparably rewarding. In all these domains, Russell's work has had a very great influence upon his contemporaries, from the beginning of the century up to the present day. In the English-speaking world at least, there is no one, with the possible exception of his pupil Ludwig Wittgenstein, who had done so much in this century, not only to advance the discussion of particular philosophical problems, but to fashion the way in which philosophy is practised.

As he relates in his autobiography, Russell was led to take an interest in philosophy by his desire to find some good reason for believing in the

---

[1] 'Bertrand Russell as a Philosopher' was originally given as a 'Lecture on a Master Mind' at the British Academy on 8 March 1972.

truth of mathematics. Already at the age of eleven, when he had been introduced by his brother to Euclidean geometry, he had objected to having to take the axioms on trust. He eventually agreed to accept them, only because his brother assured him that they could not make any progress otherwise, but he did not give up his belief that the propositions of geometry, and indeed those of any other branch of mathematics, needed some ulterior justification. For a time, he was attracted to John Stuart Mill's view that mathematical propositions are empirical generalizations, which are inductively justified by the number and variety of the observations that conform to them, but this conflicted with the belief, which he was unwilling to relinquish, that mathematical propositions are necessarily true. Taking the necessity of the propositions of formal logic to be relatively unproblematic, he chose rather to try to justify mathematics by showing it to be derivable from logic. This enterprise, in which he had been antici- pated by Gottlob Frege, required, first, the discovery of a method of defining the fundamental concepts of mathematics in purely logical terms, and secondly, the elaboration of a system of logic which would be sufficiently rich for the propositions of mathematics to be deducible from it. The first of these tasks was carried out, among other things, in *The Principles of Mathematics*, which Russell published in 1903, when he was just over thirty years of age, and the second, in which he had the assistance of Alfred North Whitehead, in the three monumental volumes of *Principia Mathematica*, which appeared between 1910 and 1913.

How far Russell and Whitehead succeeded in their attempt to reduce mathematics to logic is a question into which I shall not enter here. That there has been a junction of mathematics with logic is not disputable, but whether this is to be regarded as an annexation of mathematics by logic or of logic by mathematics depends very largely on the status which one assigns to set theory. The point which I wish to make here is that both Russell's belief that the propositions of mathematics stand in need of justification and his method of justifying them, by reducing them to propositions which apparently belong to another domain, are distinctive of his whole approach to philosophy. He was a consistent sceptic, in the sense of holding that all our accepted beliefs are open to question; he conceived it to be the business of philosophy to try to set these doubts at rest, and for reasons which I shall presently give, he thought that the best way of setting them at rest was to reduce the propositions, on which they bore, to propositions which themselves were not doubtful to the same degree.

In most cases, the reason why Russell thought that the truth of a given class of propositions was open to doubt was that they referred to a type of entity of whose existence one could not be certain. He came to believe that the acceptance of any proposition, which was not simply a minuting of one's own current experience, was the outcome of some form of inference, but thought it important to distinguish between inferences which remained at the same level, in the sense that the entities which were referred to in the conclusion were of the same sort as those which already figured in the premisses, and inferences in which there was a transition to a different level. Inferences of the second type were more hazardous, just because of the possibility that the additional entities which were introduced in their conclusions did not in fact exist. Russell himself made his point very clearly in relation to his attempt to reduce numbers to classes.

Two equally numerous collections [he said] appear to have something in common: this something is supposed to be their cardinal number. But so long as the cardinal number is inferred from the collections, not constructed in terms of them, its existence must remain in doubt, unless in view of a metaphysical postulate *ad hoc*. By defining the cardinal number of a given collection as the class of all equally numerous collections, we avoid the necessity of the metaphysical postulate, and thereby remove a needless doubt from the philosophy of arithmetic.[2]

Russell referred to this as an application of what he called 'the supreme maxim in scientific philosophizing': 'Wherever possible, logical constructions are to be substituted for inferred entities.'[3] An object was said by him to be a logical construction or, as he sometimes preferred to put it, a logical fiction, when the propositions in which it figures can be analyzed in such a way that in the propositions which result from the analysis the object no longer appears as a subject of reference. Thus, classes were treated by Russell as logical fictions on the ground that the propositions in which we refer to classes can be satisfactorily replaced by propositions in which we refer not to classes but to propositional functions. Points and instants are logical fictions because the demands which we make of them are equally well satisfied by suitably ordered sets of volumes or events. The self is a logical fiction in the sense that it is nothing apart from the events which constitute its biography. In this case, the effect of adopting Russell's maxim is that we discover the principle according to which different states are to be assigned to the

[2] *Mysticism and Logic*, p. 156.
[3] Ibid. p. 155.

same self, not in fastening upon some further entity, a spiritual substance, to which they bear a common relation, but rather in drawing attention to some special relations which they bear to one another.

This last example shows that when Russell spoke of an object as a logical fiction, he did not mean to imply that it was imaginary or nonexistent. To say that Plato and Socrates are logical fictions is not to class them with fictitious entities, like Theseus or Hercules. Similarly, in the period during which Russell held that physical objects were logical constructions, he did not wish to suggest that they were unreal in the way that gorgons are unreal. What he meant rather was that they are not resistant to analysis; when they are subjected to it, they dissolve into something else. Logical fictions do indeed exist, but only in virtue of the existence of the elements out of which they are constructed. As Russell put it, they are not part of the ultimate furniture of the world.

This raises the question how we are to determine what ultimately exists. Russell employed two criteria which he handled in such a way that they led somewhat circuitously to the same result. The first criterion, as I have already indicated, is epistemological. The basic entities are those of whose existence we can be the most certain. We shall see later on that Russell interpreted this criterion in a liberal fashion, allowing it to cover not just the hardest of data, which were, in his view, the feelings, images, and sense impressions that one is currently having, but also data of this class which one remembers having had, data which are or have been presented to others, and even merely possible sense impressions to which he gave the name of sensibilia. His reason for this liberality was that it is the least that is consistent with the possibility of constructing anything worth having: his apology for it was that the entities which he postulated were not of a different order from those which are primitively given. Even so, we shall also see that he ended by finding this basis too narrow. In the picture of the world at which he eventually arrived the main elements are not even of the order of hard data, at least in any straightforward sense, but events not directly accessible to observation, in which our belief is founded on a hazardous process of inference.

The second criterion is logical. It requires that the basic entities be simple, both in the sense of being individuals, as opposed to classes, and in the sense that they be capable of being denoted by what Russell called logically proper names. To explain how this second condition operates it will be necessary to say something about Russell's theory of descriptions.

II

The Theory of Descriptions and the Theory of Types

The problems which led Russell to formulate his theory of descriptions were connected with his assumption that the meaning of a name is to be identified with the object which the name denotes. The question whether a sign is a name is thereby linked with the question whether there is an object for which it stands. In what may be called his Platonic period, which covers the publication of *The Principles of Mathematics*, Russell was extremely liberal in his provision of objects. Anything that could be mentioned was said by him to be a term; any term could be the logical subject of a proposition; and anything that could be the logical subject of a proposition could be named. It followed that the range of objects which it was possible to name was not limited to things which actually existed at particular places and times: it extended also to abstract entities of all sorts, to nonexistent things like Pegasus or the present King of France, even to logically impossible objects like the round square or the greatest prime number. Such things might not exist in space and time; but the mere fact that they could be significantly referred to was taken to imply that they had some form of being.

Russell did not long remain satisfied with this position. Not only did it exhibit what he called 'a failure of that feeling for reality which ought to be preserved even in the most abstract studies',[4] but it raised difficulties which it had not the resources to meet. For example, if denoting phrases like 'the author of *Waverley*' function as names, and if the meaning of a name is identical with the object which it denotes, it will follow that what is meant by saying that Scott was the author of *Waverley* is simply that Scott was Scott. But, as Russell pointed out, it is clear that when George IV wanted to know whether Scott was the author of *Waverley*, he was not expressing an interest in the law of identity. Again, if the phrase 'the present King of France' denotes a term, and if the law of excluded middle holds, one or other of the two propositions 'The present King of France is bald' and 'The present King of France is not bald' must be true. Yet if one were to enumerate all the things that are bald and all the things that are not bald, one would not find the present King of France on either list. Russell remarked characteristically that 'Hegelians, who love a synthesis, will probably conclude that he wears a wig.' On this view, there is a difficulty even in saying that there is no such person as the present King of France, since it would appear that the term must have some form of

---

[4] *Introduction to Mathematical Philosophy*, p. 165.

being for the denial of its existence to be intelligible. The problem, in Russell's words, is 'How can a nonentity be the subject of a proposition?'[5]

These difficulties are interconnected. They all arise from the combination of two assumptions: first, that denoting phrases like 'the present King of France' and 'the author of *Waverley*' function as names, and, secondly, that a name has no meaning unless there is some object which it denotes. In order to meet them, therefore, Russell had to abandon at least one of these assumptions, and he chose to abandon the first. His theory of descriptions is designed to show that expressions which are classifiable as definite or indefinite descriptions are not used as names, in that it is not necessary for them to denote anything, in order to have a meaning. Or rather, since Russell came to the conclusion that expressions of this kind have no meaning in isolation, his point is better put by saying that it is not necessary for them to denote anything in order to contribute what they do to the meaning of the sentences into which they enter. Russell characterized these expressions as 'incomplete symbols', by which he meant not only that they were not required to denote anything, but also that they were not resistant to analysis. The theory of descriptions was intended to show that descriptive phrases satisfied these two conditions.

The method by which this is achieved is very simple. It depends on the assumption that in all cases in which a predicate is attributed to a subject, or two or more subjects are said to stand in some relation, that is to say, in all cases except those in which the existence of a subject is simply asserted or denied, the use of a description carries the covert assertion that there exists an object which answers to it. The procedure is then simply to make this covert assertion explicit. The elimination of descriptive phrases, their representation as incomplete symbols, is achieved by expanding them into existential statements and construing these existential statements as asserting that something, or in the case of definite descriptive phrases, just one thing, has the property which is contained in the description. So in the simplest version of the theory, which is set out in *Principia Mathematica*, a sentence like 'Scott is the author of *Waverley*' is expanded into 'There is an *x*, such that *x* wrote *Waverley*, such that for all *y*, if *y* wrote *Waverley*, *y* is identical with *x*, and such that *x* is identical with Scott.' Similarly, 'The present King of France is bald' becomes 'There is an *x*, such that *x* now reigns over France, such that for all *y*, if *y* now reigns over France, *y* is identical with *x*, and such that *x* is bald.' The question how a nonentity can be the

---

[5] 'On Denoting', *Logic and Knowledge*, p. 48.

subject of a proposition is circumvented by changing the subject. The denoting phrase is transformed into an existential statement which in this case happens to be false.

Once this procedure is understood, it can be seen to be applicable not only to phrases which are explicitly of the form 'a so-and-so' or 'the so-and-so' but to any nominative sign which carries some connotation. The connotation of the sign is taken away from it and turned into a propositional function: when an object is found which satisfies the function, the same treatment is applied so that the original function is augmented by another predicate, and so the process continues until we get to the point where the subject of all these predicates is either referred to indefinitely by means of the existential quantifier or named by a sign which has no connotation at all. It follows that the only function which is left for a name to fulfil is that of being purely demonstrative. In his more popular expositions of his theory, Russell did sometimes write as if he took ordinary proper names like 'Scott' really to be names, but since he held, in my view rightly, that such proper names do have some connotation, his more consistent view was that they are implicit descriptions. Like ordinary descriptions, they can be used significantly even though the objects to which they purport to refer do not exist. On the other hand, it is a necessary condition for anything to be what Russell called a logically proper name that its significant use guarantees the existence of the object which it is intended to denote. Since the only signs which satisfied this condition, in Russell's view, were those that refer to present sensory or introspective data, it is here that he achieved the fusion of his two criteria, the logical and the epistemological, for determining what there ultimately is.

The theory of descriptions, which was at first received very favourably, has more recently met with the objection that it does not give an accurate account of the way in which definite descriptive phrases are actually used. Thus, it has been suggested that such phrases are normally understood not as covertly asserting but rather as presupposing the existence of the object to which they are intended to refer, with the result that in the cases where the reference fails, the propositions which the descriptive phrases help to express should be said not to be false but to be lacking in truth value. It has also been remarked that very often the sentences in which we intend to pick out some object by the use of a descriptive phrase are not amenable to Russell's treatment, as they stand. When we say 'The baby is crying' or 'The kettle is boiling' we do not mean to imply that there is only one baby or one kettle in the universe. The pinpointing of the object to which we are referring is supposed to be effected by the context. But if we have to insert into a sentence of this sort some predicate which the object in question uniquely satisfies the mere fact that there may be several different predicates which serve this purpose makes it at least very doubtful whether the proposition at which we arrive as the result of the analysis can be logically equivalent to that which was expressed by the sentence with which we began.

These objections would be serious if the theory of descriptions were intended to provide exact translations of the sentence on which it operates. But in fact, though Russell himself may not have been wholly clear about this, what the theory supplies is not a rule of translation but a technique of paraphrase. Its method is to make explicit the information which is implicitly contained in the use of proper names or left to be picked up from the context. It is true that the assumption from which the theory started, that the meaning of a name is to be identified with the object which the name denotes, is itself mistaken. But curiously this mistake, so far from invalidating the theory, turns to its advantage. For as a result of laying upon names a condition which the signs that are ordinarily counted as names do not satisfy, Russell arrived at what may well be the correct conclusion that names in their ordinary employment are dispensable. The thesis that all the work that is done by singular terms can equally well be done by purely general predicates is indeed contestable, but it is in any case important to distinguish between the two functions that names commonly perform, that of indicating objects, and that of holding predicates together. In the theory of descriptions, these two functions are dissociated, the work of reference being performed by purely demonstrative signs, and the work of holding predicates together by quantified variables. Since purely demonstrative signs, if they are needed at all, can be embedded in predicates, only the use of quantified variables remains to mark the subject-predicate distinction. So if, as has been suggested,[6] variables themselves can be replaced by combinatorial operators, the old distinction between subjects and predicates disappears. All that may possibly have to remain in its place is the distinction between demonstrative and descriptive signs.

Since the distinction between subject and predicate corresponds, in one of its aspects, to that between substance and attribute, it was quite in accordance with his theory of descriptions that Russell eventually came to the conclusion that substances could be represented as groups of compresent qualities. This theory was developed by him in two of his

---

[6] Cf. W. V. Quine, 'Variables Explained Away', *Selected Logical Papers*.

later works, *An Inquiry into Meaning and Truth*, which was published in 1940, and *Human Knowledge: Its Scope and Limits*, which appeared in 1948, when Russell was seventy-six years of age. An interesting feature of it is that it again marks a point at which his philosophy of logic is connected with his theory of knowledge. The elimination of substance, though consonant with the theory of descriptions, is not demanded by it. Russell might have been content to allow his quantified variables to refer indefinitely to what he called bare particulars, these being in effect the Lockean substances to which his analysis had pared objects down. If he took the further step of reducing these particulars to their qualities, it was because he shared Berkeley's distaste for the admission of what Locke could only describe as 'A something. I know not what.' Once again he sought to dispense with an unnecessary entity, not just from a liking for economy, but rather to avoid the danger of postulating what did not exist.

An important historical effect of the theory of descriptions was to bring into currency the distinction between the grammatical form of a sentence and what Russell called its logical form. This distinction is not an altogether clear one, since the notion of logical form is itself not wholly clear. There was a tendency on Russell's part to believe that facts had a logical form which sentences could copy: the logical form which underlay the grammatical form of an indicative sentence was then identified with the logical form of the actual or possible fact which would verify what the sentence expressed. This would seem, however, to be putting the cart before the horse, since it is difficult to see what means there could be of determining the logical forms of facts other than through the grammatical forms of the sentences which are used to state them. It is a matter of deciding on other grounds which forms of sentences convey their information most perspicuously. Nevertheless, the distinction between grammatical and logical form has proved fruitful in drawing attention to the dangers of our being misled by grammatical appearances. We are not to assume, because the word 'exists' is a grammatical predicate, that existence is a property of what is denoted by the grammatical subject. The fact that 'to know' is an active verb should not deceive us into thinking that knowing is a mental act. The general point which emerges is that sentences which superficially happen to have the same structure may be transformable in very different ways.

A similar influence has been exerted by Russell's theory of types. This theory was devised to deal with an antinomy in the theory of classes, which for a long time impeded the progress of *Principia Mathematica*. The antinomy arises when one predicates of a class that it is or is not a member of itself. At first sight, this may seem legitimate: for example, it seems reasonable to say, on the one hand, that the class of things which can be counted is itself something that can be counted, and, on the other, that the class of men is not itself a man. In this way we appear to obtain two classes of classes: the class of classes which are members of themselves and the class of classes which are not members of themselves. But now if we ask with respect to this second class of classes whether or not it is a member of itself, we get the contradictory answer that if it is, it is not and if it is not, it is.

Russell's solution of this paradox depends on the principle that the meaning of a propositional function is not specified until one specifies the range of objects which are candidates for satisfying it. From this it follows that these candidates cannot meaningfully include anything which is defined in terms of the function itself. The result is that propositional functions, and correspondingly propositions, are arranged in a hierarchy. At the lowest level we have functions which range only over individuals, then come functions which range over functions of the first order, then functions which range over functions of the second order, and so forth. The system has ramifications into which I shall not here enter but the main idea is simple. Objects which are candidates for satisfying functions of the same order are said to constitute a type, and the rule is that what can be said, truly or falsely, about objects of one type cannot meaningfully be said about objects of a different type. Consequently, to say of the class of classes which are not members of themselves that it either is, or is not, a member of itself is neither true nor false, but meaningless.

Russell applies the same principle to the solution of other logical antinomies and also to that of semantic antinomies like the paradox of the liar in which a proposition is made to say of itself that it is false, with the result that if it is true, it is false and if it is false, it is true. The theory of types eliminates the paradox by ruling that a proposition of which truth or falsehood is predicated must be of a lower order than the proposition by which the predication is made. Consequently, a proposition cannot meaningfully predicate truth or falsehood of itself.

But while the theory of types achieves its purpose, it is arguable that it is too stringent. One difficulty which troubled Russell is that it is sometimes necessary in mathematics to express propositions about all the classes that are composed of objects of any one logical type. But then the obstacle arises that, in the ramified theory, the functions which a given object is capable of satisfying may not themselves be all of the same type, and while there is no objection to our asserting severally of a set of functions of different types that they are satisfied by the same object, we violate the theory when we try to attribute to the object the property of satisfying the totality of these functions: for according to the theory, no such totality can meaningfully be said to exist. Russell met this difficulty by assuming the so-called Axiom of Reducibility. He said that two functions were formally equivalent when they were satisfied by the same objects; and he called a function predicative when it did not involve reference to any collection of functions. Then the Axiom of Reducibility is that with regard to any function F which can take a given object A as argument, there is some predicative function, also having A among its arguments, which is formally equivalent to F. This does, indeed, meet the difficulty but it remains open to question whether the Axiom of Reducibility is a logical truth.

A simpler reason for thinking that the theory of types may be too stringent is that very often we do seem able to speak in the same way significantly about objects of different types. For instance, we can count objects at different levels, yet we do not think that numerical expressions have a different meaning according as they are applied to classes which differ in the type of their membership. Russell's answer was that in such a case the expressions do have a different meaning. Expressions which seem to be applicable to objects of different types were said by him to be systematically ambiguous. It was because the ambiguity is systematic that it escaped our notice. The fact is, however, that were it not for the theory of types, we should have no reason for saying in these cases that there was any ambiguity.

In the face of such difficulties, many logicians have preferred to dispense with the theory of types and try to find some other way of dealing with the paradoxes which it was designed to meet. For instance, there are those who hold that the class paradox can be avoided by depriving it of its subject: they maintain that there just is no class of classes which are not members of themselves. But, whatever its status within logic, the theory has, as I said, had a very strong secondary influence. By lending support to the view that sentences to which there is no obvious objection on the score of grammar or vocabulary may even so be meaningless, it encouraged the Logical Positivists in their attack on metaphysics, and it also helped to make philosophers alive to the possibility of what Professor Ryle has called category mistakes, which consist in ascribing to objects, or events or processes, or whatever it may be, properties which are not appropriate to their type, as when dispositions are confused with occurrences, tasks with achievements, or classes with their members. My own view is that there has been a tendency to exaggerate the extent to which philosophical puzzles arise out of category mistakes, but this is not to deny the fruitfulness of the concept in the cases where it does apply.

III

Russell's Theories of Knowledge

I said earlier that one of the criteria which Russell used for determining what there ultimately is was that of accessibility to knowledge. He took as basic the entities of whose existence and properties we could be the most nearly certain, and these, following the classical tradition of British empiricism, he identified with the immediate data of inner and outer sense. In his book *The Problems of Philosophy*, which was published in 1912 he used the term 'sense data' to designate 'the things that are immediately known in sensation',[7] and made a point of distinguishing sense data both from physical objects on the one hand and from sensations on the other, a sensation being, in his view, a mental act which had a sense datum for its object. Since he saw no reason why the objects of mental acts should themselves be in the mind, he concluded that it was not logically impossible that sense data should exist independently of being sensed. If he nevertheless believed that they did not so exist, it was because he took them to be causally dependent on the bodily state of the percipient. It was also on empirical grounds that he took sense data to be private entities. This would seem in any case to follow from the assumption that they are causally dependent upon the bodily state of the percipient, but, in regard at least to visual data, Russell used the further argument that the differences in perspective, which he supposed to arise from the fact that no two observers could simultaneously occupy the same spatial position, made it very improbable that the sense data which they respectively sensed would ever be qualitatively identical.

In *The Analysis of Mind*, which was published in 1921, Russell gave up his belief in the existence of mental acts. This was partly because he had come to believe that the self which was supposed to perform these acts was a logical fiction, and partly because he had decided that no such things were empirically detectable. Since he no longer believed that there were sensations, as he had previously conceived of them, the idea of there being objects of sensations also had to go, and to this extent he also gave up his belief in the existence of sense data. But although, in his book *My Philosophical Development*, which appeared in 1959, he spoke of himself as having 'emphatically abandoned'[8] sense data at this time, the change in his view is much less radical than this would suggest. He did stop using the term 'sense datum' but he continued to speak of

---

[7] *The Problems of Philosophy*, p. 12.
[8] *My Philosophical Development*, p. 245.

percepts, to which he attributed the same properties as he had attributed to sense data except that of being correlative to sensory acts.

In any case, the question which chiefly interested him was not how sense data, or percepts, are related to the persons who experience them but how they are related to the physical objects which we think that we perceive; and on this question he consistently took the view that physical objects are not directly perceived. Here again he follows the classical empiricist tradition in relying on what is known as the argument from illusion. In *The Problems of Philosophy*, he concentrated mainly on the fact that the appearances of physical objects vary under different conditions, which he interpreted as showing that none of them can be identified with the real properties of the objects in question: but in his later writings he attached greater importance to the causal dependence of these appearances upon the environment and upon the character of our nervous systems. Thus, he was used to remarking that the fact that light takes time to travel shows that when we look at an object like the sun we do not see it in the state in which it currently is but only, at best, in the state in which it was several minutes ago. But his main argument went deeper. He maintained that since the perceptible properties, such as size and shape and colour, which we attribute to physical objects, appear to us as they do partly because of the states of our nervous systems, we have no good reason to believe that the objects possess these properties in the literal way in which they are thought to by common sense. If the attitude of common sense is represented by naive realism, the theory that we directly perceive physical objects much as they really are, then Russell's opinion of common sense was that it conflicted with science: and in such a contest he thought that science ought to be held victorious. As he put it in *An Inquiry into Meaning and Truth* in a formulation which greatly impressed Einstein: 'Naive realism leads to physics, and physics, if true, shows that naive realism is false. Therefore, naive realism, if true, is false: therefore it is false.'[9]

Whether such arguments do prove that we directly perceive sense data, or percepts, as opposed to physical objects, is open to doubt. The fact that a curtain may appear a different colour to different observers or to the same observer under different conditions does indeed show that our selection of one particular colour as the real colour of the curtain is to some extent arbitrary, but it hardly seems to warrant the conclusion that what one sees is not the curtain but something else. The fact that light from a distant star may take years to reach us does refute the naive assumption that we see the star as a contemporary physical

---

[9] *An Inquiry into Meaning and Truth*, p. 126.

object but again does not seem sufficient to prove that we see some
contemporary object which is not the star. The causal argument is
indeed more powerful. If we make it a necessary condition for a property
to be intrinsic to an object that it can be adequately defined without
reference to the effects of the object upon an observer, then I think that a
good case can be made for saying that physical objects are not
intrinsically coloured, though whether this entitles us to say that they are
not 'really' coloured will still be debatable. Even so, it does not obviously
follow that the colour which we attribute to a physical object is a property
of something else, a sense datum or a percept. If we are going to draw any
such conclusion from Russell's arguments we shall have to make two
further assumptions: first, that when we perceive a physical object
otherwise than as it really is, there is something we can be said to perceive
directly, which really has the properties that the physical object only
appears to us to have; and secondly, that what we directly perceive, in
this sense, is the same, whether the perception of the physical object is
veridical or delusive. Russell took these assumptions for granted, but
they are not generally thought to be self-evident; indeed, most
contemporary philosophers reject them.

My own view, for which I have argued elsewhere,[10] is that something
like Russell's position can be reached more satisfactorily by another
method. The first step is to remark that there is a sense in which our
ordinary judgments of perception go beyond the evidence on which they
are based: for instance, when I identify the object in front of me as a table,
I am attributing to it many properties which are not vouchsafed by
anything in the content of my present visual experience. The second step
is to assume the possibility of formulating propositions which simply
monitor the evidence without going beyond it. I call such propositions
experiential propositions and claim that they are perceptually basic, in
the sense that no ordinary judgment of perception can be true unless
some experiential proposition is true. In accordance with Russell's later
views, I conceive of the objects which figure in the propositions as
complexes of qualities rather than particulars in which the qualities
inhere. An important further point is that they are not private entities. At
this primitive level, where neither physical objects nor persons have yet
been introduced, the question whether these sensory elements are public
or private, physical or mental, does not significantly arise.

If we grant Russell this much of his starting point, then the next
question which we have to consider is whether our primitive data are, as
he put it, 'signs of the existence of something else, which we can call the

<hr/>

[10] See *The Origins of Pragmatism*, pp. 303–21 and 'Has Austin Refuted the Sense Datum Theory?'
in *Metaphysics and Common Sense*.

physical object'.[11] The answer which he gave in *The Problems of Philosophy* was that we have a good if not conclusive reason for thinking that they are. The reason is that the postulation of physical objects as external causes of sense data accounts for the character of the data in a way that is not matched by any other hypothesis. Russell did not then think that we could discover anything about the intrinsic properties of physical objects, but did think it reasonable to infer that they are spatiotemporally ordered in a way that corresponds to the ordering of sense data.

The postulation of physical objects as unobserved causes was at variance with Russell's maxim that wherever possible logical constructions are to be substituted for inferred entities, and in his book *Our Knowledge of the External World as a Field for Scientific Method in Philosophy*, which was published in 1914, and in two essays, written in 1914 and 1915, which were reprinted in the collection entitled *Mysticism and Logic*, he sought to exhibit physical objects as logical constructions. It was for this purpose that he introduced the concept of a 'sensibile' with the explanation that sensibilia are objects of 'the same metaphysical and physical status as sense data'[12] Having, as I think mistakenly, assumed that sense data had to be located in private spaces, on the ground that there could be no spatial relations between the data which were experienced by different observers, Russell took the same to be true of sensibilia. He then gave a technical meaning to the word 'perspective' which was such that two particulars, whether sense data or sensibilia, were said to belong to the same perspective if and only if they occurred simultaneously in the same private space.

The theory which Russell developed with these materials has some affinity with Leibniz's monodology. He treated each perspective as a point in what he called 'perspective-space', which, being a three-dimensional arrangement of three-dimensional perspectives, was itself a space of six dimensions. The physical objects which had their location in perspective-space were identified with the classes of their actual and possible appearances. To illustrate how appearances were sorted, Russell used the example of a penny which figures in a number of different perspectives. All the perspectives in which the appearances of the penny are of exactly the same shape are to be collected and put on a straight line in the order of their size. In this way we obtain a number of different series in each of which a limit will be reached at the point 'where (as we say) the penny is so near the eye that if it were any nearer it could not be seen'.[13] If we now imagine all these series to be

[11] *The Problems of Philosophy*, p. 20.   [12] *Mysticism and Logic*, p. 148.
[13] Ibid. p. 162.

prolonged, so as to form lines of perspectives continuing 'beyond' the penny, the perspective in which all the lines meet can be defined as 'the place where the penny is'.[14]

Russell then drew a distinction between the place *at* which and the place *from* which a sense datum or a sensibile appears. The place at which it appears is the place where the thing is of which it is an element. The place from which it appears is the perspective to which it belongs. This enabled him to define 'here' as 'the place in perspective-space which is occupied by our private world', a place which in perspective-space 'may be part of the place where our head is'[15] and it also afforded him a means of discriminating the various distances from which a thing may be perceived, and of distinguishing changes in the objects from changes in the environment or in the state of the observer.

This theory is highly ingenious, but seems to me to fail on the count of circularity. The difficulty is that if the physical object is to be constructed out of its appearances, it cannot itself be used to collect them. The different appearances of the penny, in Russell's example, have first to be associated purely on the basis of their qualities. But since different pennies may look very much alike, and since they may also be perceived against very similar backgrounds, the only way in which we can make sure of associating just those sensibilia that belong to the same penny is by situating them in wider contexts. We have to take account of perspectives which are adjacent to those in which they occur. But then we are faced with the difficulty that perspectives which contain only sensibilia as opposed to sense data are not actually perceived; and there seems to be no way of determining when two unperceived perspectives are adjacent without already assuming the perspective-space which we are trying to construct.

Another serious difficulty is that the method by which Russell ordered the elements of his converging series is not adequate for the purpose. He relied on the assumption that the apparent size of an object varies continuously with the distance and its apparent shape with the angle from which the object is viewed. But, in view of the principle of constancy, this is psychologically false. The assumption might be upheld, if apparent shapes and sizes were determined physiologically, but to do this would again be to bring in physical objects before we had constructed them.

The main source of these difficulties, in my view, is Russell's mistaken assumption that his sensory elements are located in private spaces. But for this assumption, there would be no need for the

[14] Ibid. p. 162.
[15] *Our Knowledge of the External World*, p. 92.

complicated ordering of so many perspectives. As I have argued elsewhere,[16] we can obtain the equivalent of Russell's sensibilia merely by projecting spatial and temporal relations beyond the sense fields in which they are originally given. Because of the fact that similar percepts are usually obtainable at the meeting point of similar sensory routes, we are able to postulate the existence at these points of what I call standardized percepts. We can then proceed inductively to locate such percepts in positions which we have not actually traversed. In this way we obtain a skeleton of the physical world of common sense which we can further articulate by various processes of correlation. It is true that this method will not enable us to achieve Russell's goal of exhibiting physical objects as logical constructions out of sensibilia. We shall not be able to translate propositions which refer to physical objects into propositions which refer only to percepts. We shall, however, be able to show how our belief in the physical world of common sense is constituted as a theory with respect to a primary system of percepts, and how this system in its turn is theoretically based on the data which figure in our experiential propositions, all without the introduction of any higher-level entities. And this I believe to be the most that is feasible.

Russell carried his reductionism to its furthest point in his book *The Analysis of Mind*, which was published in 1921. Largely following William James, he there maintained that both mind and matter were logical constructions out of primitive elements which were themselves neither mental nor physical. Mind and matter were differentiated by the fact that certain elements such as images and feelings entered only into the constitution of minds, and also by the operation of different causal laws. Thus the same percepts when correlated according to the laws of physics constituted physical objects and when correlated according to the laws of psychology helped to constitute minds. In their mental aspect, these elements engaged, among other things, in what Russell called 'mnemic causation', a kind of action at a distance by which experienced data produced subsequent memory images. On the view which he there took, but later became dissatisfied with, that causation is just invariable sequence, there is no theoretical objection to such action at a distance, but Russell ceased to believe in it on the ground of its being inconsistent with the principle, which he adopted in *Human Knowledge*, that events which enter into causal chains are spatiotemporally continuous. He remained faithful to the view that minds are logical constructions, without, however, anywhere giving a

---

[16] See *The Origins of Pragmatism*, pp. 239–41 and 322–3, and *Russell and Moore*, p. 65.

precise account of the relations which have to hold between different elements for them to be constituents of the same mind, and he continued to hold, as he put it in the collection of essays entitled *Portraits from Memory*, which he published in 1958, that 'An event is not rendered either mental or material by any intrinsic quality but only by its causal relations'.[17] It is, however, to be noted, first, that this is inconsistent with his earlier view that images and feelings are intrinsically mental and, secondly, that his final reason for the assimilation of mental and physical events is not that they are both constructed out of the same elements but rather that what are called mental events are identical with physical states of the brain.

This is in line with Russell's abandonment, in his later works, of the view that physical objects are logical constructions, in favour of his earlier view that they are inferred entities. In his book, the *Analysis of Matter*, which was published in 1927, there are passages which suggest that he still wanted to identify physical objects with groups of percepts, but more often he took it to follow from the causal theory of perception, which he held to be scientifically established, that we have no knowledge of the intrinsic properties of physical objects or any direct acquaintance with physical space, though he held that we could legitimately infer that it had some structural correspondence with perceptual space. Another conclusion which he drew from the causal theory of perception was that everything that we perceive is inside our own heads. This does indeed sound very paradoxical, but a case can be made for it if one accepts Russell's distinction between perceptual and physical space. For what it then comes to is the reasonable enough decision to identify the physical location of percepts with that of their immediate physical cause. The difficulty is rather that the underlying distinction is hard to accept. Neither is it clear what reasons Russell thought he had for taking the further step of identifying percepts with the events in the brain which are ordinarily thought to cause them.

The view that physical objects are known to us only by inference, as the external causes of our percepts, with the corollary that we can know something of their intrinsic properties, was fairly consistently maintained by Russell in *Human Knowledge* and other later works. One obvious difficulty with any theory of this kind is to see how we can be justified in inferring that any such external objects exist at all. We may, indeed, be entitled to postulate unobservable entities, so long as the hypotheses into which they enter have consequences which can be empirically tested, but it seems to me that a more serious problem is

[17] *Portraits from Memory*, p. 152.

created when these unobservable objects are held to be located in an unobservable space. Not only is it not clear to me what justification there could be for believing in the existence of an unobservable space, but I am not even sure that I find the concept of such a thing intelligible.

A further objection is that the causal theory of perception on which Russell relied itself seems to require that physical objects be located in perceptual space. When my seeing the table in front of me is explained in terms of the passage of light rays from the table to my eye, the assumption is surely that the table is there when I see it. It is true that we sometimes distinguish between the place where a physical object really is and the place where it appears to be, but the calculations which enable us to make such distinctions are themselves based on the assumption that other objects are where they appear to be. It is only because we start by equating the physical position of things around us with the observed positions of standardized percepts that our more sophisticated methods of locating more distant objects can lead to verifiable results.

This does not mean that we are driven back to naive realism. Even if we do not accept Russell's distinction between physical and perceptual space, it still remains open to us to regard physical objects as really possessing only those structural properties that physicists ascribe to them. We are not even deterred from regarding percepts as being private to the percipient. Having developed the common-sense conception of the physical world as a theoretical system with respect to sensory qualities, we can interpret into the system the elements on which it is founded. The physical object is set against the percepts from which it was abstracted and made causally responsible for them. The relatively constant perceptual qualities which are attributed to it come to be contrasted with the fluctuating impressions which different observers have of it, and the impressions assigned to the observers. At a still more sophisticated level, we can replace the common-sense physical object by the scientific skeleton on which the causal processes of perception are taken to depend. In this way I believe that a fusion of Russell's theories may lead us to the truth.

IV

Morals and Politics

Of the seventy-one books and pamphlets that Russell published in the course of his life, only about twenty could properly be classified as works of academic philosophy. The rest of them cover a very wide range, including as they do autobiographical writings, biographical writings, books of travel, books on education, books on religion, works of history, popularizations of science, and even two volumes of short stories; but the largest single class consists of works on social questions and on politics. From these works it is apparent, as it clearly was to anyone who knew him, that Russell held very strong moral convictions, but he was not very greatly concerned with ethical theory. Apart from an early essay on 'The Elements of Ethics', which was written about 1910 and included in his *Philosophical Essays*, his main contribution to the subject is to be found in his book on *Human Society in Ethics and Politics*, of which the ethical part was mainly written in 1945–6, although the book was not published until 1954.

The position which Russell took in the earlier essay owed almost everything to his friend G. E. Moore whose *Principia Ethica* had appeared in 1903. Like Moore he held that good is an indefinable non-natural quality, the presence of which is discoverable by intuition, that the objectively right action is the one, out of all the actions open to the agent, that will have the best consequences, in the sense that it will lead to the greatest favourable, or least unfavourable, ratio of good to evil, and that the action which one ought to do is that which appears most likely to have the best consequences. The only point on which he differed from Moore was in holding that the exercise of free will, which is implied by attributions of moral responsibility, is not only at variance with determinism but positively requires it. It is, he argued, only because volitions have causes that moral considerations can be brought to bear upon people's conduct. Russell's view of free will was similar to Locke's in that it disregarded the question whether and in what sense it is possible for us to will anything other than we do. Like Locke, he took it to be enough that our actions should be causally dependent on our choices, no matter how these might be caused.

In *Human Society in Ethics and Politics* Russell took the same view of free will and he continued to hold that one ought to do the action which will probably have the best consequences, but for the rest he forsook Moore for Hume. He still found no logical flaw in the doctrine that we can know by intuition what is right or good, but objected to it that since people's intuitions conflict it reduced ethical controversy to a mere 'clash of rival dogmas'.[18] Moreover, the fact that the things to which we are inclined to attach intrinsic value are all things which are desired or enjoyed suggested to him that good might after all be definable 'in terms of desire or pleasure or both'.[19]

[18] *Human Society in Ethics and Politics*, p. 131.
[19] Ibid. p. 113.

The definition which he proposed along these lines was that 'An occurrence is "good" when it satisfies desire.'[20] In another passage, however, he suggested that 'Effects which lead to approval are defined as "good" and those leading to disapproval as "bad".'[21] These definitions can perhaps be reconciled by making the assumption that the effects which lead to approval are those which are thought likely to satisfy desire. This leaves it uncertain whether in calling something good I am to be understood as saying just that I approve of it, or that it is an object of general approval, and if it is just a question of my own approval, whether this is on the grounds of its satisfying my own desire or of its giving general satisfaction. Russell did not explicitly distinguish between these possibilities, but in the main he seems to have held that in calling something good I am stating, or perhaps just expressing, my own approval of it, on the ground that its existence is or would be found generally satisfying. Right actions then will be those that, on the available evidence, are likely to have better effects in this sense, than any other actions which are possible in the circumstances.

This comes close to utilitarianism, the main difference being that Russell did not fall into the error of assuming that all desire is for pleasure. He was therefore able to admit that 'some pleasures seem to be inherently preferable to others',[22] without giving up his principle that all forms of satisfaction are equally valuable in themselves. At this point, however, there was some discrepancy between his theory and his application of it. In practice, he tended to look upon cruelty as inherently evil, independently of the satisfaction or dissatisfaction that it might cause, and he also attached an independent value to justice, freedom, and the pursuit of truth.

The value which Russell attached to freedom comes out clearly in his political writings. His concern with politics became increasingly practical, but he took a strong interest in political theory. Himself an aristocrat, he thought that a good case could be made for an aristocratic form of government in societies where the material conditions were such that the enjoyment of wealth and leisure was possible only for a small minority. In societies in which it was economically possible for nearly everyone to enjoy a reasonably high standard of living he thought that the principle of justice favoured democracy. He said that although democracy did not ensure good government, it did prevent certain evils, the chief of these being the possession by an incompetent or unjust government of a permanent tenure of power. Russell was

[20] Ibid. p. 55.
[21] Ibid. p. 116.
[22] Ibid. p. 117.

consistently in favour of the devolution of power and disliked and distrusted the aggrandisement of the modern state. This was one of the reasons for his hostility to Soviet Communism, as expressed in his book *The Theory and Practice of Bolshevism*, the outcome of a visit which he paid to Russia as early as 1919. If he seemed to become a little more sympathetic to the Soviet Union towards the end of his life, it was only because he had then become convinced that the policies of the American government represented the greater threat to peace.

Russell's desire to diminish rather than increase the power of the state set him apart from the ordinary run of socialists. He was, however, at one with them in wishing to limit the possession and use of private property, in seeing no justification for inherited wealth and in being opposed to the private ownership of big businesses or of land. In his books, *Principles of Social Reconstruction* and *Roads to Freedom*, which were published in 1916 and 1918 respectively, he displayed a certain sympathy for anarchism, but declared himself more in favour of Guild Socialism, a system which provided for workers' control of industry and for the establishment of two parliaments, one a federation of trades unions and the other a parliament of consumers, elected on a constituency basis, with a joint committee of the two acting as the sovereign body. Russell himself added the original proposals that 'a certain small income, sufficient for necessaries, should be secured to all, whether they work or not',[23] that the expense of children should be borne wholly by the community, provided that their parents, whether married or not, were known to be 'physically and mentally sound in all ways likely to affect the children'[24] and that 'a woman who abandons wage-earning for motherhood ought to receive from the state as nearly as possible what she would have received if she had not had children.'[25] He did not discuss how these measures could be afforded.

In his later political writings, though he continued to seek means of curbing the power of the state, Russell was more concerned with the relations between states than with questions of internal organization. Regarding nationalism as 'the most dangerous vice of our time'[26] he thought it likely to lead to a third world war which the use of atomic weapons would render far more terrible than any suffering that the human race had previously known. The only assurance that he could find against the continuing threat of such a disaster was the institution of a world government which would have the monopoly of armed force.

[23] *Roads to Freedom*, p. 119.
[24] *Principles of Social Reconstruction*, p. 185.
[25] Ibid. p. 184.
[26] *Education and the Social Order*, p. 138.

While it was obviously better that such a government be constituted by international agreement, Russell thought it more likely to come about 'through the superior power of some one nation or group of nations'.[27] It was for this reason, since it was essential to his argument that the change be peaceful, that he advocated unilateral disarmament. The difficulty was that it was no more probable that a world government would come about peacefully in this fashion than through international agreement. One cannot but admire the passion which Russell brought to the discussion of this question, and the concern for humanity which inspired him; but in his treatment of it he seems both to have overestimated the likelihood of global nuclear war and correspondingly underestimated the merits of the traditional policy of maintaining a balance of power.

Russell's writings on political and social questions do not have the depth of his contributions to the theory of knowledge or the philosophy of logic, but they express the moral outlook of a humane and enlightened man and they add to the lucidity which was characteristic of all his work a special touch of elegance and wit. His style contains echoes of Voltaire, to whom he was pleased to be compared, and of Hume with whom he had the greatest philosophical affinity. Like Hume, he could be careless in matters of detail, especially in his later work. After the years of labour which he expended on *Principia Mathematica*, he became impatient with minutiae. The hostility which he displayed to the linguistic philosophy which became fashionable in England in the 1950s was partly directed against the minuteness of its approach, partly also against its assumption that philosophy could afford to be indifferent to the natural sciences. In an age when philosophical criticism increasingly fettered speculation, his strength lay in the sweep and fertility of his ideas. He was very much a hare and not a tortoise: but it is not the most probable of fables in which the hare does not win the race.

[27] *New Hope for a Changing World*, p. 77.

NINE

The Humanist Outlook[1]

Humanism is defined in the *Oxford English Dictionary* as any system of thought or action which is concerned with merely human interests. The point of the word 'merely' here is that it excludes theology. The early humanists, who took Erasmus for their master, were believers in Christianity; but they did not think it right to apply religious tests to every form of intellectual activity. In particular, they attached an independent value to the study of the languages, literature, history and mythology of ancient Greece and Rome; it is for this reason, indeed, that classical studies still go by the name of the humanities. At the same time, they took the first step towards freeing scientific inquiry from religious control.

That the scientific movement of the Renaissance was seen as a threat to religious orthodoxy is shown by the persecution of Galileo. Nevertheless Newtonian physics was not in fact so very difficult for Christian apologists to accommodate; it could even be welcomed as lending support to the argument from design. The most serious outbreak of intellectual hostility between science and religion occurred in the nineteenth century, when the advance of geology and the theory of evolution undermined the biblical account of Creation. It was partly as a result of this conflict that the anticlerical scepticism or deism of the eighteenth century Enlightenment gave way in the nineteenth century to a broader movement of Rationalism or Free Thought, which was not merely anticlerical but hostile to any form of religious belief. Present-day humanists are in fact the intellectual heirs of those nineteenth-century freethinkers.

Freedom of thought was a form of resistance to authority. It rested on

---

[1] 'The Humanist Outlook' is an amended version of the introduction A. J. Ayer wrote for a book which he edited entitled *The Humanist Outlook* (Pemberton with Barrie & Rockcliff, 1968). The contributors to the book were/are all members of the Advisory Council of the British Humanist Association.

the principle that one should not be required to accept as dogma what is not known to be true. The adherents to this movement were not rationalists, in the philosophical sense of the term. Though they had confidence in the power of human reason, they did not believe that reason alone, unaided by observation, could discover how the world worked. They put their trust in scientific method, with its implication that every theory is liable to revision. This open, critical spirit has continued to be a distinctive mark of Humanism.

The hostility of the rationalists to religious dogmatism was not evinced only in their fidelity to the natural sciences. It extended also to questions of human conduct. This did not mean that their moral principles were necessarily different from those which were held by their religious antagonists. The difference lay in their denying that morality either had a religious basis or needed a religious sanction.

In maintaining that one cannot look to religion to supply a logical foundation for any code of morality, they were demonstrably right. The decisive argument in their favour is that no moral system can rest solely on authority. It can never be a sufficient justification for performing any action that someone wishes or commands it. Not only has it first to be established that the person in question has a legitimate claim on one's allegiance, but even when this has been established, it still does not necessarily follow that what he commands is right. Neither does it make any difference to the argument whether the authority is taken to be human or divine. No doubt the premiss that what God wills is right is one that religious believers take for granted. The fact remains that even if they were justified in making this assumption, it implies that they have a standard of morality which is independent of their belief in God. The proof of this is that when they say that God is good or that he wills what is right, they surely do not mean merely to express the tautology that he is what he is or that he wills what he wills. If they did mean no more than this, they would be landed with the absurd consequence that even if the actions of the deity were such as, in any other person, we should characterize as those of a malignant demon, they would still, by definition, be right. But the fact is that believers in God think of the goodness which they attribute to him as something for which we ought to be grateful. Now this would make no sense at all if the deity's volition set the standard of value: for in that case, no matter what he was understood to will, we should still be obliged to think him good.

It is no answer to this argument to say that the possibility of God's being anything other than good is excluded by his nature. There is, indeed, no logical objection to building goodness into the definition of

God so long as it is compatible with the other attributes which go to make up the concept. The drawback is only that it adds to the difficulty of supposing that the concept is satisfied. But so far from this proving that God's nature can serve to define goodness, it proves just the opposite. If one did not know what one understood by goodness, independently of ascribing it to God, its inclusion in the definition would not be intelligible.

Not only is it a fallacy to think that moral principles can logically depend upon the will of God: it is also a fallacy to look to human morality for a proof of God's existence. The underlying assumption is that only purely selfish behaviour is natural to man; so that if it ever happens, as it not infrequently does, that people behave unselfishly, they must be inspired by a higher power. But this assumption is false and the conclusion which is drawn from it is invalid. The assumption is false because the only criterion for deciding what is natural to man is what men actually do. Antecedently to experience, there can be no reason for expecting people to behave in one way rather than another. If experience shows that they act unselfishly as well as selfishly, we can only conclude that both types of behaviour are natural. No doubt the self-regarding impulses are the stronger, and in many persons remain so, but this does not alter the fact that many actions are motivated by concern for others. If the capacity for evil is part of human nature, so is the capacity for good.

It is not, however, enough that the capacity for good exists: we are still left with the problem of the extent to which it is exercised. The most important question here is that of moral education. One thing which is clear is that this is not an isolated problem. It is bound up not only with the question of children's health, but also with that of their material and social background. What social reforms are needed and how they can best be brought about are problems to which the solution calls for the exercise of intelligence as much as goodwill. These are questions in which we are, and ought to be, emotionally involved. But the very fact that we are emotionally involved makes it difficult for us to treat these questions scientifically. No doubt we do not rely on science alone for our understanding of human nature. In a different way this function can be admirably performed by works of art. Yet when it comes to questions of social organization, the lack of a scientific approach will tend to deprive us of the information that we need to put our good intentions into effect.

This is not to say that science can supply us with our values. We have to distinguish the question how moral principles are formed, and how they can be implemented, from the question of their justification. To the question of justification, the correct answer, in my view, is that moral principles cannot be justified in terms of anything other than themselves. We have already seen that they cannot be founded on authority, and I believe that it can also be shown that they cannot logically be derived from statements about matters of fact. That is to say, I do not think that any conclusions about the way things ought to be can be logically deduced from a set of premisses which merely report the way things are. Of course, this does not mean that we cannot appeal to matters of fact in support of some moral decision: it is only that when we take the facts as justifying the decision, the acceptance of some moral standpoint will be presupposed. For instance, in very many cases, a sufficient reason for concluding that one ought not to pursue a certain course of action is that it will cause suffering to other people: but the reason is sufficient only against a moral background in which it is assumed both that, other things being equal, suffering is evil and that one has a duty to consider the interests of others besides oneself. These are assumptions from which very few people would dissent, at least in theory, but they are not susceptible of proof, or, for that matter, of disproof. If they are to be criticized, it can only be on the basis of a different moral outlook, which will equally operate as a judge in its own cause. This is not a ground for scepticism, still less for moral nihilism. It is just that when it comes to the conduct of life, each one of us has to decide what ends he thinks it right to pursue and what principles he is prepared to stand by. I should add that there is no escaping this responsibility. Even those who surrender their independence of judgment, or those who merely go by current fashion, are tacitly making a fundamental moral choice.

In explaining how such choices come to be made, there are many social factors that have to be taken into account: and one of them, undoubtedly, is religious belief. The fact that there is no logical connection between religion and morals does not entail that there is no causal connection. On the contrary, it is historically obvious not only that religious belief has had a considerable influence in shaping man's moral outlook, but that it has operated, at times very powerfully, as a moral sanction. It is the idea of its being indispensable as a moral sanction that is implicit in Voltaire's saying that if God did not exist it would be necessary to create him. From what I have already said, it should be clear that I am not in agreement with this view. I believe that comparatively few people nowadays are at all strongly motivated either by the hope of being rewarded, or by the fear of being punished, in an afterlife: even among professed Christians there is a decline in the literal belief in hell. Yet it does not appear that the loss of this belief, or indeed the weakening of religious faith in general, has caused people to behave worse to one another. On the contrary, I think that the balance of the evidence is on the side of moral progress. In spite of the wars, the dictatorships, the cults of violence, the political and racial persecutions which have disfigured the history of this century, I believe that the average man is more humane, more pacific and more concerned with social justice than he was a century ago. This is not to say very much: we have very little ground for complacency; but since it is becoming the fashion to decry ourselves, I think it worth remarking that the belief in social progess is still empirically defensible.

If there has been a movement towards the decrease of man's inhumanity to man, it is one in which the Christian Churches have played a part. Whether, in the whole course of its history, organized Christianity has not done more harm than good is a question which it would be difficult to settle and perhaps not very profitable to argue; it is, however, fair to say, at least of the Anglican Church, that in recent times it has shown itself to be more favourably disposed towards social reform, more ready to question its moral and even theological positions, and more tolerant of other groups than it has been in the past. I think that the same is true even of the Roman Catholic Church, though to a very much smaller extent. This is one reason why I think it would be a mistake for the humanist movement to expend its main energy on an anticlerical crusade. But whatever view one holds of the extent of the political and social influence which the Churches have managed to retain, and of the uses which they make of it, one will have to take account of the reasons for its existence. This will involve a more general inquiry into the psychological and social causes of religious belief. It is important also to consider how far the needs for which the practice of religion caters are capable of being satisfied in other ways. A study of the part that might be played by imaginative literature would be a contribution to this end.

One desire which the arts are not equipped to satisfy is the desire for personal survival. Though a belief in personal survival has commonly been held as a corollary of the belief in the existence of a deity, the two are not logically connected. It would be perfectly consistent for an atheist to accept the hypothesis of life after death, perhaps on such evidence as has been assembled by the Society of Psychical Research. From a study of these paranormal phenomena, one may, however, conclude that they are explicable in other ways. This is a field in which it is especially difficult to maintain an impartial outlook, but I think I can fairly say that, apart from the logical difficulties about personal identity which are involved in the hypothesis of survival, it does not seem to me that the evidence which has been adduced in its favour is strong enough to overcome the scientific objections to which it is exposed. I take it, therefore, to be a fact that one's existence ends with death. I think it possible to show how this fact can be emotionally acceptable.

If survival is ruled out, it follows that our accounts of happiness and self-fulfilment are closed at death. This has the harsh consequence that very many people are left with an unfavourable balance, which will never be redressed. Partly for this reason, I think that it is morally incumbent upon humanists to do everything in their power to bring about the material and social conditions in which the great majority of people will have a fair opportunity of finding satisfaction in their lives, and I think that, so far as possible, their concern should extend beyond the national or professional groups of which they happen to be members, to mankind as a whole. For instance, an expert on computers might dwell on their power to economize labour; a demographer, who studies the growth of population, might emphasize the need for birth control; an agronomist, concerned with the problem of food supply, might make out a case for a world food-authority.

Underlying all such discussions is the problem of creating the moral and political climate in which the ends which we agree to be desirable can be achieved. In common with other humanists, I believe that the only possible basis for a sound morality is mutual tolerance and respect: tolerance of one another's customs and opinions; respect for one another's rights and feelings; awareness of one another's needs. It is easy to refer in a general way to the social changes which are necessary for this to come about: the spread of education, the erosion of class distinctions, the eradication of national and social prejudice, the general increase in material prosperity. It is not easy to see, in all instances, how changes of this sort are actually to be effected. Neither are they sufficient. It would be naive to assume that it is only poverty and ignorance that stand in the way of universal brotherhood. There are irrational forces in human nature that need to be better understood. Even when they are understood, there will be difficult problems about the ways in which we ought to try to master them. But, though these questions are hard, I do not think that they are intractable; and one thing which will make them more tractable is an extension of the spirit which informs contemporary humanism.

TEN

The Meaning of Life [1]

A saying attributed to Nietzsche is that since God is dead everything is permitted. I suppose that the assertion that God is dead is not to be taken literally. There have, indeed, been philosophers, as good as A. N. Whitehead and Samuel Alexander, who held that God did not yet exist. In their evolutionary metaphysics, the universe was represented as progressing towards the emergence of a deity. Anthropologists have also described religious rites, supposed by them to be connected with harvests, in which gods are slain, annually, only to be replaced or in some instances reborn. I do not, however, know of any instance in which a deity, conceived as supernatural, is thought simply to have perished, without surviving or reappearing in any form, or leaving a successor.

I may be mistaken on this point and do not attach much importance to it, since its implications do not significantly differ from those of a theory which is known to have been held, that of the Epicureans, who did believe that there were gods but thought of them as having something better to do than fuss about human beings. They were credited with living lives of unalloyed pleasure somewhere far out in space, without exercising any control over our world or anything within it. The behaviour of the material atoms by which the course of nature was regulated was not of their contriving and to take any notice of the vicissitudes of human life would only cause them pain.

I shall address myself later on to the general topic of religious belief, in very many of its aspects. The question which I first wish to eliminate is that of the connection, suggested by Nietzsche and still very widely thought to obtain, between religious belief and moral conduct. If what Nietzsche meant by speaking of the death of God was that his audience had mostly ceased to believe in the creation of the world by an

[1] 'The Meaning of Life' was delivered as the 64th Conway Memorial Lecture, 19 May 1988, at the Conway Hall, London.

omnipotent, omniscient, supremely benevolent, necessary being, his assertion was probably false at the time at which he made it. If he meant that there was no good reason to believe in the existence of any such being, I shall in due course be arguing that he was right. That is not, however, the point at issue here. The point is that even if there were such a being as Nietzsche may be thought to have envisaged, or indeed a deity of any kind, his will could not supply a basis for morality. The reason, which is purely logical, was pointed out by Plato, in his dialogue *Euthyphro*, and has been restated by a series of philosophers down to the present day. It is simply that while moral rules may be propounded by authority the fact that these were so propounded would not validate them. For let us suppose that it is possible for there to be a God and possible that he be good. Even so his goodness could not simply consist of his divinity. For if it did, then in saying that he willed what was good, his votaries would be asserting no more than the tautology that he willed what he willed. They count themselves fortunate in his goodness and regard it as warranting their gratitude, but if all that they meant by ascribing goodness to him was that his wishes were what they were, they would have nothing to be grateful for. If it were the devil that was in supreme power, what he willed, however diabolical, would have to be reckoned good.

It is no answer to this argument to protest, as some do, that God's goodness issues from his nature. For exactly the same considerations apply. A theist is at liberty to include the notion of goodness in the concept of his deity, thereby making it necessary that if there were a God he would be good, but this very manoeuvre illustrates the point that I am making. If our theist did not possess a concept of goodness, which was logically independent of the other predicates which he conjoined with it to identify his deity, the inclusion of it would add nothing to them. From the supposition that an intelligent being created the universe and continues to rule over it, nothing whatsoever follows about his moral character. In supposing this being also to be benevolent, his devotees are assuming that he satisfies their own moral standards. They can indeed argue that he is responsible for their possession of these standards, as he is, in their view, for everything else. The fact remains that the verdicts which they reach in accordance with these standards have no logical connection with the existence or character of the source from which their acceptance of the standards proceeded. To take a less dubious example, those whom we regard as well-brought up children learn from their parents and schoolteachers how they should behave. It does not follow that their moral sentiments are validated by the fact that they acquired them in this way. Nor does it follow that the teachers are necessarily protected from the moral appraisal of those whom they have taught. The children may find reasons to adopt different standards. More pertinently, they may retain the standards in question and judge that their parents and teachers do not always measure up to them.

I should think myself guilty of labouring the obvious, were it not that the simple point at issue has had such difficulty in gaining general acceptance, especially when religion is brought into the picture. Put succinctly, the point is that morals cannot be founded on authority, and here it makes no difference whether the authority be supposed human or divine.

To say that authority, whether secular or religious, supplies no ground for morality is not to deny the obvious fact that it supplies a sanction. There is a great deal to be said about the justification and efficacy of rewards and punishments, but a thorough examination of this topic would take me too far afield, and I shall limit myself, in this context, to a few remarks about the factor of religious belief. My principal reason for singling out religious belief is that it is intimately connected not logically, as we shall discover, but historically, with a question which has a strong bearing upon what I have chosen to call the meaning of life, namely that of the possibility of the continuance of one's existence, in one form or another, after death.

Both the importance attached to the concept of survival and the manner of conceiving it vary to a great extent in different religions. For instance, with the possible exception of some initiates into mystery cults, the worshippers of the Homeric gods, and indeed their Latin counterparts, took little stock of an afterlife. If they believed that their souls were destined for Hades, it was an abode of shadows, and the prospect of inhabiting it appears to have had next to no effect upon the way they lived. The remark attributed to Achilles that it was preferable to be a slave on earth than a king in the underworld might be taken to suggest that the afterlife figures in Greek mythology as something to be feared, but I think that its implication is not that a shadowy future is unpleasant in itself, but rather that it is not worth considering because of its inferiority in status to even the meanest condition of bodily human life.

The Christian religion, with its view of man's life on earth as principally a prelude to the life to come, lies at the opposite extreme, but even in Christianity as I have just described it, after the abandonment of the belief in the millennium, inaugurated by the second coming of Christ, as the triumph of Christians on earth, the differences at different periods and among different sects in conceptions of the afterlife and their effects upon conduct are very great. A striking example is the threat of hell. Nowadays, the belief that those who are divinely adjudged to have been sinners are fated to undergo an eternity of physical torment has been generally abandoned by Anglicans and to a lesser extent by Roman Catholics. Hellfire has been replaced by the mental frustration of being deprived of the sight of God, and even more mildly by the mere lack of this privilege. Nevertheless, I am given to understand that the literal conception of hellfire is still entertained by the growing number of Protestants who answer to the description of born-again Christians and there is no doubt that throughout the Christian era, at least until the present century, it was universally orthodox, promulgated with varying degrees of eloquence by the preachers adhering to different sects and at least nominally accepted by their congregations.

But can the acceptance have been more than nominal in the general run of cases? There is a distinction to be drawn here between applying the doctrine to others and applying it to oneself. The early Christian fathers applied it to Pagans: there is a passage in Tertullian in which he looks forward to the pleasure of occupying a front seat in heaven, enjoying the spectacle of his opponents suffering in hell. Are we to assume that it never occurred to him that he himself might be adjudged a sinner?

Evangelical parents tortured their children to rid them of their innate propensities to sin. Were they quite certain that all such propensities had been beaten out of themselves? Yet, if they were uncertain, how could they have faced the future with any equanimity? Dr Johnson, for all his virtues, was a Christian who believed that he stood a serious risk of being sent to hell. There were times when the fear of death brought him very close to madness. Romantic love is a strong passion and usually represented, except in American films, as being incompatible with marriage. Consequently, its physical consummation is most frequently a sin. In James Elroy Flecker's play *Hassan*, the lovers are offered a night of love at the cost of being tortured to death in the morning. They choose the night of love. Would any remotely rational couple, however enamoured, make such a choice, at the cost of being tortured for eternity?

What I am suggesting is that there has often been a discrepancy between the conscious acceptance of the Christian doctrine of eternal damnation and the conduct which such a belief might be expected to cause if it were seriously held. This is not to say that the doctrine was wholly inoperative. In the case of Roman Catholics its force was diminished by the liberating practice of confession and the power ascribed to remit the penalties for sin. There is, however, evidence that men were afraid of dying in circumstances which denied them the opportunity of receiving absolution, even if this fear did not deter them from committing the offences for which absolution was required.

The Christians for whom the prospect of incurring the rewards and penalties of a posthumous judgment ought rationally to have the strongest effect upon their conduct are the Protestants who believe that they are protected by nothing except God's mercy. For some reason which has never been made clear, they have tended to assume that their chances of prospering in the next world were inversely proportionate to their enjoyment of pleasure, especially sensual pleasure, on earth. I should add that this view did not originate with the Reformation. The earliest Christians were also apt to take the view that extreme asceticism, often carried to the point of causing oneself physical injury, found favour with their God.

Even less intelligible is the behaviour of Calvinists who have subscribed to the doctrine of predestination, according to which salvation does not depend upon one's conduct. Whatever one does, one's eventual fate is preordained from eternity. It might have been expected that persons who subscribed to this doctrine would be disposed towards hedonism. On the contrary with a very few exceptions, such as the first Lord Beaverbrook, they have been among the foremost enemies of pleasure. I suppose the explanation to be that, sharing the Puritan belief that God was in favour of asceticism, and not being entirely confident that they were among the elect, they refrained from the pursuit of pleasure as a means of bolstering their confidence. An alternative explanation which I have frivolously put forward, although it would show them to be more ingenious, and would not, in my unorthodox view, convict them of absurdity, is that they believed in backward causation. They conducted themselves as Puritans in order to have been saved.

Before I leave the topic of the effect on moral conduct of Christian belief, I ought to say that I am not suggesting that it has been wholly or even primarily utilitarian. No doubt the hope of future reward or the fear of future punishment has had some influence, if only temporarily, and especially on the behaviour of children, but I believe that this influence has been much smaller than those hostile to Christianity generally suppose. Very often people have behaved well, and badly also, as in the persecution of so-called heretics, because they believed that they were fulfilling God's intentions, irrespective of any advantage to themselves. Whether the worth of their lives is affected by the fact, if it is one, as I hope to show, that their motivation is delusive is a difficult question to which I shall return.

At this point it needs to be remarked that by no means all believers in the future life situate it in another world. There are very many persons, especially in the East, who subscribe to a theory of reincarnation, according to which one has led and will lead an indefinite series of lives on earth. Belief in this theory may well have more influence on conduct than the Christian conceptions of an afterlife, since the level at which one is incarnated in one's next life is believed to depend on one's behaviour in one's present existence. I have been told that some sects admit the possibility of one's returning to earth in something other than a human form, but as I have no idea what moral standards could be thought to govern the behaviour of what are popularly known as the higher nonhuman organisms, let alone fish or insects, I shall confine myself to the cases where the one who is reincarnated always reappears as a human being, the value of each of his successive lives, whether measured in terms of happiness, or honour, or moral worth, being determined by the character of its predecessors.

But now we confront the objection that, even in this restricted form, the doctrine is not intelligible. It might seem strange that millions of people should believe what is unintelligible but however strange it may seem, there is no doubt that it frequently happens. The Christian doctrine of the trinity affords another example. In the case which we are considering, the difficulty is to give a sense to saying that anyone is identical with a single person, let alone a series of persons, who died before he was born. One could perhaps just imagine a person's living discontinuously. He might perhaps vanish for a period and then reappear, perhaps with no consciousness of where he had been, but not greatly changed in appearance, retaining his old memories, recognizing his surroundings and the persons that he had known. But this would be a strange mode of persistence, not reincarnation.

It is indeed possible to imagine circumstances in which it would be possible to give a sense to saying that one was the same person as someone who had lived and died long ago. To revive an example that I used in an earlier work,[2] suppose that someone now living claimed to have been Julius Caesar and supported his claim by asserting that he remembered Caesar's experiences: and suppose that not only did his description of the experiences agree with all the known facts, but new discoveries were made which confirmed his account of events in Caesar's life that were hitherto unknown to us. In that case, we should probably adjust our concept of memory in such a way as to allow for the possibility of one's 'remembering' experiences that one never had. It

[2] *The Problem of Knowledge*, p. 194.

would, however, also be open to us to alter our concept of personal identity, dispensing with the requirement of physical continuity, and putting the onus on memory, supported perhaps by the possession of similar talents or a similar character. It is important to realize that this would simply be a question of a linguistic distinction. To borrow Quine's useful phrase, there is no 'fact of the matter' in such a case.

If we enter into the realm of science fiction, allowing the possibility of brain transplants, teletransportation, fusion and so forth, we are likely to attach less weight to spatiotemporal continuity, and more to memory and similarity of character. The far-reaching implications of such thought experiments have been brilliantly developed by Derek Parfit in his book *Reasons and Persons*. Parfit is reductionist, in the sense of insisting that the ascription of personal identity over time must depend entirely upon the character of the experiences which form the links in the chain. There is no call, and no warrant, for a substance, a soul, to be the owner of the experiences. It is worth noting that Buddha, who is widely regarded as the foremost authority for the doctrine of reincarnation, also took this view. What is not so clear is that Buddha always insisted that there had to be criteria for determining that series of experiences which were separated in place and time belonged to the same self. Yet this was essential for his theory to be intelligible. Someone who says 'I used to be Julius Caesar' or 'Florence Nightingale' or both, without establishing any connection between her present experiences, and those, is literally talking nonsense.

An oddity of Buddhism at least is that one would expect its doctrine of reincarnation to be allied with a sense of the value of life. And indeed, as we have remarked, the quality of one segment of a person's life is believed to determine the value of the starting point of the segment which succeeds it. Nevertheless, life as such, at least as experienced by a self-conscious being, is regarded as being at best a necessary evil. The summit of moral achievement is admission to Nirvana; implying, both in Buddhism and Hinduism, release from the cycle of reincarnation, with a consequent loss of the sense of self-identity and of all desire. In Buddhism this is supposed to yield 'absolute blessedness': in Hinduism, absorption into Brahman, the impersonal divine reality of the universe. I confess that I cannot conceive what a state of absolute blessedness would be like if one had no desires to be satisfied and no awareness that one had attained it. So far as the reality of the universe goes, I suppose that I already form part of it, inasmuch as I exist; and I have no objection to its being called impersonal, if this means that it is not a person, though I balk at calling it divine. I have no trouble at all with the notion of the loss of the sense of self-identity. On the contrary it is something that I expect to occur to me, if not within the next decade, at least not very long after that.

Notice that I have avoided speaking of the loss of the sense of self-identity as something that I am due to suffer. This could, indeed, happen, if my mental condition were sufficiently abnormal. This loss of the sense of self-identity is that which results from being dead, and being dead is not something that one suffers, because one is no longer there to enjoy or suffer anything. As Wittgenstein expressed it, in one of his best sayings 'Death is not an event in life: we do not live to experience death.'[3]

Is it because they fail to take this into account that many people who do not expect to survive, and therefore are not affected by the fear of having to atone for their sins, or merely passing into a worse state of existence, are nevertheless afraid of death. They regard it as somehow terrible to cease to exist. I was tempted to quote Claudio's famous speech from *Measure for Measure*, but with the possible exception of the line 'To lie in cold obstruction and to rot' it is too strongly infected with the fallacy that death is a state of wretchedness that one undergoes.

The rational attitude is that attributed by Boswell to David Hume, whom Boswell reports as saying to him 'that he was no more uneasy to think that he should *not be* after his life, than that he *had not been* before he began to exist', prompting Dr Johnson to exclaim that Hume was either mad or insincere. Yet, if one comes to consider it, why should it worry me more, if at all, that I shall not be alive in the year 2050 than that I was not alive in the year 1850. The way things are going indeed, the latter, at least for Englishmen in comfortable circumstances, might well prove the better time to have lived. In the very long, perhaps infinite history of the universe, there is a relatively minute period that contains my life. Apart from the character of the experiences that I undergo, which are of course affected by the nature of my material and social environment, why should it matter to me at what points in the four-dimensional continuum this minute stretch begins and ceases?

I have to confess that when I have put this argument to my friends, they have tended not to find it convincing. They may be willing to admit that for some people at least, and in certain moods even for themselves, it would not have been a misfortune never to have been born, but having embarked on life, they take it almost as a grievance that they are going to be deprived of it. The prevalence of this attitude is borne out by the fact that the death penalty has generally been considered the most severe of punishments, a view commonly though

---

[3] *Tractatus Logico-Philosophicus*, 6.4311.

not universally shared by those who are in danger of having it inflicted on them. Yet is it obviously preferable to spend many years, perhaps the rest of one's days, in prison, under conditions which are almost certain to cause more pain than pleasure, than to be freed of the possibility of continuing to experience one or the other?

A similar peculiarity is that murder should be reckoned the most heinous of crimes. Is it always the case that the murderer, even if he is not caught, comes off better than his victim? Even though it is partly fiction, I think it fair to take the play of *Macbeth* as an example. Would any rational assessor prefer Macbeth's fate to Duncan's? 'Thou hast it now: King, Cawdor, Glamis, all . . .' and much good did it do him. And what about Duncan? 'After life's fitful fever, he sleeps well.'

Macbeth died too, eventually. So do we all, though nowadays few of us in battle. And this is a relevant fact, that we all do die. A feature of the general attitude to murder and to capital punishment appears to me to be the universal assumption, manifestly untenable when it is brought to light, that in putting an end to a man's life, one is taking something away from him that he would possess for as long as he pleased, if not for ever. It is as though we believed ourselves to be robbing him of immortality. What we are doing is shortening his life. And how much harm does this do him, if it does him any harm at all? Clearly there is no general answer to this question. It depends on his mental and physical condition, the type of society in which he lives, and his position within it, the work, if any, in which he is employed, the range of his desires and his capacity for satisfying them, his vitality, his age. It is not only for personal reasons that I consider this last factor to be important. I quote three stanzas of a well-known poem by A. E. Housman, who in fact lived to the age of seventy-seven, just the age that I am now.

> Loveliest of trees, the cherry now
> Is hung with bloom along the bough,
> And stands about the woodland ride
> Wearing white for Eastertide.
>
> Now, of my threescore years and ten,
> Twenty will not come again,
> And take from seventy springs a score,
> It only leaves me fifty more.
>
> And since to look at things in bloom
> Fifty springs are little room,
> About the woodlands I will go,
> To see the cherry hung with snow.

I cannot claim that I have spent more than a negligible fraction of my last fifty-seven springs going out of my way to look at things in bloom. I am not even sure that I should immediately recognize a cherry tree if I saw one. Nevertheless, the moral of the poem is one that I can appreciate. I am not a stranger to the feeling that the average span of life is too short to allow one to do all the things that one wants to do, to visit all the places that one wants to visit, or the same places often enough, to saturate oneself sufficiently in painting, or music, or literature, if they are where one's enjoyments lie, perhaps even to complete the work that one feels oneself capable of doing.

But now I must enter two caveats. The first is that my last paragraph was written from the point of view of a member of a privileged minority. Opportunities for travel, for acquiring pictorial skills and visiting galleries, for making and listening to music, for reading a wide variety of books have indeed increased very markedly in many Western countries in the last thirty years, but they are still rather narrowly circumscribed. Not many people can afford to take long holidays and the majority of holiday-makers are reported to prefer taking their own culture with them to enlarging their view of life. Not many people receive the education which disposes them to attach value to the arts. Not that they are the only domain in which one might reasonably ask for more. Anyone who takes an interest in anything at all, in science at any level, even if he only reads about it, in sport as a player or observer, in gardening, in social life, even like the speaker in Housman's poem, in nothing more than the passage of the seasons, may complain that life is too short for his interest to be exhausted.

But, even with this addition I maintain that we are still talking about a privileged minority. The vast majority of the human race, in Asia, in Latin America, in Africa, in the so-called underclasses of the more affluent Western societies, are far too fully occupied in waging a losing struggle to achieve a tolerable standard of living for it to be rational for them to wish their miseries prolonged. Perhaps they do wish it, nevertheless. Perhaps they never lose the hope that things will take a turn for the better. In some cases the myth of reincarnation may play a role. I claim only that they can have no good reason to wish that life were longer than it is.

> The trivial round, the common task
> would furnish all we ought to ask;
> Room to deny ourselves; a road
> To bring us, daily, nearer God.

This quotation from John Keble's hymn 'The Christian Year' was intended to assure its readers or performers that they were not required to retire to a 'cloistered-cell'. What is interesting is the implication, persisting in mid-nineteenth century High Anglicanism, that life should not be altogether pleasurable. There has to be some self-denial, apparently for its own sake, or perhaps because it is what God requires. Here there is indeed a suggestion that a reward lies in store, though it is left unclear what relation the certainty or quality of the reward bears to the length of the trivial round. What is implied is that once the end is secured, the sooner the trivial round stops the better. I think that this is a pervasive feature of mid-Victorian piety, though not often made explicit. If that is so, it is odd that they seemed never quite to make up their minds whether death was a blessing or a misfortune. In either case, they clothed it with ritual trappings, which on the whole have not persisted.

I come now belatedly to the second of my two caveats and that is the onset of age. Obviously I am not concerned with the truism that people grow older as the years pass, but the fact that they almost inevitably deteriorate, both physically and mentally. There are indeed societies where the aged are honoured. It is, or used to be, preferable in old age to be a Chinese than a French peasant, underfed by your daughter-in-law and entrusted with the care of the geese. Still even the Chinese patriarch was not protected from 'grey hairs and the loosening of teeth', let alone more serious physical disabilities. There are those, presumably enjoying some financial security and not in any fear of lacking warmth or nourishment, who profess to value the calm and detachment of old age. I think that it was Sophocles who is said to have congratulated himself on outgrowing sexual desire. This is not an attitude that I should wish to share. From my own experiences I judge it to be true that as one gets older, one tends to live with less intensity. One is more prone to the mood of Mallarmé's 'La chair est triste, hélas, et j'ai lu tous les livres': even one's aesthetic sensibilities become less keen. It seems to me absurd, however, to regard these as compensations of age.

Are we then to welcome the fact that doctors are said to be on the verge of finding ways of combating the hardening of the arteries, so that the average expectation of life is likely to be increased? Is this desirable? Not if it amounts to no more than an addition to the number of decrepit centenarians. It would be different if some method were found of arresting the process of ageing. If my condition remained what it was in the prime of my life, I should have no objection to living a greater number of years. Perhaps this would be true of most people, at any rate those whom I have described as belonging to the privileged minority. In the case of those for whom life at its best is disagreeable I can see no reason why they should wish it prolonged.

If the average expectation of life were markedly increased, it would be necessary to limit the number of new births. The general opinion is that life is a good in itself but it is a good which is dependent on the possession of it being fairly strictly rationed. Otherwise Malthus comes into his own and the value of life is swamped by the misery of living.

There are many ways in which a person's life may come to have a meaning for him in itself. He may find fulfilment in his work, though this cannot be guaranteed to last until old age. The same is true of the satisfaction which some people find in their domestic lives, with the factor of children and grandchildren playing its part. The English, of all classes, have not been noted in the past for the affection which they have commonly shown towards their children, or indeed received from them, but there have been exceptions and they may be on the increase. There are hobbies, like chess or stamp collecting, which may become a passion. I am not suggesting that these activities are of equal worth but only that they may be equally absorbing. Some people are absorbed in making money, presumably in most cases for the sake of the luxury, prestige, or power that the possession of it brings, but in some cases simply for its own sake; I know of a man who having set himself the goal of making a million pounds by the time he had attained a relatively youthful age could think of nothing better to do than set out to make another. His life might have been more interesting if he had been less sure of success. It lacked the spice which the fear of ruin gives to the life of the gambler. Again, I am not saying that the life of a gambler is morally preferable to that of a shrewd investor but only that it may be a life of greater intensity.

One of the most conspicuous elements in what counts and has long counted in many societies for most people as a meaningful life is the pursuit and still more the acquisition of fame. This has increased its importance in the present century because the improvement of communication, the diffusion throughout the world of many of the same programmes on television and the cinema, has spread fame much more widely. It is also ephemeral. Pop stars drop out of fashion and questionnaires reveal a surprising ignorance of what one might have thought were household names. I wonder, for example, what percentage of Asians could name either the Prime Minister of England, or the President of the United States. I think it might turn out to be surprisingly small.

In general, people who desire fame also wish to be thought to deserve it. They wish that their work should be esteemed by those whom they regard as persons best qualified to judge it, preferably in their lifetime when they can be awarded honour and gratified by praise, but also after their death. Sometimes those who are neglected in their lifetime take consolation in the thought that its merits will eventually be recognized. 'On me lira vers 1880,' said Stendhal in the 1830s and how right he was. Of those who are recognized in their lifetime, I think many attach more importance to the hope that their work will endure and their names be honoured as the authors of it.

Yet there is something irrational about this. It is comprehensible that if one has created an outstanding work of art, of whatever kind, or hit upon an original scientific theory, or written good poetry, or a novel of unusual depth, or even made some contribution to philosophy, one should wish the outcome to continue to be appreciated. But why should it matter that one's name be attached to it? After all one is not going to know anything about it. One runs no risk of suffering the humiliation of Max Beerbohm's Enoch Soames or the triumph that he would have felt if he had found a eulogistic record of his name in the British Museum's catalogue. All the same it does matter. I have the hope that some of my work will continue to be read after my death, perhaps even here and there in a hundred years' time. Yet I do not care at all for the idea that it will be attributed to one of my colleagues, however much I may like or admire him. Perhaps I should prefer that someone else should get the credit for my work, than that it should vanish without trace, but I cannot honestly say that this is a matter of indifference to me. If the work survives, I want my name also to survive as its author. Yet it is not a pleasure that I shall enjoy. I shall have no means of telling whether it has survived or not.

Nevertheless, my friends and my children and my grandchildren, if I have any, will know that it has survived; and the belief that they will take pride in the fact is a source of satisfaction to me. I think that this is true, though its importance may be overestimated. A childless curmudgeon may equally relish the thought of his posthumous fame. Moreover, it is a motive which does not reach far into the future. I care a great deal for my son, my stepdaughter and her three-year-old child, but the idea that persons in the twenty-fourth century will take any pleasure in my being their ancestor carries no weight with me. It is a matter of indifference to me, and I expect to most other people, if they think about it honestly, whether or not their family line continues for another three hundred years.

So far, I have been speaking about the satisfaction that people receive for the character and conduct of their personal lives. But for the most part when questions are raised about the meaning of life, they do not look for an answer at this level. The problem which is posed is much more general. Does the existence of the universe serve any purpose, and if it does serve a purpose, does the existence of human beings enter into it? There is a tendency to assume that an affirmative answer to the first question entails an affirmative answer to the second, but this need not be so. If any sense can be made of the statement that the universe has a purpose, then the purpose could be one in which the existence of human beings played no part. Admittedly, those who cleave to the superstition of determinism, are committed to holding that the original organization of the world causally necessitates the emergence of human beings, but even they are not obliged to attach value to this outcome. They could regard us as an excrescence on the scheme of things.

Nevertheless the vast majority of those who believe that the universe serves a purpose do so because they take this as conferring a meaning on life. How far down in the scale of organisms are they prepared to go is not always clear. The hymnodist Mrs Alexander boldly strikes out with 'All things bright and beautiful, All creatures great and small, All things wise and wonderful, the Lord God made them all.' The first and third lines seem to allow for a good many omissions, but perhaps the second line makes up for them. Everything after all must have some size.

We must not overlook the last line of the stanza. Not all theories that the world has a destiny are theistic. There are conceptions of the governance of all things, and of men in particular, by an impersonal fate. Nevertheless, the notion of human life as owing its meaning to its playing its part in a grand design is most commonly associated with the belief that the universe was created by a being of supernatural intelligence, and it is this belief that I now intend to discuss.

Let me begin by saying that I totally reject it. In my youth, when I published my first book, I argued with some force that the concept of a transcendent deity was literally nonsensical. Now I am prepared to be a little more conciliatory. I am, indeed, in doubt, whether the notion of an incorporeal subject of consciousness is logically coherent, but as a follower of Hume I am prepared to envisage a series of experiences which are not linked in the ordinary way with experiences of a physical body. The problem which he and the rest of us have failed to solve is to fashion an adequate criterion of identity for such a series. But let that pass. The hypothesis then would be that the course of nature, including the emergence of human beings and the vicissitudes of their individual lives, was planned by the owner of this disembodied consciousness. There are indeed, difficulties about time, since a series of experiences presumably occurs in time and therefore must be antecedent to whatever our cosmologists light upon as the first physical event, if any.

The series of psychical events, if deified, presumably had no beginning, which is not an easy conclusion to accept. But the difficulties of embracing either side of Kant's antinomy that the world had or that it had not a beginning in time are notorious, and they are not lessened by assuming time to start off with the world's alleged creator.

Fortunately, we need not become entangled in them. The hypothesis of there being a creator, even if it is allowed to be intelligible, fails through its being vacuous. To have any content it would need to specify the end for which the world was designed and the way in which various features of it promote this end. But this it does not even attempt to do. The so-called argument from design owed its popularity to the occurrence of teleological processes within the world; the adaptation of animal and human organs, such as those of sight and hearing, to their functions, the pollination of flowers, the dependence of parasites upon their hosts, phenomena now explained, more or less adequately, by the theory of natural selection. What was overlooked, except by some philosophers such as Hume in his *Dialogues Concerning Natural Religion*, was that the analogy of a watch and a watchmaker, or a building and its architect, apart from its internal imperfections, since neither watchmakers nor architects are incorporeal, simply does not apply to the universe as a whole. From what we know of it, the universe bears no resemblance to a clock or any other artefact. It has some structure, since anything that we are capable of describing must have some structure or other, but not any structure that the hypothesis of a creator prescribes. Whatever happens, the believer in the creator is going to say that that was what was intended. And just for this reason his hypothesis is vacuous.

'It can't all just be a fluke,' a young philosopher said to me the other day. On the contrary a fluke is all that it can be. I do not know how much that goes on is capable of explanation. I suspect rather less than we are apt to assume. But let us be optimistic. Let us suppose that we command a physiological theory which accounts for all the phenomena of consciousness in terms of processes in the central nervous system, and let us suppose that this theory is derivable from some biochemical theory, and so along the line until we come to relativity theory and the subatomic theories of contemporary physics. And let us suppose that we realize Einstein's vision of integrating them. What have we then? A set of formulae that are at best contingently true. They happen to account for the phenomena, as they are so far known to us, and maybe they will continue to do so. Or maybe they will need to be modified, as their predecessors have been. It makes no difference which way it goes. In either case the phenomena are what they are and the theories are adapted to them. Both could logically have been otherwise.

Suppose now, what we have seen to be false, that sense could be made of ascribing these theories to the intentions of a supernatural being. That too would make no serious difference. We should still end up with a fluke. For the fact that the world was ordered in the way it is rather than some other, if not due to the limitation of his capacity, must simply be put down to his whim.

Though they commonly go together, religious belief and belief in an afterlife, not taking the form of reincarnation, are logically distinct. I know of two atheists, both of them Cambridge philosophers, one of whom, J. Ellis McTaggart, was quite certain that he would survive, since he held the strange metaphysical view that everything in the world was a disguised immortal soul, and the other, C. D. Broad, whose interest in psychical research led him to believe that there was about an even chance of his surviving. What is curious about Broad is that he had no wish for this to happen. He thought poorly of this world and believed that the next world, if there was one, was quite likely to be even nastier.

I cannot claim to have gone deeply into the subject of psychical research, but such evidence as I have seen of what it has yielded has not seemed to be strong enough to overcome the main objections to the idea of one's surviving one's death; first the unsolved logical difficulty of defining personal identity in anything other than physical terms; and perhaps more importantly the abundant evidence which goes to show that all our conscious experiences are causally dependent upon our brains. I have already admitted that we do not have a set of well-established psychophysical hypotheses which correlate experiences one to one with states of the brain but the evidence for the overall, dependence of consciousness upon the brain is very strong.

Even if life had a meaning in the sense that we have just been discussing, it would not be known to the persons who had faith in it, nor would they have any inkling of the part that their own lives played in the overall plan. It might, therefore, seem surprising that the question was so important to them. Why should it matter to them that they followed a course which was not of their own choosing as a means to an end of which they were ignorant? Why should they derive any satisfaction from the belief that they were puppets in the hands of a superior agent?

I believe the answer is that most people are excited by the feeling that they are involved in a larger enterprise, even if they have no responsibility for its direction. This is a dangerous propensity since it makes them easier to manipulate, and so facilitates the growth of political and religious fanaticism. On the other hand, it can also serve the promotion of good causes, such as the agitation in favour of the victims of political injustice, or the organization of relief for the inhabitants of areas of famine. The case of war is an interesting example. I can speak, from experience, only of the second Great War, and only from an English point of view. I took part in it first as a soldier and then as a member of departments of intelligence. I suppose that I spent no more than half my time in England but it included the period of the blitz and that in which the V1 rockets were replaced by the V2s. The feature of this war, which concerns my argument, is that the civilian population was involved in it to a greater degree than in any previous war and certainly to a greater degree than they ever will be again, if our present strategy is maintained. As a result, it was apparent that they were living with a greater intensity, and also displaying in manner and action a greater amount of fellow feeling than they previously had or would have again. It may sound shocking, but I honestly believe that, with the exception of those who suffered personal injury or personal loss, especially in the form of death or maiming of those whom they loved, most English people enjoyed the war.

This is allied to the fact that if we take the intensity with which a life is lived as a criterion of its being meaningful we shall find no very close correlation between meaningful lives and those that we consider morally estimable. The same will be true if we attribute meaning to the lives of those who pass for having been great men or women, especially if their greatness consisted in their power. I do no know whether Lord Acton was justified in saying that great men are almost always bad, but it is certainly not the case that they have always been good. We need only think of Alexander the Great, Augustus Caesar, Jenghis Kahn, Cesare Borgia, Martin Luther, Peter the Great, Catherine the Great, Louis xiv, Florence Nightingale, John Pierpont Morgan, Lord Beaverbrook and David Lloyd George. I have avoided bringing the list up to date with Hitler and Stalin, in order to avoid the question whether we are going so to construe greatness that causing an inordinate amount of evil strips one of the title. There will still be no denying that they were major historical figures and I suspect that, on the whole, they were satisfied with their lives, Hitler at least until his last days and even then he seems to have seen the collapse of his fortunes more as the failure of the German people than his own; Stalin quite probably until the very end, since even if he was poisoned he was not aware of it.

In the realm of the arts, the disparity is not so flagrant, but still there is no positive correlation between being a great artist and an amiable man. Wagner is perhaps the most obvious counterexample. There is little correlation between goodness and happiness. If virtue is said to be its own reward it is because it so often acquires no other. As the Psalmist put it, it is the ungodly whom one sees 'flourishing like a green bay-tree'. In speaking of the ungodly I am not straying into deism. I am not even thinking of major criminals, who quite often come to grief, but of the multitude of minor villains who appear to have come to the fore in recent years, persons skilled in sharp practice on the stock exchange, hooligans, racists of one or other colour, persons whose principal aim is not merely to keep up with the Jones's but to outstrip them without being too scrupulous about the means.

The obvious disparity between virtue and prosperity in this world troubled the philosopher Immanuel Kant. He believed that there ought to be another world in which this balance would be redressed and thereby discovered a motive for believing in a God who would bring this about. I use the word 'motive' rather than 'reason' because, much as I dislike Kant's moral philosophy, I have too much respect for his intelligence to suppose that he regarded his pious hope as a serious argument. After all, it was Kant who first demolished the tricky ontological argument for the existence of God, the surprisingly durable pretence that the existence of a necessary being can be established by smuggling the factor of necessity into some grandiose concept, and went on to dispose with equal ease of the argument from design and the argument to a first cause.

My reasons for disliking Kant's moral philosophy are not only technical, inasmuch as he never succeeds in finding a way to bring his goodwill into action, but also moral. I do not care for the supremacy which he accords to the sense of duty over every human sympathy or principle of altruism. In his theory, indeed, it is only the sense of duty that counts. This is because he believed, mistakenly, that to act or fail to act in accordance with it lies in our power, in a way that the possession of the motives for other forms of action and our responses to them do not. In fact, actions done from a sense of duty are no less subject to causal conditioning than any others. Does the extent to which our actions are causally conditioned rob them of their moral value? I think not. I think that acts of cruelty or kindness are ugly or attractive in themselves, irrespective of their being correlated, in some measure, with states of our central nervous system, or explicable, however vaguely, in terms of our genetic endowment and the stimuli to which we have been subjected. This question is more difficult when it is directed towards the agent. Our ordinary moral judgments imply that he could not only have acted but in many cases chosen otherwise and it is not entirely clear to me what this means. I am inclined to think that the concept of desert which is included in our notion of moral responsibility is incoherent, but this is not a question into which I can enter here.

If I say that there are no such things as objective moral values, this is not to be taken as a profession of moral nihilism. I am not endorsing any moral principle that anybody happens to hold, still less alleging that all actions are morally neutral. On the contrary, I have strong moral sentiments and am anxious that other people should share them and act upon them. In saying that moral values are not objective, I am maintaining only that moral terms, while as it were, commenting on natural features of the world, do no themselves describe them. One consequence of this is that moral argument, in so far as it is not a dispute about some matter of fact, say, an agent's motive or the physical character of his action, is possible only on the basis of some common sentiment. For this reason, it is commonly *ad hominem*. One endeavours to convince one's opponent that his standpoint commits him to endorsing a course of action of which one is sure that he cannot honestly approve.

Evidently, there is no general answer to the question what constitutes a meaningful life. A life lived in one culture at a given social and economic level which satisfies one person might well fail to satisfy another who dwelt in a different or even in the same environment. Treating the question subjectively one can say, platitudinously, that it is a matter of the degree to which one achieves self-fulfilment. Treating it objectively, it is a matter of one's standing in one's society and the historical influence, if any, that one exerts. We have seen that the results of these different viewpoints need not coincide either with each other or with what we humane and liberal persons would regard as morally commendable.

I conclude with a question to which I do not know the answer. How far should our judgment of the worth of a person's life be affected by the fact that we take it to be based upon an illusion? Let us take the example of a nun, belonging to a strict order, leading a life of austerity, but serene in the performance of her devotions, confident that she is loved by her deity, and that she is destined for a blissful future in the world to come. If this example is considered to be too subjective, we can allot her a position of authority in the convent and locate her at a time and place when abbesses were historically important. It makes no difference to the problem. The question is whether it matters that the deity in whose love she rejoices does not exist and that there is no world to come.

I am inclined to say that it does matter, just as G. E. Moore in the last chapter of *Principia Ethica* goes so far as to say that 'a merely poetical contemplation of the Kingdom of Heaven *would* be superior to that of the religious believer, if it were the case (as he in fact thought it was) that the Kingdom of Heaven does not and will not really exist.'[4] I suppose that he was and I am yielding to what he called 'a strong respect for truth'. But what is our argument? It is not as if there were some end that the nun's life is failing to achieve. So far as one can survey the Universe *sub specie aeternitatis* one has to agree with Macbeth. It *is* 'a tale, told by an idiot, full of sound and fury, signifying nothing'. What is wrong with this quotation is its aura of disillusionment. It is not that we are sentenced to deprivation. It is open to us to make our lives as satisfying as our circumstances allow. But to return to the nun. It would indeed be terrible for her to discover that the point of her life was nonexistent. But *ex hypothesi* this is something that she will never know.

[4] 2nd edn., p. 495.

ELEVEN

That Undiscovered Country[1]

My first attack of pneumonia occurred in the United States. I was in hospital for ten days in New York, after which the doctors said that I was well enough to leave. A final X-ray, however, which I underwent on the last morning, revealed that one of my lungs was not yet free from infection. This caused the most sympathetic of my doctors to suggest that it would be good for me to spend a few more days in hospital. I respected his opinion but since I was already dressed and psychologically disposed to put my illness behind me, I decided to take the risk. I spent the next few days in my stepdaughter's apartment, and then made arrangements to fly back to England.

When I arrived I believed myself to be cured and incontinently plunged into an even more hectic social round than that to which I had become habituated before I went to America. Retribution struck me on Sunday, May 30. I had gone out to lunch, had a great deal to eat and drink and chattered incessantly. That evening I had a relapse. I could eat almost none of the food which a friend had brought to cook in my house.

On the next day, which was a bank holiday, I had a long-standing engagement to lunch at the Savoy with a friend who was very anxious for me to meet her son. I would have put them off if I could, by my friend lives in Exeter and I had no idea how to reach her in London. So I took a taxi to the Savoy and just managed to stagger into the lobby. I could eat hardly any of the delicious grilled sole that I ordered, but forced myself to keep up my end of the conversation. I left early and took a taxi home.

That evening I felt still worse. Once more I could eat almost none of

[1] 'That Undiscovered Country' was written while A. J. Ayer was recuperating at 'La Migoua', his house in France, in the summer of 1988. It appeared in the *Sunday Telegraph* on 28 August 1988 under the title 'What I saw when I was dead . . .'. The version printed here is almost identical, with only one or two amendments made by him in May 1989.

the dinner another friend had brought me. Indeed she was so alarmed by my weakness that she stayed overnight. When I was no better the next morning, she telephoned to my general practitioner and to my elder son Julian. The doctor did little more than promise to try to get in touch with the specialist but Julian, who is unobtrusively very efficient, immediately rang for an ambulance. The ambulance came quickly with two strong attendants, and yet another friend, who had called opportunely to pick up a key, accompanied it and me to University College Hospital.

I remember very little of what happened from then on. I was taken to a room in the private wing, which had been reserved for me by a specialist, who had a consulting room on the same floor. After being X-rayed and subjected to a number of tests which proved beyond question that I was suffering from pneumonia, I was moved into intensive care in the main wing of the hospital.

Fortunately for me, the young doctor who was primarily responsible for me had been an undergraduate at New College, Oxford, while I was a Fellow. This made him extremely anxious to see that I recovered; almost too much so, in fact, for he was so much in awe of me that he forbade me to be disturbed at night, even when the very experienced sister and nurses believed it to be necessary.

Under his care and theirs I made such good progress that I expected to be moved out of intensive care and back into the private wing within a week. My disappointment was my own fault. I did not attempt to eat the hospital food. My family and friends supplied all the food I needed. I am particularly fond of smoked salmon, and one evening I carelessly tossed a slice of it into my throat. It went down the wrong way and almost immediately the graph recording my heartbeats plummeted. The ward sister rushed to the rescue but she was unable to prevent my heart from stopping. She and the doctor subsequently told me that I died in this sense for four minutes, and I have had no reason to disbelieve them.

The doctor alarmed my son Nicholas, who had flown from New York to be at my bedside, by saying it was not probable that I should recover and, moreover, that if I did recover physically it was not probable that my mental powers would be restored. The nurses were more optimistic and Nicholas sensibly chose to believe them.

I have no recollection of anything that was done to me at that time. Friends have told me that I was festooned with tubes but I have never learned how many of them there were or, with one exception, what purpose they served. I do not remember having a tube inserted in my throat to bring up the quantity of phlegm which had lodged in my lungs. I was not even aware of my numerous visitors, so many of them, in fact, that the sister had to set a quota. I know that the doctors and nurses were surprised by the speed of my recovery and that when I started speaking, the specialist expressed astonishment that anyone with so little oxygen in his lungs should be so lucid.

My first recorded utterance, which convinced those who heard it that I had not lost my wits, was the exclamation 'You are all mad.' I am not sure how this should be interpreted. It is possible that I took my audience to be Christians and was telling them that I had not discovered anything 'on the other side'. It is also possible that I took them to be sceptics and was implying that I had discovered something. I think the former is more probable as in the latter case I should more properly have exclaimed 'We are all mad.' All the same, I cannot be sure.

The earliest remarks of which I have any cognizance, apart from my first exclamation, were made several hours after my return to life. They were addressed to a French woman with whom I had been friends for over fifteen years. I woke to find her seated by my bedside and started talking to her in French as soon as I recognized her. My French is fluent and I spoke rapidly, approximately as follows: 'Did you know that I was dead? The first time that I tried to cross the river I was frustrated, by my second attempt succeeded. It was most extraordinary, my thoughts became persons.'

The content of those remarks suggests that I have not wholly put my classical education behind me. In Greek mythology the souls of the dead, now only shadowly embodied, were obliged to cross the river Styx in order to reach Hades, after paying an obol to the ferryman, Charon. I may also have been reminded of my favourite philosopher, David Hume, who during his last illness, a 'disorder of the bowels', imagined that Charon, growing impatient, was calling him 'a lazy loitering rogue'. With his usual politeness, Hume replied that he saw without regret his death approaching and that he was making no efforts to postpone it. This is one of the rare occasions on which I have failed to follow Hume. Clearly I had made an effort to prolong my life.

The only memory that I have of an experience, closely encompassing my death, is very vivid. I was confronted by a red light, exceedingly bright, and also very painful, even when I turned away from it. I was aware that this light was responsible for the government of the universe. Among its ministers were two creatures who had been put in charge of space. These ministers periodically inspected space and had recently carried out such an inspection. They had, however, failed to do their work properly, with the result that space, like a badly fitted jigsaw puzzle, was slightly out of joint.

A further consequence was that the laws of nature had ceased to function as they should. I felt that it was up to me to put things right. I also had the motive of finding a way to extinguish the painful light. I assumed that it was signalling that space was awry and that it would switch itself off when order was restored. Unfortunately I had no idea where the guardians of space had gone and feared that even if I found them I should not be able to communicate with them. It then occurred to me that whereas, until the present century, physicists accepted the Newtonian severence of space and time, it had become customary, since the vindication of Einstein's general theory of relativity, to treat space-time as a single whole. Accordingly I thought that I could cure space by operating upon time.

I was vaguely aware that the ministers who had been given charge of time were in my neighbourhood and I proceeded to hail them. I was again frustrated. Either they did not hear me, or they chose to ignore me, or they did not understand me. I then hit upon the expedient of walking up and down, waving my watch, in the hope of drawing their attention not to my watch itself but to the time which it measured. This elicited no response. I became more and more desperate, until the experience suddenly came to an end.

This experience could well have been delusive. A slight indication that it might have been veridical has been supplied by my French friend, or rather by her mother, who also underwent a heart arrest many years ago. When her daugher asked her what it had been like, she replied that all that she remembered was that she must stay close to the red light.

On the face of it, these experiences, on the assumption that the last one was veridical, are rather strong evidence that death does not put an end to consciousness. Does it follow that there is a future life? Not necessarily. The trouble is that there are different criteria for being dead, which are indeed logically compatible, but may not always be satisfied together.

In this instance, I am given to understand that the arrest of the heart does not entail, either logically or causally, the arrest of the brain. In view of the very strong evidence in favour of the dependence of thoughts upon the brain, the most probable hypothesis is that my brain continued to function although my heart had stopped.

If I had acquired good reason to believe in a future life, it would have applied not only to myself. Admittedly, the philosophical problems of justifying one's confident belief in the existence and contents of other minds has not yet been satisfactorily solved. Even so, with the possible excepton of Fichte, who maintained that the world was his idea but may not have meant it literally, no philosopher has acquiesced in solipsism, no philsopher has seriously asserted that of all the objects in the universe, he alone was conscious. Moreover, it is commonly taken for granted, not only by philosophers, that the minds of others bear a sufficiently close analogy to one's own. Consequently, if I had been vouchsafed a reasonable expectation of a future life, other human beings could expect one too.

Let us grant, for the sake of argument, that we could have future lives. What form could they take? The easiest answer would consist in the prolongation of our experiences, without any physical attachment. This is the theory that should appeal to radical empiricists. It is, indeed, consistent with the concept of personal identity which was adopted both by Hume and by William James, according to which one's identity consists, not in the possession of an enduring soul but in the sequence of one's experiences, guaranteed by memory. They did not apply their theory to a future life, in which Hume at any rate disbelieved.

For those who are attracted by this theory, as I am, the main problem, which Hume admitted that he was unable to solve, is to discover the relation, or relations, which have to be held between experiences for them to belong to one and the same self. William James thought that he found the answers with his relations of the felt togetherness and continuity of our thoughts and sensation, coupled with memory, in order to unite experiences that are separated in time. But while memory is undoubtedly necessary, it can be shown that it is not wholly sufficient.

I myself carried out a thorough examination and development of the theory in my book *The Origins of Pragmatism*. I was reluctantly forced to conclude that I could not account for personal identity without falling back on the identity, through time, of one or more bodies that the person might successively occupy. Even then, I was unable to give a satisfactory account of the way in which a series of experiences is tied to a particular body at any given time.

The admission that personal identity through time requires the identity of a body is a surprising feature of Christianity. I call it surprising because it seems to me that Christians are apt to forget that the resurrection of the body is an element in their creed. The question of how bodily identity is sustained over intervals of time is not so difficult. The answer might consist in postulating a reunion of the same atoms, perhaps in there being no more than a strong physical resemblance, possibly fortified by a similarity of behaviour.

A prevalent fallacy is the assumption that a proof of an afterlife would also be a proof of the existence of a deity. This is far from being the case. If, as I hold, there is no good reason to believe that a god created or presides over this world, there is no good reason either to believe that a god created or presides over the next world, on the unlikely supposition that such a thing exists. It is conceivable that one's experiences in the next world, if there are any, will supply evidence of a god's existence, but we have no right to presume on such evidence, when we have not had the relevant experiences.

It is worth remarking, in this connection, that the two important Cambridge philosophers in this century, J. E. McTaggart and C. D. Broad, who have believed, in McTaggart's case that he would certainly survive his death, in Broad's that there was about a 50 per cent probability that he would, were both of them atheists. McTaggart derived his certainty from his metaphysics, which implied that what we confusedly perceive as material objects, in some cases housing minds, are really souls, eternally viewing one another with something of the order of love.

The less fanciful Broad was impressed by the findings of psychical research. He was certainly too intelligent to think that the superior performances of a few persons in the game of guessing unseen cards, which he painstakingly proved to be statistically significant, has any bearing on the likelihood of a future life. He must therefore have been persuaded by the testimony of mediums. He was surely aware that most mediums have been shown to be frauds, but he was convinced that some have not been. Not that this made him optimistic. He took the view that this world was very nasty and that there was a fair chance that the next world, if it existed, was even nastier. Consequently, he had no compelling desire to survive. He just thought that there was an even chance of his doing so. One of his better epigrams was that if one went by the character of spiritualistic seances, life in the next world was like 'a "Pleasant Sunday Afternoon" at a Nonconformist chapel, enlivened by occasional bump-suppers'.

If Broad was an atheist, my friend Dr Alfred Ewing was not. Ewing, who considered Broad to be a better philosopher than Wittgenstein, was naive, unworldly even by academic standards, intellectually shrewd, unswervingly honest and a devout Christian. Once, to tease him, I said: 'Tell me, Alfred, what do you most look forward to in the next world?' He replied immediately: 'God will tell me whether there are *a priori* propositions.' It is a wry comment on the strange character of our subject that this answer should be so funny.

My excuse for repeating this story is that such philosophical problems as the question whether the propositions of logic and pure mathematics are deductively analytic or factually synthetic, and, if they are analytic, whether they are true by convention, are not to be solved by acquiring more information. What is needed is that we succeed in obtaining a clearer view of what the problems involve. One might hope to achieve this in a future life, but really we have no good reason to believe that our intellects will be any sharper in the next world, if there is one, than they are in this. A god, if one exists, might make them so, but this is not something that even the most enthusiastic deist can count on.

The only philosophical problem that our finding ourselves landed on a future life might clarify would be that of the relation between mind and body, if our future lives consisted, not in the resurrection of our bodies, but in the prolongation of the series of our present experiences. We should then be witnessing the triumph of dualism, though not the dualism which Descartes thought that he had established. If our lives consisted in an extended series of experiences, we should still have no good reason to regard ourselves as spiritual substances.

So there it is. My recent experiences have slightly weakened my conviction that my genuine death, which is due fairly soon, will be the end of me, though I continue to hope that it will be. They have not weakened my conviction that there is no god. I trust that my remaining an atheist will allay the anxieties of my fellow supporters of the British Humanist Association, the Rationalist Press Association and the South Place Ethical Society.

TWELVE

Postscript to a Postmortem[1]

My purpose in writing a postscript to the article about my 'death' is not primarily to retract anything that I wrote or to express my regret that my Shakespearian title for the article, 'That Undiscovered Country', was not retained, but to correct a misunderstanding to which the article appears to have given rise.

I say 'not primarily to retract' because one of my sentences was written so carelessly that it is literally false as it stands. In the final paragraph, I wrote: 'My recent experiences have slightly weakened my conviction that my genuine death . . . will be the end of me.' They have not and never did weaken that conviction. What I should have said and would have said, had I not been anxious to appear undogmatic, is that my experiences have weakened, not my belief that there is no life after death, but my inflexible attitude towards that belief. Previously my interest in the question was purely polemical. I wished to expose the defects in the positions of those who believed that they would survive. My experiences caused me to think that it was worth examining various possibilities of survival for their own sakes. I did not intend to imply that the result of my inquiry had been to increase the low probability of any one of them, even if it were granted that they had any probability at all.

My motive for writing the original article was twofold. I thought that my experiences had been sufficiently remarkable to be worth recording, and I wished to rebut the incoherent statement, which had been attributed to me, that I had discovered nothing 'on the other side'. Evidently, my having discovered something on the other side was a precondition of my having completed the journey. It follows that if I had discovered nothing, I had not been there; I had no right to imply that there was a 'there' to go to. Conversely, if there was evidence that I

[1] 'Postscript to a Postmortem' appeared in the *Spectator*, 15 October 1988.

had had some strange experiences, nothing followed about there being 'another side'. In particular, it did not follow either that I had visited such a place, or that I had not.

I said in my article that the most probable explanation of my experiences was that my brain had not ceased to function during the four minutes of my heart arrest. I have since been told, rightly or wrongly, that it would not have functioned on its own for any longer without being damaged. I thought it so obvious that the persistence of my brain was the most probable explanation that I did not bother to stress it. I stress it now. No other hypothesis comes anywhere near to superseding it.

Descartes has few contemporary disciples. Not many philosophers of whatever persuasion believe that we are spiritual substances. Those who depart so far from the present fashion as not to take a materialistic view of our identities are most likely to equate persons with the series of their experiences. There is no reason in principle why such a series should not continue beyond the point where the experiences are associated with a particular body. Unfortunately, as I pointed out in my article, nobody has yet succeeded in specifying the relations which would have to hold between the members of such a series for them to constitute a person. There is a more serious objection. Whatever these relations were, they would be contingent; they might not have obtained. But this allows for the possibility of there being experiences which do not belong to anybody; experiences which exist on their own. It is not obvious to me that this supposition is contradictory; but it might well be regarded as an irreparable defect in the theory.

If theories of this type are excluded, one might try to fall back on the Christian doctrine of the resurrection of the body. But, notoriously, this too encounters a mass of difficulties. I shall mention only one or two of them. For instance, one may ask in what form our bodies will be returned to us. As they were when we died, or when we were in our prime? Would they still be vulnerable to pain and disease? What are the prospects for infants, cripples, schizophrenics, and amnesiacs? In what manner will they survive?

'Oh, how glorious and resplendent, fragile body, shalt thou be!' This body? Why should one give unnecessary hostages to fortune? Let it be granted that I must reappear as an embodied person, if I am to reappear at all. It does not follow that the body which is going to be mine must be the same body as the one that is mine now; it need not be even a replica of my present body. The most that is required is that it be generically the same; that is, a human body of some sort, let us say a standard male model not especially strong or beautiful, not diseased, but still subject to the ills that flesh is heir to. I am not sure whether one can allow oneself a choice with respect to age and sex. The preservation or renewal of one's personal identity will be secured in this picture, by a continuity of one's mental states, with memory a necessary, but still not a sufficient, factor. I am assuming now that these mental states cannot exist on their own; hence, the need for a material body to sustain them.

I am far from claiming that such a scenario is plausible. Nevertheless it does have two merits. The first is that we are no longer required to make sense of the hypothesis that one's body will be reconstructed some time after it has perished. The second is that it does not force us to postulate the existence of a future world. One can live again in a future state of the world that one lives in now.

At this point it becomes clear that the idea of the resurrection of the body had better be discarded. It is to be replaced by the idea of reincarnation. The two are not so very distinct. What gives the idea of reincarnation the advantage is that it clearly implies both that persons undergo a change of bodies and that they return to the same world that they inhabited before.

The idea of reincarnation is popular in the East. In the West it has been more generally ridiculed. Indeed, I myself have frequently made fun of it. Even now, I am not suggesting that it is or ever will be a reality. Not even that it could be. Our concept of a person is such that it is actually contradictory to suppose that once-dead persons return to earth after what may be a considerable lapse of time.

But our concepts are not sacrosanct. They can be modified if they cease to be well adapted to our experience. In the present instance, the change which would supply us with a motive for altering our concept of a person in such a way as to admit the possibility of reincarnation would not be very great. All that would be required is that there be good evidence that many persons are able to furnish information about previous lives of such a character and such an abundance that it would seem they could not possess the information unless they themselves had lived the lives in question. This condition is indispensable. There is no sense in someone's claiming to have been Antony, say, or Cleopatra, if he or she knows less about Antony or Cleopatra than a good Shakespearian scholar and much less than a competent ancient historian. Forgetfulness in this context is literally death.

I should remark that even if this condition were satisfied, our motive for changing our concept of a person would not be irresistible. Harmony could also be restored by our changing our concept of memory. We could introduce the ruling that it is possible to remember experiences that one never had; not just to remember them in the way that one remembers facts of one sort or another, but to remember these experiences in the way that one remembers one's own.

Which of these decisions would lead us to the truth? This is a senseless question. In a case of this kind, there is, as Professor Quine would put it, no fact of the matter which we can seek to discover. There would indeed be a fact to which we should be trying to adjust our language; the fact that people did exhibit this surprising capacity. But what adjustment we made, whether we modified our concept of a person, or our concept of memory, or followed some other course, would be a matter for choice. The most that could be claimed for the idea of reincarnation is that it would in these circumstances be an attractive option.

This time let me make my position fully clear. I am not saying that these ostensible feats of memory have ever yet been abundantly performed, or indeed performed at all, or that they ever will be performed. I am saying only that there would be nothing in logic to prevent their being performed in such abundance as to give us a motive for licensing reincarnation; and a motive for admitting it as a possibility would also be a motive for admitting it as a fact.

The consequence of such an admission would be fairly radical, though not so radical as the standbys of science fiction such as brain transplants and teleportation. Less radical too than the speculations of mathematical physicists. These speculations titillate rather than alarm the reading public. Professor Hawking's book *A Brief History of Time* is a best seller. Perhaps the reading public has not clearly understood what his speculations imply. We are told, for example, that there may be a reversal in the direction of the arrow of time. This would provide for much stranger possibilities than that of a rebirth following one's death. It would entail that in any given person's life a person's death preceded his birth. That would indeed be a shock to common sense.

Index